THE FINAL DAYS
OF
MICHAEL HUTCHENCE

Mike Gee

OMNIBUS PRESS
LONDON · NEW YORK · PARIS · SYDNEY

Contents

Michael Hutchence was going through a lot. The last time I saw him was in a club in New York about two or three years ago. I didn't know whether he was married then or had a girlfriend – this was before I moved to Holland where I read about him all the time.

I was upset when I read about the Paris MTV Awards where he got grief from the guy from Oasis. Michael shouldn't have been in that position – being threatened publicly and backstage.

When I saw him there in that club that night, the first thing I thought was why is he alone and he was looking at women like he'd never had one before. He was looking like everything was unobtainable and bright and shiny and he couldn't get it. I think, maybe, he was high.

But he was living the same way every day he was living. I think he was living a silent desperation.

He wouldn't know what he was feeling. He had low self-esteem which is very normal for a musician of his age who was trying to compete at his age – it can all come down on you.

You can either put up with it or you can run.

– Dee Dee Ramone to the author, April 2, 1998

Preface

February 1998: So why write a book about a man who committed suicide? It's a good question and good place to start. I sometimes wonder myself.

Michael Hutchence wasn't a friend, he was an acquaintance; INXS aren't friends – they are acquaintances. But we go back some ways: 20 years to small town Perth, Western Australia, when the Farriss Brothers played the pub circuit fronted by a scrawny, gangling, smouldering teen who already had star splattered all over him as he slithered and strutted the small stages amid the beer undertow, pash, grope and racket of a session.

To be frank, I didn't want to write this book when it was first offered to me. I felt I'd be a traitor to Michael's memory and to the band: the funeral had been a month earlier – a strange, almost mystical affair. Claustrophobic, a cauldron of sweat and emotion intensified by Sydney's unseasonable tropical take on weather. Mountainous clouds built around the cathedral beforehand and the fury broke – and in the tradition of many native races cleansed – as the coffin of the rider on the storm was carried from its doors. Even in death Hutch played out a grand finale. If Jim Morrison had appeared in a chariot and whisked him away it wouldn't have been that much of a surprise.

Suicide was a surprise. Suicide is – no matter which way you look at it – a cop out, especially when there's a child involved. There is no rationalization to be had here. Even the mountain of evidence that suggests Michael Hutchence was under massive pressure and suffering the kind of depression that's alleviated by taking the controversial prescribed drug, Prozac, isn't enough to say "well, you have to understand . . ."

So why write this book? For the memory of the good guy, the gentle guy, the deep, thoughtful, funny/sad, shy, philosophical guy I met along the way – the guy Michael most often was; the bloke beneath the superstar skin. Then for the chance to expose the lies and misinformation that followed his death (and dogged him through the last years of his life), and the tactless, thoughtless actions of the press: some of the journalistic community distinguished themselves by emulating the very worst aspects of the paparazzi-style modus operandi that was so condemned, only months earlier, in the wake of the death of Princess Diana. There are many good people in this community, skilled, thoughtful, intelligent, compassionate men and women, but there are others who – blinded by insensitivity, ego and journalistic ambition – display little respect for privacy, dignity or individual emotion. So why write this book? Perhaps to say that we should not accept this revelling in cheap sensation, death and suffering any longer and ask for a better deal – the whole picture of life.

Finally, for you to experience something of a life sadly wasted – in the end not even elegantly, and to share what it was that INXS and Michael achieved, the country they grew up in and its music, the importance of their struggle, success and soundtrack to Australia, and their place in the modern muse worldwide. To tell a grand story with an awful ending.

If you will, as you read this book, think of this: the only thing that distinguished Michael Hutchence and Paula Yates from you or me is that they were famous. Yes, they were hedonists; yes, they took drugs; yes, they drank; yes they got it off and got it on, regularly. How many of you don't? Who reading this likes it both ways, maybe 20 times a week, is into bondage, group sex, telephone sex, has it off with an inflatable, goes home every night and tokes on a joint or three, swallows some pills, can't sleep without some kind of fix, drinks during the day, knows they're an alcoholic but can't face it, has casual affair one, two, three – and rationalizes them, is a sadist, masochist, voyeur? If you were famous, your story would not be that much different from the one you're about to read. And everybody else would want to revel and wallow in it. How would you feel? Where would you run? How would you hide? How would you cope with continual persecution and judgement?

The death of Michael Hutchence is a tragedy and the events

after his death a sad indictment of how facile and superficial this modern world has become. If his death is to have any meaning then perhaps it should be by taking one small, squalid, horrible moment and act, and applying it to the bigger picture. That's up to you. Then again, you may just revel in the sensation, sex, drugs and rock'n'roll that's portrayed here. I would ask you don't. There is nothing cool about it at all. Michael Hutchence was – in his own words – just a man. Let him be that and remember the music, the words, the impossible to articulate buzz that came with his great performances or the feeling when a song lifted, seduced, befriended, calmed, amused, touched or ripped through you. Remember him as a part of INXS, a family: without them Michael had no platform on which to perform.

We expect so much, too much, of our idols, icons, stars – in all the arts. We devour them, own them without knowing them, take away their space, time, freedom because we adore them. And in doing so, more often than not, we destroy what we love most. A common condition when it comes to man, hey? So when you read this think also of every performer, artist, actor, sculptor, painter, and of the will to succeed, to create, to express, to love. The right to dream, dare to be different and go for it. And think of every person on this planet.

Michael Hutchence and INXS touched many, many millions of people. Remember that. I do.

And, yes, I still feel like a traitor, sometimes; maybe I always will. That's my problem.

– Mike Gee, Sydney, Australia

Everybody thinks they own part of you.

It is difficult because you talk to everybody but you can't actually talk to anybody about what you want to talk about . . . It's only what they want to talk about and I imagine he became very fucking lonely because he had nobody else to talk to. What do you do? You talk to a million people a day but none of them are your friends.

What are you left with? You've got a big house, big car, a lot of money . . .

The point is he [Michael Hutchence] couldn't go anywhere because everybody knew who he was, especially with Paula Yates and the split-up with Bob Geldof. That was the biggest thing in Britain you could imagine. For six months you couldn't pick up a paper in Britain without seeing Michael Hutchence and Paula Yates or something about them . . .

In the end you're constantly trying to please everybody else but yourself and you're just leaving yourself out there.

He was having a relationship with someone who was involved with somebody else and his parents would have approved of something or somebody else and he was trying to please them, them and them, just to keep the peace and you're left in the middle with fuck all.

– Stuart Cable, Kelly Jones and Richard Jones of Stereophonics
to the author, April 1998

Credits

Books are not made by one person. And believe me, they are made. They are the result of timing, dedication, consideration and a splendid pile of coincidences all falling into place in fate's lap at the right time. There were several times when the likelihood of this book ever being written was truly in doubt. That it was is the result of persistence, patience and faith from several people who should know better. Firstly, I'd like to thank Melissa Elsley of Music Sales in Sydney who got me into this in the first place. When I first met Mel I knew she was trouble. Mel is confident, mouthy and gives as good as she gets. In the past six months, she's listened to me endlessly dribbling on over the phone, lunch and coffee. She's also woken me up way too early on so many occasions I've lost count. This, she says without a hint of shame, is her revenge. Melissa's been my publicist, troubleshooter and constant source of energy and belief. Without her none of this would ever have happened. Melissa suggested to her boss, Chris Charlesworth, noted former rock writer himself and guru of Omnibus Press in England, that I write this book. The fact that he agreed after one 10,000km phone call is a mark of the nature of the man. I thank him for his trust and hope I've honoured his judgement. To everybody else at both companies who've been involved in any way in the production and publication, thank you. To my old scaly mate Roland McAdam, CD-ROM pioneer, a special tug on the locks for having the guts to come out and stand-up for his old friend, Sir Bob Geldof: nobody else would. It provided a desperately needed balance. After Michael's death his closest friends and inner circle around INXS rightfully respected the band's silence and made themselves unavailable for comment but to those who talked to me off the record (you know who you are) and pointed me in different directions, thank you. To the members of the INXS list on the internet, thank you for your support - especially after I'd once gone off about people writing books like this about Michael. Your endless belief in the band and the man was a constant reminder of the power of INXS' music to affect people; your grief a genuine reminder of just how special Michael was to many people, fans, onlookers. To Jon Casimir, friend and fellow musicophile, thanks for getting the U2 experience down pat and your intuitive comments. To everyone else in *The Sydney Morning Herald* internet section – Des, Pierre, Richard, Charlotte, Hattie, Ben, Rob, Stephen – who had to cover for me when I went missing in action (Mel's fault) during the birth and writing of the book, you're all insane – the best kind of people. I'd like to take this chance to thank all the people in all the record companies, touring and publicity agencies, who over the years have supported me with interviews, favours and friendship. Special thanks to Michael Parisi, Mark Pope, Michelle Hunter, Chrissie Camp, Bo Martin, Matt Medcraf, David Catterall, Sylvia Potalivo, and everybody at Warners who have always looked out for me and trusted me, Sue McAullay, Brooke Harry, Amanda Urquhart, Rina Ferris, Michael 'the legend' Chugg and Barbara Dennis at Frontier Tours, and to John Woodruffe and Keith Welsh (ex-bass player of Flowers and Icehouse) at The Music Network, and all the editors of all the publications in Australia and overseas who have continued to publish me over 25 years. To Shawn Deacon for understanding. To the big man of Australian music, Peter Rix, and all at ARIA, thanks for entrusting me with the show scripts for the past couple of years. The experience gave me the confidence to go ahead with this project. To all the bands and artists who gave so generously of their time, thought and emotion over the years: sincerely thank you, it's been a pleasure and an honour. To my mother, Betty, and late father, Jim Gee, see I eventually did something, somewhere, sometime, just like you knew I always would. That it took me 44 years is no fault of yours. Still haven't cut my hair though. To my brother Chris: consider that anything is possible. Finally, to two very special people. Firstly, my long-time business partner and friend, Jayne Elizabeth Margetts, with whom I embarked on a rather uncertain journey some seven plus years ago: I wouldn't have got here if you hadn't been there. Jayne's a Scorpio which says everything; she's also got a heap of guts, ton of tenacity, a big warm heart she likes to hide and more talent than she actually believes she has. Finally to Wendy Cavenett, my girlfriend for six years, other business partner and the only person who actually wants to live with me: this book also would not have been written without your constant presence, support and prodding. Your belief in me is astounding and your ability to organise my entire life into something remotely functional irreplaceable. Wendy's now getting published in all the right publications like Black & White – she's a better writer than me – but I know when this is published nobody will get a bigger buzz. I am eternally grateful, Bendette, for all the tea, coffee, clean clothes and zillion other things you do and I don't. This book is as much yours as mine. And I love you heaps. To anybody else I've forgotten, excuse me, the old memory isn't as strong as it used to be – at least, that's my story and I'm sticking to it. Let's rock.

1

Underneath The Colours

Michael Hutchence was a star. He didn't know how not to be a star. He was that rare thing: a Morrison, a Jagger, a Hendrix. A natural showman who embodied the great rock stance and pose, the moves, the sexuality (God, he dripped that). When Michael Hutchence took to the stage, he didn't just perform, he became part of the stage, the body of the music; it rippled through his lean, muscled body, ground itself in his balls and worked its way through his torso. His hands were expression, instruments that opened and caressed and carved and executed, his lips and his eyes were the focus of yearning, pain, come on and go down. He made girls and women want him and want him badly. He made boys and men wish they could make girls and women want them that way, that easily, that specially. He was cocky, aggressive, angry; gentle, understanding and friendly. He was bigger than life and he played on it. Even when INXS were having a bad night – and they had them, it was worth a ticket just to watch Hutch strut his stuff. He preened, camped, slithered, strode the stage in control and in the spotlight.

He always seemed that way. That was the public Hutchence, but like many of his contemporaries his private nature was at odds with the so-called wild man of rock tag he got landed with. Booze, drugs, women, money, sure, Mike had it all . . . yet he never rammed it down your throat, never expected anybody to kiss his ass, lick his boot heels.

He was also Australia's only true rock'n'roll superstar. Sure, there are names that may be as big, careers that embraced massive international success: the brothers Gibb, Olivia Newton John, Peter Allen, groups such as Men At Work, Midnight Oil, AC/DC, the Little River Band and Air Supply, latterly silverchair and Savage Garden. With the exception of silverchair, Midnight Oil and AC/DC – they were kindly, middle-of-the-road acts most mums and dads would be happy to share on a Saturday night with a bottle of wine.

Perhaps, one day, blond-haired, attitude-laden, intense, Daniel Johns of silverchair might become the superstar Michael was. And you don't know whether to feel sorry or happy for him. Superstar is a condition, a lifestyle, a way of being, and very few can handle it. But Michael, he not only handled it, he loved it. He was the one – worldwide. And one is the loneliest number you can ever be. He was proudly Australian and ever a gypsy. He roamed the world but never forgot his beginnings. This was a restless spirit, an adventurer, a romantic – deeply so, a total lascivious hedonist. Contradictions and extremes abounded in Michael yet as he finally sang, he was just a man and he knew it.

Once when we were talking about fame I mentioned The Kinks' song 'Celluloid Heroes', with its lyrics about the stars whose names are written in concrete along Hollywood Boulevard. He looked at me in the way he most liked – he kind of fixed you with his eyes then homed in on whatever they found . . . if you could match his gaze. "The real heroes are out there each night. All the kids, the mums and dads, our families and friends, the people who make the whole thing work for us. Anybody who buys the records and listens. You know what I hate – I hate people who come up to me with a record or programme or something and say 'Could you just sign this: it's for my friend'. And you know it's for them. It's so false. They just want the signature for their own little ego trip and you know they aren't a real fan. They just want to impress people. Doesn't matter that they hate the music, never go to a show and couldn't give a damn if we ever made another record. The real fans – they *are* amazing. They stick with you. That autograph becomes part of their life. But in a way – when you're on-stage it's quite strange because there are moments when you look at that sea of faces and they're adoring you and want to connect and be part of it and you're up there pulling it all off and almost laughing – not at them but just at the unreality of the situation."

Michael Hutchence always had that human touch, that genuine ability to look beyond the obvious and see the seam and fold of what lay underneath – except, sometimes, when it came to himself. He saw families within families – that whole extended infinite circle of contact spanning outwards from the band at the centre was a gestalt made of infinite families. And he was part of one of the most enduring families in rock – INXS. A bunch of guys who came together as kids and never changed a member – and it's hard to think of another band that endured so long without a sacking, a split or splinter.

The story of INXS began in 1971 when Kirk Pengilly and his best mate Tim Farriss formed Guiness, a high school band that even auditioned nine-year-old Jon Farriss for the drummer's chair and booted him out because of his age.

By the time Guiness split, the third Farriss, Andrew, already had a band up and running with a couple of teens named Garry Gary Beers and Michael Hutchence. It seemed obvious: Tim and Kirk joined, Jon – by then 16 – got the drummer's gig. Fuelled by faith and belief, the pilgrimage to the top stuttered into life.

How Hutch ended up in the band is already the stuff of lore. Born in Sydney at about 5am on January 22, 1960, the first child of Kelland and Patricia Hutchence (who already had a daughter, Tina), Michael Kelland Frank Hutchence spent most of his early years in Hong Kong where his father moved the family for business reasons. He grew up around other expatriate children, gained a brother, Rhett, and attended the favoured school, the King George V. In 1972 the family moved back to Sydney settling in pleasant suburban Belrose. Everything was nice. Nice is one of those icky words. But nice it was. A proper start, good start, as they say in the text books.

His first day at Killarney Heights High School wasn't looking so good though and it was only the intervention of a kid named Andrew Farriss that saved him from a painful initiation by a bunch of older kids. They became mates – and before their teens were over started writing songs together: Andrew the music, Michael the words. A creative partnership that became one of the longest and strongest in rock.

But Hutch tells the story of these years better than anybody else, and did so in December 1984 to *The Sydney Morning Herald*.

"If you have a one-bedroom home in Hong Kong you have a servant. We had servants. We had a woman in Hong Kong for seven years and she was like a mother. I'm still really sloppy.

"Dad the capitalist was working for Haig Scotch and then ended up in the rag trade . . . The first school I went to (on returning from Hong Kong) was horrifying. Here I was a little English brat from Honkers arriving at Killarney Heights, which was one of the worst schools in Australia. It didn't have that cocoon of gentility of Hong Kong, suddenly you were on your arse. And on the first day I had a fight. It was a totally new mentality and I had to learn that.

"Strangely though I could never understand the concept of racism. I know that sounds really sick with the colonial attitude but all my friends were Chinese, Americans and Portuguese or English – from everywhere in the world. Hong Kong was very transient, you lose friends all the time and you had to constantly make new ones – you're never that close.

"I had a little folk band with a couple of people and we used to do Peter, Paul and Mary. I think that was when I was about 12.

"In Sydney we lived in Belrose. It was a good time actually. My parents got divorced when I was 16 – my mum's a very independent professional . . . and my father's very traditional. They got divorced and he went to the Philippines. I went to the States and lived for a year in LA when I was 15 with my mother. She was doing make-up, lifting all those wrinkles for Beverly Hills people before they went to parties.

"I used to spend most of my time by myself and listened to music and started writing prose, tons of it. It was very flowery, very descriptive, but I never really associated it with music. To me it was separate. It was just a way of getting something out of me because I didn't have many friends and I just totally enjoyed it. I'd just lie on my bed and write, and in LA I was getting into drugs and subverting what I was supposed to do with my life, as far as my father was concerned especially.

"Back home my friend Andrew was getting into music and I arrived back a 'cool cat'. He had his little band and I started hanging out and just used to sit down and watch. All that happened was Andrew needed someone to sing while he was testing out the drummer and said 'do you want to sing along for a while', and I started doing it, really badly, at 17.

"We had this thing called 'The Circle' and it was a very cliquey group. We'd listen to Deep Purple and Status Quo and drive around in panel vans screwing our heads off. This was out in swimming pool and Volvo land. We were into mysticism, and recorded really strange stuff, experimental.

"We started off with a remarkably naive attitude, and belief and faith. It was like being the three musketeers or something. If you have that in a band, it's an unbelievable situation.

"It is a horrible grind if I look at it now with a totally different perspective. I mean you don't have anything to eat all day, you load your equipment up stupid steps, set it all up, do your sound check, do your show, get paid $10, load it all down and get home at three in the morning. But you're so into it you don't even notice.

"It was very idealistic, it was a way of expressing stuff that I had in my head. I like writing it down and converting it and singing it.

"If you write a song you think, 'That's not a bad song', and then you think, 'Well, maybe I can write a better one than that'. If you think you've made it or think you've got to the end, then it's all over because then it becomes boring doesn't it?

"The drugs and sex and stuff is all true. It's easy to indulge. People want you to do that, people love seeing people slowly die, they're very insect-like. There's a strange curiosity watching a person fall to bits, and how they cope. It's very cannibal in one sense."

It's a revealing and blunt statement and worth remembering. The growing adult picturing the excitable boy who left for Perth, Western Australia, when the Farriss family moved there in early 1978 taking Jon with them. At Tim's instigation the band decided to go as well.

Hutch got in a car with Kirk and drove the 3279 kilometres to the other side of Australia "with a Tupperware container of Chinese chopped vegetables ready for the wok in the desert".

Perth is the most isolated city in the world. It isn't in the desert but is near enough to being surrounded by it. The nearest major city, Bunbury, is some 170km south, the nearest northwards, Geraldton, is 500km away. It's paradise lost if you can stand the now extreme conservative Liberal politics and want to live in a bubble.

In 1978 it was still swinging on the tail end of the Seventies mining boom that had made WA a very rich state, full of fat millionaires. Many of the idle rich would fall into disgrace in the Eighties and Nineties as "bottom-of-the-harbour" asset disguising and tax avoidance schemes were uncovered alongside a web of political intrigue. Shady involvement with the business elite would eventually disgrace a Labor Government and send some of its members to jail.

Perched on the beautiful Swan River about 12km from the coast, Perth is strikingly healthy. The air is clean, the water is clean, the coastal beaches are blue ocean, sparkling sand and legendary pleasuregrounds. Sun, sand and surf; the maxim for laid-back reverence. The rest of the country tries to ignore Perth, except when a major sporting event occurs there. There is a ridiculously strong East-West rivalry which is almost as pointless as the rivalry between Melbourne and Sydney.

When the Farriss Brothers Band arrived, Perth was at a cultural nexus. A year or so earlier, British punks – the genuine article – had begun arriving with their emigrating-to-a-new-life parents. Skinhead or mohawked, bovver-booted, leather-jacketed, pierced and completely displaced, they had no idea what to do. A Perth slum was the equivalent of a middle-class suburb in the turf they'd so recently vacated. There was no reason to kick heads in, smash up phone boxes, loot stores or trash pubs in the name of anarchy. They lasted until the ruling bikies decided enough was enough: one evening the worst of Perth's skinheads were virtually wiped out as a force when they needled the until-then-patient bikers once too often. Born to be wild came down hard and vicious.

Perth was so removed from anarchy that even the students never gave a toss about anything. Once the Vietnam war had ended, the campuses slipped into lethargy, inter-faculty wars occurring only over such world-shattering issues as who could put on the best piss-up.

But the punks inspired bands who played in a few dark, soggy-carpeted pits where the new wave festered and eventually spread

17

into the well-established hotel and campus circuit where until then blues, boogie and rock ruled. Bands like The Triffids, Mannikins, Victims, Cheap Nasties and Scientists emerged. Campus radio championed their rites and those of the overseas icons who were delivering an instant – if somewhat short-lived revolution – in the UK. Or so it seemed to us.

Yet despite its isolation, international tourists flooded through Perth on their Australian tours: Elvis Costello in his winkle-pickers, a sullen Lou Reed, Wreckless Eric, Madness and Blondie, who put Perth on the world map when Debbie Harry commented on the quality of the city's cocaine.

Drugs were a matter of fact. Marijuana plantations in the south-west had long been producing some of the country's finest ganja – and in great quantities. Importers ensured a regular supply of the legendary DP (Durban Poison) from South Africa and quality acid: the home brew was a bit dodgy. Mescaline, uppers, downers, smack, purple hearts, opiates . . . it was a regular supply and easily obtainable.

Into this environment the Farriss Brothers Band fitted like a glove, their parents settling into well-to-do Nedlands, just a few minutes walk from the University of WA, in a friendly, large, back-street house with a typically big barbecue backyard.

A 10-minute drunken stagger away was the Broadway Tavern, not a big barn like some of Perth's legendary rooms on the pub circuit such as The Raffles, Nookenburra and Charles Hotel, but a bar with a bluesy crowd and vibe, where it was possible on most nights for 200+ customers to just lay back, get smashed and stoned and listen to the band playing for their life.

Getting those days in focus is difficult. The exact date in '78 the Farriss Brothers Band entered the somewhat fuzzy personal picture is lost in the haze and daze. But it was at a Broadway Tavern session, maybe a sundowner. The muffled sound coming from inside wasn't instantly recognisable, neither were the faces of the group as we paid to enter. The music was nothing remarkable: new wavish pop with a definite XTC bent, a touch of The Members or Department S maybe, some bubbly mainstream pop that smelt suspiciously of Bowie and some funky rock rhythms and riffing. This was a band that was still sorting out its personality and character. What was remarkable

18

was the skinny mainframe out front who seemed lost in some sort of semi-epileptic fit of his own making. Michael Hutchence – a kid who three years earlier was worried and embarrassed by his severe acne problems – didn't seem too hung up. Somehow we ended up in front of this curly-haired streak who close-up looked a lot younger than he did from a distance. He seemed possessed and dispossessed, yet already was learning how to work a crowd. And he could sing some. A big, yet velvety, husky voice. It didn't pitch right all the time and his top end was rough but time and experience would take care of those problems. One that could jump out at you or sit with you. That night I reckon the Farriss Brothers Band and the bar broke even. In other words half the crowd got pissed, chatted and forgot about the group. The other half, late teen college girls in particular, hung around watching.

A few weeks earlier a much bigger name interstate mob had played with far less interest from the same pack. There was something going down that session, some of that chemicrazy natural reaction stuff where the hormones, male and female, get jumbled up with the aural and visual feed and – stimulated by either the drug and/or drink of choice – produce a positive feed to whatever degree of consciousness remains. The get-off factor. The higher the better. Later the get-off factor for INXS would rival that of U2. Get-off doesn't get much bigger. But that's down the track.

Ten years later, in the guise of editor of *Revue*, the weekly music section of the *West Australian*, Perth's only daily newspaper, I visited the Farriss parents, Jill (who sadly passed away a few years ago) and Dennis in that same beautiful house in the back streets of Nedlands. *Kick* had just gone to No 3 in the US, the first single off it, 'Need You Tonight', to No 1. Their sons were one-half of arguably the biggest band in the world.

That they allowed a perfect stranger into their home, and shared two hours of their time, never hiding an emotion, shining with pride, recounting story after story, most on the record, is as good a reflection as you'd find of the family INXS. Out came the photo albums that weren't tucked away in impossible to reach places, and we were back there again, a decade earlier and before. Boys becoming men. Ray Davies' "stars in every

19

street". Hutch had hollow legs, they said. At family barbecues he would eat and eat and never get fat. The Farriss family regarded him as a fourth son. And they remembered how shy and lacking in self-confidence he was in those early days.

Their rehearsal room was a small bedroom in which they crammed and jammed. How they fitted in is hard to imagine. In 1988 that room had a couple of gold discs on the wall, and there were others elsewhere in the house. Rock is born in similar bedrooms and garages all over the world; that's part of its romance and enduring spirit. In that old suburban home the trace of INXS' beginnings still eked out of the walls, as if the music had been captured in the brick. The photos were of everyday people who wanted to better themselves. That's what seeing the Farriss Brothers Band in 1978 was really about. It all sounds soppy and romantic and idealised but when you're 16, 17, 18 and you're making music and that's all you want to do then there are no limits, only the thrill – and the devil – inside.

Taking whatever gigs they could get, the Farriss Brothers Band found itself playing WA's north-west mining towns, where the miners and their families were starved of live music. Tough country, tough people and tough lessons. A year of such gigs and endless rehearsals and the Farriss Brothers Band returned to Sydney, like any band of their age, and started looking for their ticket to ride.

Australian music had a lot of ticket riders at that time. The second coming was underway with two streams running parallel to each other, occasionally intersecting. The big names were bold aggressions sparked by the punk splatter but retaining their Australian suburban and urban roots. Born and bred of the Australian pub circuit – said to be the hardest, and best, learning ground in the world, an endless round of gigs up and down the coast, a 3000km shuffle from Adelaide to Melbourne to Sydney to Brisbane and all points in between – were traditional rockers like Midnight Oil, Cold Chisel, The Angels, Dragon and Rose Tattoo. Closer to the raw punk and new wave were the legendary Saints, fronted by Chris Bailey and Ed Kuepper, whose seminal 'I'm Stranded' single predated UK punk by a year; the menacing, depraved Boys Next Door who became The Birthday Party who became Nick Cave and The

Bad Seeds; Flowers, led by trippy Iva Davies on his way to Icehouse and becoming one of Australia's finest songwriters; cerebral pop stars The Go-Betweens from Brisbane, who would later become more popular in England and Europe as indeed would Kuepper and Bailey; the glam-orous Teenage Radio Stars whose implosion with that of Jab would give birth to The Models; the always underestimated but seminal Flaming Hands; an infant industro-electronic SPK; and the timeless, indefinable X. If there was a surf god and barbecue king then it was Richard Clapton whose 1975 smash *Girls On the Avenue* was bested only by the finest east coast sand'n'surf set to date, 1977's *Goodbye Tiger*. A few years later Clapton would produce INXS' second album *Underneath The Colours*. And in their own world – but best of all – were the mighty Split Enz headed by the Finn brothers, Tim and Neil: already a cult sensation in the UK after being championed by Phil Manzanera and touring in 1976 and '78, the Enz were a year shy of *True Colours*, the album that would cross the zany art-rockers over to a pop market and make them Australia's biggest drawcard. Years later Crowded House would arise from the mid-Eighties ashes of the Enz and become one of the most celebrated pop bands in the world.

Point is, it wasn't going to be easy. Everywhere there were independent labels mailing out so much coloured vinyl that black became a radical statement, all of them releasing records by wannabes of varying intent and ability, most of whom would, of course, flutter briefly then die in their own feedback.

In this cornucopia of raging slabs the Farriss Brothers Band somehow came to the attention of the manager of Midnight Oil, Gary Morris, a whirlwind of a bloke whose passion for music and absolute devotion to his bands is as legendary as most of the acts he's managed. At the second Australian Record Industry Awards (ARIA) in 1987, Morris, representing multiple winners the Oils, delivered one of the moments in ARIA lore. "We do have room service in Australia, Bryan," Morris said, indicating Bryan Ferry's casually rumpled tuxedo. "You could have ordered an iron." Ferry was resplendent in the latest crushed-linen look set off by lapis-lazuli cufflinks and had even tied his own tie. Now fondly remembered as a prime example of Antipodean yobbo-ism, Morris happily stands his ground still:

"I'm a true yobbo and proud of it. A yobbo can walk a straight line." He can also talk and did – for 20 minutes – while accepting one of Midnight Oil's awards at the fifth ARIAs in 1990. His selected topics included the downfall of Western Civilisation.

INXS would become three times best group ARIA winners (1986, 1988 and 1991) and 1988's Outstanding Achievement Award winners for the phenomenon that was *Kick*.

Morris renamed them INXS at the suggestion of one of Midnight Oil's road crew, although conceptually he fancied the notion of "inaccessible", even suggesting they do no interviews and perform behind bars. However, Morris' commitments to Midnight Oil, whose brilliant, politic, heartland star was just beginning to rise, meant he couldn't give the youngsters the time they really needed. So he got a young manager and agent named Chris Murphy to check 'em out. CM Murphy needed just one look. He'd been searching for a group he could take all the way to the top and in INXS he found them. It's strange how often that happens. A few years later a young record company deputy director at LA-based indie IRS Records, Jay Boburg, would travel all the way to New Orleans to see an unknown band named R.E.M. perform before an audience of five and sign them on the spot. They would stay six albums, leaving only when they got just too big for the label to handle.

On the other side of the world every move being made by the Farriss Brothers Band and INXS was literally paralleled by a similarly unknown young Irish group. In 1977 the Feedback were playing Rolling Stones and Beach Boys covers in Dublin bars. They then changed their name to the Hype before Bono, The Edge, Adam Clayton and Larry Mullens finally settled on U2 in 1978. After winning a talent contest in Limerick that year, they were spotted and signed by manager Paul McGuinness and subsequently signed to CBS Records Ireland, releasing their début EP *U2:3* featuring the track 'Out Of Control' in 1979. Neither knew it then but their paths were already marked to intersect in 1988 when *Kick* and U2's *The Joshua Tree* would be the two biggest records in the world and the associated tours would criss-cross the US and Europe hot on one another's heels. Bono and Michael Hutchence would become great friends and neighbours in France; and Bono would play a significant role in his friend's life – before and after.

In Sydney, C M Murphy signed INXS to the indie Deluxe which was distributed through RCA and the first INXS single, 'Simple Simon' backed with 'We Are The Vegetables', hit the racks in May 1980, just nine months after their live début at the Ocean-view Hotel, Toukley. 'Simple Simon' isn't one of the great début singles in the history of rock. A rather immature and loose piece of quirky new wave pop, 'Simon' was as simple as he was forgettable; their second single 'Just Keep Walking' wasn't. Not that it was a masterpiece but there was a strut and pace to it, a delivery that got it on the turntables and made it a reasonable introduction to their début album *INXS*, that, sadly, lived up to the title of its final track, 'Wishy Washy'.

But the third single, now that was the goods. It wasn't original but it was a mighty, swaggering cover of a Sixties classic, 'The Loved One', by The Loved Ones who featured Gerry Humphries, brother of Barry Humphries – now adored universally as Dame Edna Everage, then as the foul-mouthed Ozzie half-wit-come-cliché Barry Mckenzie. 'The Loved One' was a barrel-chested, cock-busting bluesy swamp of a song with fat chords and a genuinely sex bomb Hutchence vocal. Grunt and grind, INXS let 'The Loved One' sashay and swing its butt big and broad and grand. 'The Loved One' gave INXS their first top 20 hit. Six years later it would be properly immortalised when they re-recorded it for inclusion on *Kick*.

Murphy, meanwhile, was working his charges endlessly, the time-honoured Australian way. In 1981, INXS played 280 gigs, criss-crossing the country on the Fear And Loathing Tour, The Campus Tour, Stay Young Tour and Tour With No Name.

The next single, 'Stay Young', was an even better original and the only real hit on *Underneath The Colours*, INXS' second album, produced by Richard Clapton and released in October 1982. Stronger than the début, it was still a patchy affair with Clapton doing a reasonable job of tying a lot of loose ends together and disguising the band's let's-try-everything-and-see-what-works approach. The patented funky bottom end was coming on a little stronger but INXS still appeared a band with too many ideas and not enough focus. Still, it went to No 15. The second single (and last on Deluxe), 'Night Of Rebellion', came and went in a blink and is now worth $100 (Australian) on the collector's marketplace.

Clapton, a frizzy-haired, bouncy, larrikin poet with a killer voice and a larger than life nature, told Toby Cresswell in the January '98 edition of *Juice*, "Chris (Murphy) tricked me into coming down to the Paddington Green Hotel in late 1981. There were about nine middle-aged guys there to get a drink, and there was Murphy pacing up and down. INXS came out and at the end of the first set I went into their dressing room raving and raving and we hit it off.

"There was this passion. To come out and be playing for me and Chris and nine drunks just blew me away . . . "

Later, Clapton comments, "When I first knew Michael he had absolutely no confidence." Outsiders never guessed. Clapton blew the album's budget getting the right atmosphere for the vocals.

Phil Mortlock, the Australian head of WEA Records when INXS signed with their first 'major' in July 1982, wasn't as convinced. In *The Bulletin* (October 4, 1988) he recollected, "They were support to Cold Chisel and I just remember thinking how young they all seemed. I saw Midnight Oil for the first time around then, too, and they struck me as if they'd been performing all their lives. INXS were just like a bunch of kids. What I didn't detect then was the strength and determination I'd discover later."

He got an indication when Murphy arrived in his office with the single and video before WEA had even finalised the deal.

Three months later, the Mark Opitz produced *Shabooh Shoobah*, the band's third set and crucial first for WEA, arrived to critical acclaim, a top five slot and went gold – much faster than its predecessors. *Shabooh Shoobah* is really the first real INXS record, the album that defined a better part of their sound and began to pull together all the strains that had blown like fluffy clouds – some said a virus – through their music.

More importantly, *Shabooh Shoobah* opened and closed with a couple of killers, 'The One Thing' with its instantly recognisable guitar chord intro, thunderous Jon Farriss bouncing rhythm and centrepiece vogueing, heavily percussive chorus, and 'Don't Change', a beautiful melody and harmony roped together on a big ballad, irresistible and destined to become an anthem and fan favourite. The band took off on the 78-date Una Brilliante Band De Musica Amenizara Espectacula Tour – yeah, and it's still almost impossible to spell.

Ever seen a ghost? No. Well, watching INXS on that tour was like seeing ghosts . . . the ghosts of the Farriss Brothers Band. The faces and forms were familiar, still young but older and worn in, skin that had seen some highways and pitstops and then some but that's all that remained. In their place was a tough, rehearsed but still raw and edgy professional band. INXS for the first time looked the part. Hutchence had grown into his own psyche. Now he carried the sneer of one coming to terms with his own potential. His movements were even more sexual, his command poised and controlled; and there was that great rush and wash of energy between band and audience that Ray Manzarek of The Doors would tell me, years later, is the *ultimate* sensation – that to and fro force that builds and builds as the twin vampires in a room feed off each other, a great spirit out of control, sweeping everything along in its path, lifting possibilities and potential. INXS didn't pull it off every night, then neither did The Doors but twice I saw and felt the irresistible surge, knew that it wouldn't be long before Hutch and co. were big in Japan, America, Britain, Europe. It was there on that tour. Murphy had taken them the long way round and the band had done the rest.

The great years of INXS were beginning and backstage, post-show, you sensed even they, their minders and crew knew it. There was an optimism, a sense of growth, a confidence, a down-to-earth friendliness and a band that knew how to party. And girls queued up outside stage doors. Young, pretty, well-bred and not so well-bred girls. Bra-less, knickerless, sweaty, obsessed girls. Amidst them professional groupies looking for another notch on the bed post. In the late Eighties I spent an evening talking to a beautiful, intelligent, 30-something woman who for a decade had pursued her fantasies. As she said, "They (her men of rock) were lonely, a long way from home, looking for a little company and warmth. They came and went." The names she rattled off were as astounding as they were several supergroups long. She waited for Michael but he never came – not that year or any thereafter.

In January 1983, INXS signed to Atlantic Records for North America, making their début with 'The One Thing' single which immediately grabbed high rotation play on MTV and ended up making it to number 30 on the charts. *Shabooh Shoobah* followed to a warm critical reception. *Rolling Stone,* most famously, called it "novel in approach and stirring in execution . . . amid the current plague of identical synth-pop records, *Shabooh Shoobah* is no ordinary song and dance". The US tour kicked off in March, the first show played to an audience of 24 in a San Diego bar, two months later hitting the famous The Ritz in New Yawk City and finishing in California at the US Festival where INXS were second-up in front of 150,000 people. They were good enough to earn an encore.

The best story of the tour comes from Grant who told Toby Cresswell about the end result of supporting the fab all-girl pop group The Go-Gos: "Six boys/five girls – you can work it out. I'd ring up the road manager and say 'I'm missing a couple of guys', and he'd say, 'I think they're travelling on our bus today'. The next day he'd ring up and say, 'Have you seen Belinda?' " In the early Nineties I finally got around to asking the settled, married and well-established solo performing Belinda Carlisle about that tour. She laughed demurely, but refused to elaborate further.

Murphy and Grant had pulled it off; turned the rules upside down. As writer Clinton Walker observed in *The Bulletin* (October 4, 1988), "Murphy's huge gamble was to push an Australian band overseas before it had even 'made it' at home, but he never doubted the promise of INXS. He was only half-joking in 1982 when he said that he was taking the band overseas 'whether they were wanted or not'."

The MMA power base might have been surprised when as a result of a chance meeting with producer Nile Rogers – who already had credits with Chic, David Bowie, Duran Duran and Power Station under his belt – the band found themselves, in September 1983, in the legendary Power Station studios in NY where they cut 'Original Sin' in just two takes, much to Rogers' surprise. What Rogers didn't know at the time was that the band didn't think he was actually producing a session and were equally surprised to find it all down on tape. Add backing vocals from Darryl Hall of the then hugely successful Hall & Oates and 'Original Sin' was the biggest rumble in the INXS jungle yet – and their first Australian No 1.

By now INXS were on a roll – you see it in music from time to time. An outfit that's ahead of the game, rolling without questioning, going with instinct and confidence. Each release is better than its predecessor, the tours sell out bigger, faster and the band shows no sign of losing their spunk and fat-frying energy. Keeping to a schedule from hell, INXS cut their fourth album, *The Swing*, at England's Manor Studios with Nick Launay at the dials. Sessions began in September and the finishing flourishes were added in Australia in December.

New Year 1984 opened with 'Original Sin' at No 1 and yet another Australian tour. *The Swing* went straight in at No 1 on the Australian charts. Here is the archetypal INXS album, perhaps one of their three finest: for the first time the body of songs was nearly as strong as its standout cuts; the greatest weakness of *Shabooh Shoobah* is that they weren't. Launay implicitly understood INXS' greatest strengths and the album's title reflected the burbling funk underbelly he and the band pasted throughout the set.

The opening quintet of 'Original Sin', 'Melting In The Sun', 'I Send A Message', 'Dancing On The Jetty' and the title track was a searing rumble of pure visceral energised funk rock, through which Andrew Farriss and Hutchence wrought all the pop sensibilities they knew made great music. 'Burn For You' was a perfect Michael love song.

It didn't take a degree in music to realise that their songwriting skills had reached a new level. Of all the INXS albums, only *Kick* and *Welcome To Wherever You Are* match *The Swing* for its sheer energy and continuity. At the time though, critics ankletapped INXS. In the great tradition of Australian rock, INXS were running into the tall poppy syndrome and paying the price. Not that it mattered overseas where they were just getting bigger and bigger and bigger. And controversial.

Yeah, it is hard to imagine INXS ever being controversial but take a closer look at Hutchence's lyrics and you'll find all matter of comment slipped in. Growing up well off and wanting little, Mike had always rejected airs and graces as had the rest of INXS: they were writing and thinking about the common people a long time before Jarvis Cocker of Pulp wrote his marvellous anthem. And they were looking at what affected the you and I of this world. The more they travelled and saw, the more the lyrics pictured some of Michael's growing concerns.

'Original Sin' upset touchy America and brought about some remarkable reactions. The inspiration for the song came while the band was touring the deep South of the States. "We were watching kids playing on a front lawn of a house," Michael said at the time. "It was a black neighbourhood so there were a lot of black kids playing, and just one white kid. And everyone was getting along just fine. I thought, every day those kids wake up, the possibility is they'll be a little more prejudiced than the day before."

So an innocent song about racial prejudice and kids seeing their fantasies slip away enraged the crank factor, particularly in the extremely conservative mid-west Bible belt where DJs playing the song attracted death threats from the Ku Klux Klan and the Young Nazi party. At one show a protester threw a .45 revolver on stage.

Are these the kind of lyrics you'd kill for? *"Dream on black boy, Dream on white girl, And wake up to a brand new day, To find your dreams have been washed away . . ."*

Hutchence was unconcerned by the uproar, more pleased than sorry, only regretting that the fuss slowed sales of *The Swing* in the US where it eventually peaked at No 52. "I don't think one thin page of words can change the world," he said, "but it can push things around. It made all the right people angry."

Murphy and Grant wouldn't have been unhappy either, especially when *Billboard*, the American music industry paper, got involved in the furore and backed the band, lambasting DJs who didn't play the song and – in gentler words – accusing them of being gutless. Such publicity is hard to get at the best of times.

Elsewhere 'Original Sin' topped the French and Argentinean charts, went close in several other European countries, including Germany, and made the sextet superstars in Japan where

28

the fans – once they're on-board – will go to any lengths to get to know their band.

"They will work part-time jobs for most of the year, then book plane flights for the whole tour months in advance – following the same schedule. I don't know how they find out," Hutchence told Sheryle Bagwell in an interview in *The Australian* (June 1, 1985).

"What do these girls want from the band?" she asked.

"Sex – no fantasy I suppose," answers Hutchence. "It is probably very personal for each one but it seems each believes that there is some golden string of rapport, an attachment like an umbilical chord between themselves and you. We don't downplay these people at all. In fact, there is a stigma attached to them that shouldn't be there."

1985 opened with three blockbuster summer concerts, the largest of which – in Adelaide at Football Park for the Year of the Youth – drew a sell-out 20,000 punters and blistering performances from Hunters & Collectors and the headliners. The talk next day was of Hutchence rolling around the stage and just how tight his jeans were.

Even more significant than the 'hang of Hutch' was news that noted producer Chris Thomas would come to Australia to produce their fifth album, *Listen Like Thieves*. Thomas is big league. The man who began his career as engineer on The Beatles' *White Album* had by then worked with Pink Floyd, Bowie, Pete Townshend, Roxy Music, The Sex Pistols, and former rock journo Chrissie Hynde's glorious The Pretenders. Most recently, he's worked on Pulp's 1995 classic *Different Class* and its excellent, much darker, less commercial follow-up *This Is Hardcore*. Coincidentally, Pulp are another band who had to wait a decade (and then some) before they broke through.

Sessions started in March at Sydney's Studios and were completed in August at Air Studios in London. In between time INXS played for Live Aid at the Sydney Entertainment Centre in a performance that was, of course, beamed around the world. Thirteen years later, the irony is as obvious as it is sad. Live Aid made Robert Frederick Zenon Geldof, born October 5, 1954, Dun Laoghaire, County Dublin, the most celebrated man in music. And rightfully so. Shocked by the terrible pictures of the Ethiopian famine he saw on television, Geldof put his mouth where his heart was and organised the astonishing Band Aid aggregation of stars and superstars that recorded the single, 'Do They Know It's Christmas'. Selling more than 3 million copies, thanks to Geldof's foresight in maintaining financial control of every aspect of the record's production, manufacture and distribution, it netted famine relief more than 96p of the £1.35p retail price.

If Geldof had stopped there it would have been enough but, of course, he knew it wasn't. Somehow he strong-armed the world's rock luminaries to stages in London and Philadelphia with cuts to elsewhere in the world, and then linked the whole globe by television. Where were you the day of Live Aid? Chances are you were one of the estimated 1,000,000,000 pie-eyed in front of the screen watching Sade, Queen, Bob Dylan, Neil Young, The Cars, Beach Boys, Pat Metheny, Santana, Madonna (how well I remember her youthful early set), Kenny Loggins, Bryan Adams, Crosby Stills and Nash, Eric Clapton, Judas Priest, REO Speedwagon, Page and Plant, Status Quo, Elvis Costello, Bryan Ferry, Sting, Paul Young, Adam Ant, Simple Minds, U2, The Who (marvellous), Paul McCartney, Mick Jagger, Tina Turner, Elton John, Spandau Ballet and David Bowie. Phil Collins even made it to both stages thanks to Concorde.

The biggest television audience of all time pledged more than 50 million pounds. Live Aid stands tall as one of the greatest musical events of all time, rivalled perhaps only by Woodstock in name and fame, but in achievement unsurpassed before or since.

Throughout it all Geldof remained dignified, eloquent, funny and humble. He still was a few years later, on a perfect summer morning when he made me coffee in the penthouse suite of a hotel overlooking the still ocean that kicked gently at Scarborough Beach, a 10-minute drive from Perth. Dressed simply in a ripped T-shirt, baggy pants and a pair of those hotel towelling thongs, and wearing a four-day growth, Geldof was all deeply set, heavily rimmed eyes that picked their mark; he moved with a gentle stagger. At one stage he sat down and started picking articles out of the pile of papers that sat on the suite's balcony table. Each demonstrated a wrong, an ill in the world. A political disgrace. A crime against humanity, or simply against a small group of people somewhere in the vast melee of the title fight for survival. It was easy to understand why they called him Saint Bob. The silent strength of character and depth of thought Geldof revealed that day were unspoken reminders of what he had achieved.

Years later the long string of fate that was unwound that July day in 1985 when the world stopped for rock'n'roll at its most powerful and universal would wrap itself round Michael Hutchence and become a significant part of a terrible tragedy that left a trail of broken hearts, shattered lives, press innuendo and a world wondering why.

2

Dogs In Space

Recently, somebody was speculating seriously – again – that rock is dead. Great blocks of news print were devoted to analysis, definition and conclusion. The outbreak of what's become one of the oldest known recurring viruses to affect the bloated beast that is contemporary music was set off by a very small downturn in CD sales for the previous financial year. The industry rippled, trying to absorb the 'shocking' news that profits were down the odd million or three; 'serious' music observers pulled out the obituary and updated it. All bollocks, of course; rock isn't dead, nor is it about to die. Sure the beast has plenty of fat and some rather unattractive sores but dead . . . if it is there are an awful lot of phantoms out there and they're cutting some damn innovative and empowering music in their misty morph state.

What has changed, though, is the way rock presents itself and deals with its public. In the days before the technological revolution sliced through the Eighties, opening up the computer games market, before sport became a colossus, extreme sports took a chunk of the youth market and before records represented a big dollar outlay in comparison with other forms of entertainment, music loved its fans, pandered to and solicited them with all kinds of collectible jewels, special pressings, events. Sadly, that's mostly history. Economics took care of it a while ago.

And without fans, rock will eventually die. Fandom is a wonderful thing. Bands need all the fans they can get. Sadly, fans are now forgotten by the giant combine harvester that is today's record industry, munching its way through the cornfields of cash each year, chewing up sales as fast as it can and spitting out more and more CDs in the hope that somebody's gonna like the taste. Some companies try harder than others, many just don't try at all.

Now fans have to look after themselves. They're still out there but they've had to change mediums. Many diehard fans are in space now, cyberspace, where there are thousands of lists dedicated to thousands of bands, where fans e-mail each other about band-related matters 24 hours a day, seven days a week, or visit their chat group and discuss why their cat is named Hutch, their dog Pengers, their goldfish Jon, how much is that 12″ white label version of 'Mystify' really worth, the complete tour schedule for 1986. Good stuff, fan stuff. Best of all it's global.

The INXS List is one of the biggest groups on the 'Net and they've had a hard time of it recently. But join them and you'll find a group of people from 15-50 with a wealth of knowledge and a rather remarkable sense of concern and friendship. Tad obsessive, at times, but, hey, that's what fans are.

And in any book about Michael Hutchence, the fans have to be right up there. That he would have wanted. He would have also told the industry and those analysts to 'get a life' in not so many words. INXS have always looked after their fans. It comes from their no-bullshit take on life. Frauds, posers and fakes have never been big in INXS country. Hopefully, that comes across somewhere in all of this rattle and hum about life, death and the grand mystery.

Intermission
11.54pm, March 10, 1998: Tonight the Buffalo-born, DIY, punky, curly-locked, singer/songwriter Ani DiFranco played the Metro Theatre in Sydney, a lovely room that holds 1600 and remarkably was sold out. DiFranco, who from the start has run her own record label, Righteous Babe, distributing and promoting her entire catalogue – eight studio albums, a compilation, a double live set in nine years – crosses brute verve and adept plucking on the acoustic guitar with outspoken, politic and observational songs through which she talks her intimate tales – much like the legendary storyteller Utah Phillips with whom she recorded the spellbinding and life rich *The Past Didn't Go Anywhere* album. DiFranco spoke, laughed and sang of her first abortion at 17, of moving to NY when she was 18 and going to the Knitting Factory where John Zorn, Marc Ribot, Eliott Sharp spank the avant further out of shape, and visiting the Not Room

on the first floor – so small it isn't really a room – to listen to the poets because "in Buffalo we too had words in long columns where every second verse ended in a rhyming sound"; she found every poem laced with sexual innuendo and death and passion; even poems about children and dogs. She sang about lust and love – lustily and with love, betrayal and simply saying "fuck you" to boys who took her girl for granted.

Invariably, interviews with musicians, if they are long enough and good enough, end up with a session of "have you heard?". One of my Michael Hutchence interviews ended up in a rather deep-seated discussion about arguably the greatest female singer/songwriter of them all, Joni Mitchell. Amidst his record collection there used to be a signed copy of Joni's definitive crossover album *The Hissing Of Summer Lawns*. That led to a mumble about female singer/songwriters. Going for the one-up, I admit, I mentioned Ani DiFranco, then just four albums into her reasonably well-kept-secret cult career. Michael lowered his sunglasses and said, "She's good. That song 'What If No One's Watching', I like that. The idea of what if when we're dead, we are just dead?" His ears were well-tuned.

Supporting Ani was fellow singer/songwriter Dar Williams, a more traditional, no less exuberant, mid-twenties woman with attitude and something to say, who in both look and lyrical substance leans closer to the great Joni. Dar ended by thanking her computer list. "There's a thing called the Dar list and some of its members are here tonight. Isn't that so amazing, a hemisphere away from where I live my life there's all these fans thanks to the computer."

Which kind of supports the opening rant.
End Of Intermission

So how come a new chapter, right here, not even halfway through the INXS story? Surely, it would be better to begin the second chapter on the high of *Kick* and relate the slow downward spiral thereafter? True, and I thought about that, there's a certain poetry and nicely balanced ten years on either side. But it doesn't take into account that with *The Swing*, INXS ended their apprenticeship.

The big league – and despite their successes they hadn't

cracked the US or UK yet – was tantalisingly close. INXS were about to graduate; they just didn't know on which day. The watershed proved to be 'What You Need', the second single in the US (and the first in Australia) off *Listen Like Thieves* which arrived in November 1985. Critics got sweaty about it; why is harder to say. *Listen Like Thieves* is the growth hormone INXS needed to ingest before they could make *Kick*. Leaving the writing now almost entirely to Andrew Farriss and Hutchence, the album is closer to their live sound but reeks of a producer getting to know the act, and the act pawing at something they knew was there but just wouldn't come out.

The first single in the US, 'This Time', was pretty pop but not particularly memorable and staggered to No 81. US *Rolling Stone* disagreed: "INXS rocks with passion and seals the deal with a backbeat that'll blackmail your feet." Heaven knows what they thought when 'What You Need' hit the stores and left 'This Time' in the vortex of its jungle juiced, big beat, slap in the face funk out. Strut your stuff boy, shake those tail feathers girl. And, be careful, bam, slam, ooh that rifferama chorus got you again. No 5, thank you. INXS were *beeg* time, this time.

'What You Need' also gave *Listen Like Thieves* the big boot – up the charts. It fell one notch short of the top 10 which seems fair enough in retrospect, although at the time everyone was hanging out for it to bust double figures, and sold more than one million copies in the US. Spanking the Yanks (or Brits, for that matter, but specially the Yanks) at their own game is something Australians love. It's also small-minded stuff and an admission of a far deeper social malaise that afflicts the country: it has a weak culture of its own, constantly borrows from others and fights to deny any focus on its only true culture: that of its native people, the Aborigines. As a result there's a mine of psychological disasters at play: for many years no matter how good a homegrown act might be, unless they succeeded overseas they were still seen as lesser individuals; then when they did succeed overseas, more often than not they became victims of the tall poppy syndrome and were accused of selling out. This was, of course, pure crap and more to do with the subliminal notion that Australia is actually artistically inferior to the rest of the big people's world – America and Europe.

This stupidity has waned in recent years as Australia becomes more cosmopolitan and multi-cultural – despite the efforts of a shrinking percentage of its citizens and some rather out-dated, old and not-so-old politicians – but its radio networks are still obliged to play a set quotient of Australian music and peddle bad international music at the expense of good local.

It was something Michael Hutchence felt deeply about and something that came up in every conversation we had. By March 1986, when INXS took a break from the roads they'd been careering up and down for the past six months, there was a whiff of it in the air. Later it would become an annoyance which Hutchence would rail against, as he did the treatment of the Aboriginal people. Michael loved music, all music, as long as it was good. He would talk happily about world music, the sounds and rhythms that drew him and the emotion in roots music, whether it be Irish, Aboriginal, Jamaican, Indian or Native American.

When INXS returned to their roots – the clubs and pubs – on the Get Out Of The House Tour in April 1993, we spent an hour one afternoon talking by a hotel pool in the port town of Fremantle, where the America's Cup yacht race had been held after the now-disgraced local entrepreneur Alan Bond had snatched it from the Americans.

During the interview, Hutch kept returning to the young bands INXS had selected in each city to open the shows, how keen he was to get more involved with working with young up-and-comers, how astounded he had been to return to Australia and find so many quality young outfits. As it turned out that wasn't to be but his words still hold true today, "Pride, believe in yourself. Don't listen to what people say. Australian music is as good as the music anywhere in the world. Australians have to stop being so fucking insular. You know, Australian rock journos, a lot of them piss me off because they just don't know what they're talking about. They don't get out of Australia, they have no idea of just how many awful bands there are in the States, how many totally crap records are released, they don't see that, don't see anything but what the record companies hold up before them. And radio, what's happened to radio here? They've got to be made to play more homegrown music."

Sadly, that included INXS music by then. No such problems though in 1986. You couldn't escape 'What You Need'. The question the title begged was personally answered in different ways by the band members. Andrew Farriss produced Australian singer/songwriter – and INXS tour backing vocalist – Jenny Morris' single 'You're Gonna Get Caught' which went Top 10 and gold, Tim did what Tim has always done – went fishing – and Michael starred in the Richard Lowenstein directed *Dogs In Space*.

Lowenstein holds a bigger-than-some space in INXS history. He'd been drawn into the family when Gary Grant went looking for him after Hutchence, enthralled by the stunning video to Hunters & Collectors' seminal 'Talking To A Stranger', a rough, tough, jagged rock, tribal funk undercut spellbinder that ran some seven-minutes, suggested he'd be the ideal director for the video for 'Burn For You'. Lowenstein appropriated an avant garde approach to the rock video; 'Talking To A Stranger' is a blur of out of focus bodies and faces, lights, fires and windswept beaches and cliffs. The very primitive essence of the song is dragged to the fore and the viewer is swept along with action as if they're riding a camera on tracks.

Lowenstein recalled in *The Bulletin* article his first and much earlier impression of INXS: "I wasn't a fan, no. It was at the Crystal Ballroom in Melbourne and I thought they were just like a bad imitation of The Ears, especially the lead singer."

Again, fate would have the last laugh. *Dogs In Space*, based loosely around the story of The Ears, featured Hutchence in his first lead role. So who the hell were The Ears? Today, they are long forgotten but between 1979 and 1981, the sextet of Mick Lewis, Carl Manuel, Charles Meo, Cathy McQuade, Sam Sejavka and Gus Till, gained some notoriety as arty punks on the Melbourne circuit, releasing just two singles 'Leap For Lunch' (on an unknown label) and 'Scarecrow', a 7" (MISS26) on Missing Link in 1981.

Now, and this is where it gets funky, The Ears may have been a short-lived affair but what about their members? Sejavka, the vocalist, was supposedly the inspiration for Hutchence's character, and went on to play in mid-Eighties indie cult, twisted poppers Beargarden with Manuel, before becoming an award-winning script and play writer. In 1990, he wrote the script for the film, *Earth Bound,* and in '92 the stage play, *In Angel Gear.*

Meo ended up a few years later in Melbourne shockabilly, post-Iggy and Captain Beefheart big band Olympic Sideburns, but left in 1984. McQuade left a much bigger mark, forming the funk-base, post-disco, Deckchairs Overboard in Sydney, and leaving a handful of singles, a self-titled album and mini-album. An early member was Paul Hester, getting in some practice for when he graduated to the Crowded House stool.

But the man we're really interested in is keyboardist Gus Till whose next gig (briefly) was The Models, a popular chart success in Australia with whom INXS would play in early 1987 on the Australian Made concerts. Till then joined Manuel and Meo in Beargarden, leaving in 1986 – the year he ended up playing on the sessions for Michael Hutchence's 'Rooms For A Memory' single, a cover of the old Whirlywind track that was lifted off the *Dogs In Space* soundtrack. The musical director for the film was Ollie Olsen, a Norwegian avant-gardist and sound visionary who would become the other half of Max Q in 1989 and form Australia's most influential electronics label Psi Harmonics, one of whose acts would be the world-recognised The Third Eye. Till played on the Max Q album, became Olsen's partner in The Third Eye and produced the 12″ version of 'New York, New York' for Ecco Homo in 1990. Ecco Homo was really the recording name for video-maker Troy Davies and John Clifford. In 1988, Olsen produced their début 12″ 'Motorcycle Baby' and Hutchence worked on the session.

Blinded by detail? Don't be. What's important is that out of *Dogs In Space,* Michael would develop his more avant and electronic interests and also gain a reputation as a musician who could actually act. There's more. The initial Lowenstein contact for 'Burn For You' would also result in Michael meeting a hero who would become one of his closest friends, the extraordinary and peerless, Nick Cave.

Filming for 'Burn For You' began in North Queensland – Lowenstein interrupting a trip to the Cannes Film Festival after finishing his first feature, *Strikebound* – and ended in Europe.

Cresswell writes in the *Juice* article, "During that trip Lowenstein and co-director Lyn Marie Milburn took Hutchence backstage at a Birthday Party show and introduced him to the band. Although Hutchence was by then selling many times more records than Cave, the INXS singer was in awe. For the hour it took for a taxi to collect the party, Hutchence lay on his back staring at the sky, delighted that he had finally met Nick Cave."

Thirteen years and a few months later Cave will become godfather to Michael and Paula Yates' daughter, Tiger Lily, and 14 years later will unleash a heartbreaking rendition of 'Into My Arms' at Michael's funeral.

Lowenstein, meanwhile, had big plans for Hutchence whom he described as "like the projection of all my repressed desires to be a rock singer". *Dogs In Space* was just an idea in Lowenstein's head at the time but the satire of his student years in Melbourne set in a rundown squat in 1978 with Hutchence as Sam, a heroin-addicted punk, earned a wealth of hyperbole: "With its M.A.S.H.-like forests of dialogue and its tragic denouement (Sam's girlfriend takes her first shot of heroin and dies of an overdose), *Dogs In Space* was a justly-acclaimed portrait of punk Down Under, of lopsided anarchy, of doomed youth in excellent weather", gushed David Cavanagh in the *Brisbane Courier-Mail* (November 12, 1994) during an interview with Hutchence in his old stone villa in the south of France.

Cavanagh continues, "Hutchence and his fellow actors, enjoying themselves and unable to get out of character, lived in the house for two months. He left only when a telex arrived informing him that INXS' song 'What You Need' had become a huge hit in America. Even now, he remembers those two months in Melbourne as one of the happiest periods of his life.

" 'We just couldn't stop being in a movie,' Hutchence says. 'But it was a true story, I played a friend of mine: "Sam" has now gone on to be an award-winning playwright, believe it or not.' "

I reckon, and have since 1989 after I first heard the Max Q set with Ollie and friends, and was swamped by Mike's blistering industro-funk and electronic blitzkrieg, that somewhere in that record and in *Dogs In Space* lies the essence of the man. Shoot me down if you like, it's a gut sensation and it ain't new.

Dogs In Space was also such a fitting metaphor. INXS were about to become dogs in space. The rest of 1986 is full of more touring (everywhere) and the release of two more singles, the title track from *Listen Like Thieves* which only made it to 54 in the US but cracked the UK top 50 – the first time the band had done so, even if it was only No 46. 'Kiss The Dirt (Falling Down The Mountain)' failed to crack the top 100 Stateside and topped at 54 in the UK. Despite the success of 'What You Need' at the beginning of the year and the ensuing tours, INXS still had not cracked either of the big two markets. And if you don't think that spelt pressure you don't know the music biz. *Listen Like Thieves* might have sold a million copies but as many dollars and more were spent in touring and promotion.

Incredibly, the band didn't stop. That is take a long break, not just six weeks here or there, but six months, a year. INXS had been working six years straight at this point. Yes, nerves were fraying. But they also knew how close they were to going over the top. Over Christmas 1986/New Year '87, INXS head-lined the Australian Made tour, an extraordinary celebration of Australian music that played in each of the six capital cities with a bill of eight Australian bands: INXS, Jimmy Barnes, Divinyls, The Models, Mental As Anything, Triffids, The Saints and I'm Talking.

Australian Made landed in Perth at Subiaco Oval on January 10, 1987 – a pleasantly warm, perfectly blue skied, hazy kind of day. The soft burbling funk of I'm Talking, the first band to feature now leading solo artist Kate Ceberano (who has the lithe and spunky slice of pop called Pash circulating this March '98 instant), seemed to marry their friendly rhythms with the warmth of the day. Kate's the sexiest, nicest, most intelligent, big girl in the world, with a smile that eats up her face – and she's got a voice to die for. At the other end of the 'she' zone is Chrissie Amphlett, the Joan Jett of Australian rock who throws back sex in the face of her lecherous fans by dressing up in a school-girl outfit and flashing her panties and bra in their faces. The Divinyls – based around Amphlett and guitarist Mark McEntee, were by then already one of Australia's more success-ful acts in America where they were joined in the line-up for one tour by Frank Infante, formerly of Blondie. Chrissie's as rock as it gets, but get her alone and you'll find a perceptive and shrewd woman who's always known where she's going. Late afternoon, they were a roar the sound system struggled to make sense of as they cranked out hits such as their anthem 'Boys In Town', 'Casual Encounter', 'Good Die Young', 'Hey Little Boy' and 'Science Fiction'.

The biggest dent in the aural canals came when Barnesy – Jimmy Barnes – appeared on stage. The legendary lead singer of Oz rock icons, Cold Chisel, who split in 1984 and recently reconvened 13 years later, has long had the most tortured tonsils this side of Brian Johnson of AC/DC. In full flood Barnes approximates a 747 taking off in your left ear drum and an hour later landing in your right. Beloved and idolised Barnes threw in the best set I've ever seen him play, a storming, gargantuan, thundercloud of a set that sent the crowd into delirium.

INXS had to follow their mate. They came on in white suits with flared trousers. They sucked. They were abysmal. They tried too hard and seemed totally out of sync. Michael minced so much he made sense of all the gay rumours about him – and that's like saying Julio Iglesias is a woman-hater. In fact, the only time the set caught alight was when Barnes joined them for a storming version of the old Easybeats track, 'Good Times', which he and the band (minus Tim Farriss) had recorded as a special single before the tour began. As Michael and 'Jummy' traded verses and chorus and the band thrashed away behind them, there was an "it-was-great moment". It was the only one. Australian Made was the worst INXS show I ever saw. Back-stage they didn't seem too concerned but they didn't seem too happy. Michael look tired and wan. Only Kirk buzzed round with his normal charm.

Soon afterwards recording of INXS 's next album began with Chris Thomas producing again. Sessions were split between Rhinoceros studios and Studio de la Grande Armée in Paris, with Bob Clearmountain mixing at Air Studios in London.

So begins one of the most remarkable chapters in Australian music history. It is hard to put into words what INXS achieved over the next two years and two albums; it is as colossal as it is a mark of sheer dedication, stamina and willpower. Until this point in time only the Bee Gees – whose Australian-ness was based on an adopted sons escape clause – and Olivia Newton-John had really broken the world charts apart, while Air Supply,

41

the Little River Band and to a lesser extent Men At Work had all done well, particularly in the US. When it came to long standing world domination Australia's lone champions were that mighty thunderclap AC/DC whose lore amongst metal heads had reached legendary proportions.

On October 16, 1987, INXS began their Calling All Nations world tour in the US. Three days later, their sixth album *Kick* was released. By January 1988, INXS had their first US No 1 – 'Need You Tonight' – one of the last songs to be recorded. It began one of the great chart runs of any band on the *Billboard* Top 100, six top 10s in a row.

Following 'Need You Tonight', 'Devil Inside' (reached No 2), 'New Sensation' (5), 'Never Tear Us Apart' (7) and the *X* album singles, 'Suicide Blonde' (9) and 'Disappear' (8), left INXS duking it out with U2 for the tag of world's biggest band: there were no other competitors. U2's near perfect *The Joshua Tree* and its critically-maltreated live 1988 follow-up *Rattle & Hum* both topped the US and UK albums charts while the singles 'I Still Haven't Found What I'm Looking For', 'Where The Streets Have No Name' and 'Desire' made it to 1, 13 and 3 respectively in the US and 6, 4 and 1 in the UK.

INXS also finally cracked the difficult British market, where reviewers in the trade press had for years taken delight in bashing most Antipodean outfits. 'Need You Tonight' gave them their first top 5 single making it to No 2 after 'Never Tear Us Apart' had capped at No 24. 'Mystify' went to No 14 and 'Suicide Blonde' to No 11.

Strangely – some would say perversely – while America slowly fell out of love with INXS after the September 1990 release of *X*, the UK got the message. 'Disappear', which hit the stores in November 1990, would prove the last top 20 single for INXS in the US and while *X* made it to No 5 and sold exceptionally well again, the follow-up, the very ordinary live album, *Live Baby Live*, sold slowly (for INXS) struggling to reach No 72 while August 1992's critically-acclaimed studio set, *Welcome To Wherever You Are*, failed to crack the top 10 and had to settle for a peak of 16. A year and two months later *Full Moon, Dirty Hearts*, arguably the worst INXS album in a decade, reached no higher than No 53.

But by then the Brits were in love with the band. Extraordinarily, *Live Baby Live* had made it to No 8, one spot higher than *Kick* three years earlier, *X* splitting the pair looked like a No 1 but stopped short at 2. *Welcome To Wherever You Are* remedied that and gave the band their first UK No 1 album. *Full Moon, Dirty Hearts* made a mockery of the critics who panned it mercilessly, going all the way to No 3, the same position attained by *INXS – The Greatest Hits* in November '94.

If comparisons must be made and the truth be told, there's no doubt U2's star has well exceeded that of INXS, both creatively and in popularity, in the mid-and late Nineties. *Pop* (1997) is one of the quintessential releases of the decade and shows a band 20 years on restating themselves by drawing upon all the elements of their work to create their most complete, exciting, mature and satisfying album since *The Joshua Tree*.

That is to take nothing away from INXS, there are different circumstances at work in the histories of the two bands. But rock is both cyclical and repetitive when it comes to generational ignorance. There are kids buying records today for whom the only Beatles have been the ones crawling around outside; The Grateful Dead are people who have been buried or cremated properly; The Who are precisely that. Even more sadly in the glut of bad techno and dance covers which now foul the airwaves, many kids believe the songs they are hearing are original. They have no sense of the history or the heritage of rock. That needs to be worked on, and was a problem of which Michael was conscious although he drew a broader picture, believing it afflicted all the arts.

What happened to INXS in the Nineties post-*Kick* is now happening to U2. While massively popular, the recent U2 tour of Australia highlighted an interminable problem for any mega-successful act – how do you overcome the popularity of your back catalogue, those hit singles that won't go away and the audience that ages with them?

The Sydney Morning Herald's music critic Jon Casimir believes it's a question that even U2, who exist in a stratosphere well outside the usual norms and whims of rock, now has to answer. Casimir, who attended the launch of U2's Pop tour in Las Vegas and saw their Sydney show some 10 months later, remarked on how the set list had changed dramatically. In March 1998, the band opened with a burst of old gold blockbusters and the set contained far less of their newer material and more concessions to the simple conventions of rock; gone, for instance, was The Edge's karaoke version of 'Daydream Believer'. Worse still was the audiences polite response to and refusal to buy into anything post-*The Joshua Tree.*

Casimir pointed out that even Bono – as definitive and crowned a figure in rock as there is – felt he had to explain why U2 had been trying to push their own boundaries outwards for the better part of a decade: "If it keeps it interesting for us, then it won't be bullshit for you."

INXS faced exactly the same dilemma after *Welcome To Wherever You Are,* something Tim, Michael and Kirk all spoke about on separate occasions during the past five years. It's necessary to understand that rock bands, especially big rock bands, face a time when they reach what the chairman of ARIA, Peter Rix, once eloquently described to me as "the top of the mountain". From there they begin a slow, and hopefully graceful, slide down the other side.

What is wrong, Michael would say, is that people assume that white rockers are dead in their boots when they're 40. It is accepted that blues and jazz musicians are just hitting their peak at 50 or 60 yet white rock and pop stars get neutered as early as 30.

Elvis Costello, the most informed and knowledgeable gentleman I've ever interviewed when it comes to music, summed it up thus, "In your twenties you can be cutting edge and groundbreaking; in your thirties – if you are lucky – you are relevant, if you aren't you are just ignored or too old for it; then the day you turn 40 you suddenly become a national treasure. What I'll be when I'm 50 I'm not sure – probably some mad eccentric nutter – but it is as meaningless as it is a rather sad reflection of how both the industry and society deals with age and judges its artists."

The internationally celebrated Perth-based blues guitarist Dave Hole, well into his mid-forties and 25 years of the blues, told me a few years ago, "In America I'm the new kid on the blues block. I'm just earning my spurs. If I was white rocker I'd be a has-been by now."

The double standard – as ridiculous as it sounds – is quite deadly and hits often when its victims are also going through one version or another of mid-life crisis (and that's a bitch). You can work out the permutations. Michael described it as "pure ignorance and conditioning" but he also remarked that people are creatures of habit and don't adapt well to change, particularly in their icons. Rock critics, on the other hand, demand constant progression.

By the middle of 1988 INXS were icons and more. Superstars is such a slug of a phrase but it's applicable to the behemoth that INXS had become. Prior to *Kick*'s release the album's recording sessions were tense affairs, often riven with drama as the band and Thomas – a man of considerable self-belief – fought it out. Gary Grant told Cresswell (*Juice*, January '98), "The days before *Kick* the band was almost gonna break up. The band hadn't yet cracked the mega album and everyone was pretty frazzled. I know that there had been well over a million dollars spent in advances for tour support. *Listen Like Thieves* had done a million copies and the next thing was *Kick*."

All up INXS spent 16 months on the road touring their finest recorded hour – including a US tour broken into four legs. Jon Bon Jovi, the veteran stadium rocker, faced his own nightmare that year on a world tour that seemed to him endless. "When it gets over a year, it gets insane," he told me in 1995. "We'll never do tours that long again. To understand just what it's like, imagine getting on and off a plane, in and out of limos, buses, changing hotels, every day or second day for 500 days with maybe a one or two week break here or there. And everywhere you go people want a piece of you, want you to do interviews, have advice for you, want to help you. Man, it becomes very weird and very strange."

According to Cresswell it did for INXS: ". . . The last stages of the *Kick* tour were putting great stresses on the band. Pengilly had barely seen his first child, born that year. Jon Farriss developed a knee condition which affected his drumming, while Hutchence succumbed to the pressures of the road by flipping out a little. For a time he travelled separately from the group, only showing up at gigs and disappearing again immediately after the show. One of the luxuries of being a

45

successful band was the presence of a drug roadie who could make sure the group was sorted and Hutchence developed a brief affection for ecstasy.

"Every show INXS played was followed by a party – and they could hit it hard. Lowenstein recalls being in Prague before the Berlin Wall came down where the only alcohol available was Polish vodka at $1 a bottle. He was woken in the middle of the night to see Jon Farriss stuck in the elevator with the doors opening and closing on his head. Richard Clapton recalls the evening when Hutchence was staying at the Park Hyatt Hotel in Sydney and decided, sometime after midnight, to abseil up the side of the city's most expensive hotel accompanied by a group of friends and a ghetto-blaster. That kind of behaviour could carry on for months on end."

And his hedonistic pursuits were . . . his hedonistic pursuits. A feature by Steve Dougherty and Todd Gold in *Woman's Weekly* of August 16, 1988 began: "When five of the six members of the hot Australian rock band INXS arrived at their hotel in Calgary, Canada, after a sell-out concert, a block of squealing high school girls in prom dresses ditched their dates to ogle the stars, all squealing the same question:

" 'Where's Michael?!' "

"At that moment, Michael Hutchence, the band's leonine lead singer, stepped out of a white stretch limo. He was wrapped in a long white bathrobe and a long-legged blonde girl named Johnnie. As the pair hustled through the lobby, flustered teens gasped and burbled, 'My God! It's him!'

"INXS guitarist Kirk Pengilly maintained an air of dignified calm. 'We've gotten use to it,' he said, deadpan. 'We've learned to hate him.' "

There are plenty of stories like that. So what? Apart from moralists who probably aren't reading this anyway, any other man or woman probably has a similar tale or two of their own youthful – and maybe not-so-youthful – pursuits to tell, though it's doubtful if such events occurred with the regularity that Hutch appeared to enjoy.

Eventually, INXS returned to Australia in November '88 to a hero's welcome and a triumphant sold-out tour. By then they'd whipped U2 at the MTV video awards where they walked away with five gongs and were looking at worldwide sales for *Kick* of six million plus. Today, it has sold more than 11 million and remains the band's biggest selling record.

So what was so special about *Kick*? Simply, it is the only INXS album that doesn't contain any fillers. *Kick* is consistently excellent from beginning to end. Not only does it contain INXS' most poignant anthem, 'Never Tear Us Apart' – arguably their finest song, and the hits 'New Sensation', 'Devil Inside' and 'Need You Tonight', but the album tracks are charismatic, strong, dynamic and offset the popular picks perfectly – in pace, substance and atmosphere. 'Calling All Nations', 'Tiny Daggers', 'Mediate', 'Mystify' and 'Guns In The Sky' all stand as fine reminders of just how good an album band INXS could be, contrary to a school of thought in certain circles that always labelled them as a singles band.

With the exception of some of the tracks on *Elegantly Wasted,* their comeback album a decade later, *Kick* is also the closest INXS came to capturing their live sound in the studio. It isn't all the way there but with a little imagination the mist that tends to blanket the majority of their LPs lifts. Why nobody ever figured out how to record them perfectly is a good question, as much as it is a source of frustration to some fans. It's also a hint that INXS in the studio presented producers with a less predictable than usual equation. They weren't just punk, funk, rock, pop . . . they swung. Their music was a swing and it comes at you from different directions. Hutchence, as one of the world's pre-eminent vocalists, needed emphasis, but the band deserved better than they sometimes got. On *Kick*, INXS do.

The show was a blow – a wind of sound blasting everything that stood in its way, the bottom end a thick turbulence that body punched the solar plexus, the keyboards, guitars, sax smoke on the waters and Hutchence . . . Hutch was suitably Byronesque, a much used metaphor that for once was entirely appropriate. Mad, sexy, drunk with stardom Michael.

Sitting in the Perth Entertainment Centre – a 7,500 seater with hard-to-mix acoustics like most large venues of its type – on November 8 for the first night of three, it seemed more than a decade since those Broadway Tavern days. Here was a fitting finale to a splendid rage around the world that netted 174 dates in 421 days. Calling All Nations lived up to its name – it went round and round and round and round some more, visiting every developed country in the globe, America no less than four times and most European countries twice. And not far behind or not far ahead were U2; from arena to arena, festival to show, they circled each other like electric warriors.

Intermission

8.59pm, March 14, 1998: In a special lift-out feature in today's *The Australian* newspaper celebrating 40 years of Australian rock music since Johnny O'Keefe's 'The Wild One' was released in March 1958, 20 Australian music writers voted their top 10 Australian albums and top 40 singles of all time. First place in the album category was a three-way tie between Crowded House's self-titled début, Midnight Oil's *10,9,8,7,6,5,4,3,2,1* and *Kick*; the only INXS single to make the singles list was 'Original Sin' which tied for 24th place. Top Australian all-time No 1 single was shared – fittingly – by The Easybeats 1966 anthem, 'Friday On My Mind' and The Saints 1976 punk ravish '(I'm) Stranded'. You'd be hard-pressed to argue. Third all on its own was the Ross Wilson-led Daddy Cool's hippie era anthem 'Eagle Rock' – at early Seventies outdoor festivals and weekend shows this was the number to light the 'numbers'. Three world success stories came in next: at No 4, 'Cattle and Cane' by the critically-adored The Go-Betweens (featuring Grant McLennan, Robert Forster and Lindy Morrison) while 'I Got You', the Split Enz pop crossover smash from 1980 and Yothu Yindi's vital, tribal and groundbreaking 'Treaty' (1990) shared fifth spot.

That *Kick* came in equal first is as fitting as it is a PA stack sized surprise, particularly as INXS bashing has been a bit of a sport over the last 12 months (kick an icon if you think they're going down is an Australian tradition). It also probably says more about *Kick* than another hundred or so words would so let's move on.

End of Intermission

So what did INXS do on their holidays that spanned nearly all of 1989 and continued on and off through the recording sessions that began in November for *X* and ran through to the final mix by Michael and Chris Thomas in London in May 1990? Michael, restless as ever and looking for new sensations, recorded the *Max Q* set with Ollie Olsen. Here was a pair: Ollie was renowned for his fondness for altered states and Michael wasn't exactly a virgin in that regard. What resulted was a shiver-me-timbers barrage of electronic pulsebeat, rock riffs and dancecore rhythms. Michael was justifiably proud of *Max Q* – named after Ollie's dog – and several times spoke of his frustration at the way it was underplayed. How and why are best explained by those in management and record company at the time. Who didn't and never have. *Max Q* has always been an unspoken affair that was richly consummated then left standing with just a loin cloth. If it's Hutch you want, then go find a copy and listen. He's in there; in deep.

"It's two people from opposite – yet not so dissimilar – ends of the musical spectrum coming together, and a case of sticking it up anybody that didn't get it," he told me at the time. "Just because I'm a pop star and Ollie an underground figure, people immediately started to judge and try to interfere. I've always said that I'm never going to let the pressure, the industry or anything else stop me doing what I want to. We wanted to make an album that took some real chances and we did. What people around me were worried about was that if I screwed up and *Max Q* got bad reviews there would be some fallout onto INXS." It didn't, there wasn't.

Undeterred Michael took off on another tangent – his next feature film, *Frankenstein Unbound,* which he began filming later that year. Directed by one of the kings of B-grade horror movies, 62-year-old Roger Corman, and starring a classic cast of masters, misfits and headcases – John Hurt, Raul Julia, Jason Patric, Bridget Fonda, Catherine Rabett and Nick Brimble, *Frank* attracted a "Competent but uninspired" review from *Variety*. In other words, it succeeded at its loose camp horror ambition. For Corman, whose previous credits included such cult classics as *Attack Of The Crab Monsters, A Bucket Of Blood, She Gods Of Shark Reef* (particularly low grade excellence, around the Z-mark) and *Teenage Caveman*, it was a chance to get back in the big league with a $10 million 20th Century Fox flick. Michael played Percy Bysshe Shelley opposite Patric's Lord Byron.

In late '94, Hutchence was still full of Frankenstein – and his uncelebrated ability to do 'voices' – when David Cavanagh interviewed him in France (*Brisbane Courier Mail*, November 12, 1994): "Me and Jason (Patric) had this really clear idea," he recalls, "and it had nothing to with what anybody else wanted. We played it with beards. Roger called me [his voice becomes clipped, mechanical], 'Mike. I tend to think Percy Shelley was rock. Star. Would you like to do. It? [*Hungover thespian*] 'uh . . . yeah.' So I ended up in Lake Como in Italy, two weeks of filming. Jason was trying to do Byron like Mel Gibson because Byron was a motherfucker . . . he was an expert marksman; he used to get up every morning and sit on his lake and he had a menagerie of [*Olivier playing Henry V*] baboons! and lions! and Tigers! and peacocks! in a giant cavalcade that came down from London. [*Steven Berkoff*] Forty carriages full of animals! He was one of the richest men in England. [*Hopelessly vague rock star*] . . . And Percy was on the dole. My theory was that Shelley wasn't so foppish. Percy was hangin'. Ligging. And in awe of Byron, of course, and couldn't do a damn thing around him, except translate Latin. But Byron would sit on his lake and people would line up on the other side with binoculars and watch him in his villa – all the mad shenanigans, with 16-year-old wives running around nude, and writing *Frankenstein* and shit – and he'd . . . *pook!* . . . shoot them. That was the opening sequence: Byron taking potshots at his fans. It was beautiful . . ."

Cavanagh continues, "As with *Dogs In Space*, Hutchence found it difficult to come out of character. Filming completed, he and Patric set off around Italy on the trail of the real-life Shelley and Byron, armed with vast compendia of information about the pair's exploits."

"We lost it completely," Hutchence giggles. "We'd spend an entire day with a word. Like . . . green. [*Aristocratic ponce*] Green, green, green, green. That's what they'd do. Sit around with Dr Whatsisname giving them opium, doing 'green' for a day."

And it was in the last third of '89 that Michael Hutchence fell for Kylie Minogue and Kylie Minogue fell for Michael Hutchence and the long lens of the paparazzi protruded, sharp and focused, into his life – as it turned out, for good. More on that later.

Elsewhere, the remaining members of INXS were living a slightly saner version of the life shuffle. During 1989 and the gaps in 1990, Kirk and Tim went into the studio to produce the début set by the edgy, intense and articulate, keyboard-drive, guitar smeared, Sydney outfit Crash Politics, Andrew produced (and toured with) Jenny Morris' excellent second album *Shiver* which produced three hit singles – the world music tinted shuffle 'Saved Me' (recommended), 'She Has To Be Loved' and 'Street Of Love' – and sold more than 200,000 copies in Australia. Garry Beers hooked up with – and co-produced the début album, *Here's Looking Up Your Address*, for – Absent Friends, a fun group which got serious for a while, and included old mates from the lately disbanded The Models – Andrew Duffield, Sean Kelly and Roger Mason, the fine-boned, beautiful, expatriate Canadian singer/songwriter Wendy Matthews and Mark Callaghan and Geoff Stapleton of GANGgajang, arguably Sydney's definitive suburban and surf set pop outfit. Jon wrote songs, relaxed, but also appeared on the Absent Friends album.

By the time INXS reunited they faced two mountains to climb: the balance in the band had changed and would need an overhaul and they had to follow-up a massively successful album. Neither of which is particularly easy.

Picture this: you've been with the same bunch of people for virtually 10 years, shared just about everything there is to share, recorded six albums, become one of the biggest bands in the world, done some of this, a lot of that, put your mind through a mangle, dealt with incalculable pressure, endless press, inescapable politics, got to the point of exhaustion yourself on your last tour, then suddenly stopped dead in your tracks. The normal reaction is a three-week (minimum) physical meltdown, followed by another month of feeling like your brain has been washed by unknown covert forces. Eventually, you pick up the pieces of normality, repair and reinstate relationships of all kinds, start to do some stuff on your own ... and then you've got to want to do it all over again.

Ed St John in *INXS: The Official Inside Story of a Band on the Road* (Mandarin, 1992) which chronicles in detail the X Factor tour of 1990/91 (123 dates in 286 days) pictures the mood of the band at the time: ". . . As Kirk Pengilly puts it, 'For the first time since we'd left high school, we actually had the opportunity to function as individuals.'

" 'In a sense, INXS split up after the *Kick* tour', says Jon Farriss. 'We all sort of went "Goodbye, I don't know when I'll see you again", and walked away from it. It was a wonderful break because it was the first taste any of us had of real personal freedom.

" 'It was also the first time that any of us had felt in control of our own lives. Up until then we'd done things because we had to do them rather than because we chose to. So when we all got back together again it was a very conscious decision. We weren't fulfilling an obligation, we were doing it because we wanted to.'

" 'When you are constantly around one another – the way we'd been for 10 years, you really influence each other in so many ways,' observes Michael Hutchence. 'On a long tour you can actually lose track of the differences between everyone and sort of merge into one person with the same tastes in music and clothes and everything.

" 'Of course when we all got back together it was like putting the band together from scratch. We came back as virtually new people, with new tastes, new interests and new friends' . . .

"Kirk Pengilly remembers their first months back together as being somewhat tense and difficult. 'There was a lot of pressure on the band to deliver something as successful as *Kick*,' says Kirk, 'and also an internal pressure as to whether the band would still work – so we went through a period of trying to establish where we sat with each other.

" 'It was quite a difficult album for us to make, although I think some of that might have been because we weren't getting on well with Chris Thomas. But ultimately we were very proud of the album we made.' "

Fresh from a holiday as an unknown (a novel experience) in Northern Thailand, Michael was even more graphic in an article by Chris Blanche in *The Daily Telegraph* (March 29, 1990): " 'This is the first time we've actually had a break, been able to go off and say, wait a minute, who am I, what do I really like and what do I want to go on doing.

" 'So we've come back and it's been good in that it's distracted us from our past success. We've almost had to reform the band, which is great and really hard because we're having basic ideological musical arguments again. But it's important and the sparks fly.' "

When *X* was released on September 21, 1990, it was obvious to anybody except the most diehard fan that if the sparks had flown they didn't necessarily ignite all the time and tended to spray in different directions.

X is a patchy album. It was in many ways a typical follow-up to a blockbuster in that it attempted not to sound like a blockbuster but ended up sounding like one anyway. But it has some great moments. The single, 'Suicide Blonde', with its Richard Lowenstein directed video was a fine, bouncy, typically funky, sexy (and sex sold big-time for INXS) pop bluster with a great Hutchence vocal. The fine opening track 'Disappear' is even better, particularly its happy-go-lucky intro and keyboard melody and backdrop through which guitars strum and Jon pounds out a toe-tapping beat, and 'Lately' is near-perfect stereotypical INXS pop, again with a killer melody. 'Bitter Tears' was an okay single but it never really grabbed the international market. 'Who Pays The Price', 'Know The Difference', 'On My Way' and 'Hear That Sound' are stocking material, though if you haven't listened closely 'Faith In Each Other' is *X*'s most underestimated moment. But *X*'s two gems rate amongst INXS' finest songs: 'The Stairs' spends nearly five minutes working up an atmosphere into a storming rock dance (listen to the guitar lines that lead into the body of the song – beautiful stuff), the whole band gels together in the movement, and Hutch sings an understated vocal over the top. 'By My Side' is a sister piece to 'Never Tear Us Apart', built almost symphonically by Andrew with one of Mike's best lyrics: sad romantic poignancy. "Here comes the clown, his face is a wall, no window at all. In the dark of night, these faces they haunt me, but I wish you were so close to me, in the dark of night, by my side . . ."

At his funeral on November 27, 1997, 'By My Side' would be played at the beginning of the service and 'Never Tear Us Apart' at the end. Nothing could have been more fitting – except to have Michael there singing them. Then again, he was.

The X Factor tour saw the band play some legendary shows: on January 12, 1991 in Mexico before 50,000 – plus another 1,000 armed guards brought in to contain the fevered Latinos – they became the first band to play the country since The Doors 20 years earlier; a week later at Rock in Rio, 100,000 gathered in the capital of Brazil; on February 16 they played a sold out show at Madison Square Garden, the most famous of US venues; and on March 11 when tickets went on sale for their forthcoming Australian tour, box offices around the country were besieged – in Sydney, 22,000 tickets sold in 20 minutes.

The tour opened in Perth on April 15, 1991, at a sold out Perth Entertainment Centre where INXS were stunning to watch – world-class staging and lighting – but just didn't seem quite on song. A year later, St John revealed in his book that a few days before the Australian leg was due to begin, Michael began losing his voice: " 'When I had all the problems with my throat on the Australian tour I went to see a Sydney throat specialist who is one of the very best in the world,' " Michael says. " 'He looked at my throat, and then asked to see how much work I'd done over the past five years. So we pulled out a few bits of paper and showed him our touring itinerary since the mid-'Eighties.

" 'He took one look at this and said I was incredibly lucky to have any voice left at all. He said what we'd done was ridiculous, and I think I agree with him.' "

However, a seven-week break in the tour schedule allowed the chords to recover enough for the band to round off the tour in style, returning to Europe where they headlined the Rock Am Ring Festival in front of 50,000 in Cologne and were joined on stage by Dave Stewart of Eurythmics fame for a version of 'Suicide Blonde'. On July 7, INXS made their Eastern Bloc début in Budapest, Hungary, before flying back to England for one of the biggest shows they would ever play: Summer XS in front of 72,000 screaming fans in a sold-out Wembley Stadium on July 13. The penultimate X Factor show (the tour ended on July 16 in Glasgow) was taped for *Live Baby Live* (as were previous shows in Philadelphia, Chicago, New York, Paris, Toronto, Dublin, Glasgow, Rio De Janeiro, Montreal, Spain, Switzerland, Sydney, Melbourne and Las Vegas) and filmed by

David Mallett for a video that would come out simultaneously with the album.

Next day, perversely, INXS were in London's Metropolis Studios where they recorded 'Shining Star', a song Andrew had written on the road. It came out as a single on October 21 to herald the November 11 release of *Live Baby Live* on which it was oddly placed as the fifth track. Who knows why? It's not even one of Andrew's better songs and whatever early flow the album struggles to realise is cut short. Live albums are notoriously hard to get right and rock history is littered with live disasters – mostly because so many lose the spontaneity and rawness of the sound in the production suite. And, of course, there are those who should never have recorded a live album because they just can't cut it on stage.

In fan land, though, live albums are a staple diet – the more the better, which leads to a worldwide network of tape trading, particularly on the internet lists. The bigger INXS got, the more they were bootlegged, particularly during the Calling All Nations and X Factor tours. Today, they're hard to find. However, there's a couple I've heard that sound better than *Live Baby Live*, which is really murky, uninspiring and suffers from bad editing. Sadly, it fails to capture the power of INXS at their most effervescent, and instead portrays them as rather tame white boys doing their funky soulful rock thang.

The latter stages of the X Factor tour, though, were among the best times on the road for the band. They seemed to cruise through everything that was going on and became closer, rather than distanced, by the ceaseless motion. *X* went on to sell more than four million copies, less than half the sales of *Kick* but INXS were still sitting on top of the world.

It wouldn't stay that way.

3

Welcome To Wherever You Are

The pretty hate machine begins here. Rock had been working up to something for a while and finally discovered what it was: angst. 1991 was the year the gut caved in. Suddenly, everybody was feeling sorry for themselves. The oh-woe-is-me-generation arrived on the back of one of the greatest albums of all time: *Nevermind* by Nirvana. Generation X was born in media offices around the world and grunge screamed out loud. 'Smells Like Teen Spirit' was the best anthem anybody had recorded in a decade and *Nevermind* with its punk veins and hard rock stomach made Kurt Cobain the de-facto spokesman for thousands upon millions of disenchanted and spiritually empty kids worldwide, particularly in America.

However, grunge was realistically dead as a force and movement the moment 'Smells Like Teen Spirit' became an anthem. Soon the teen spirits were owned and on their way to becoming the '90s equivalent of Bon Jovi. And they couldn't go on with it. Soundgarden have now broken up, Alice In Chains are a huge question mark unable to complete a follow-up to 1995's eponymous titled set because of lead singer Llayne Staley's continuing drug problems. Pearl Jam with a new album, their fifth, *Yield*, should be the leaders. But they sound uncertain, like a band grasping for direction. Some of *Yield* even tries its hand at Americana. Why is hard to say. Pearl Jam will never be Arizona's Giant Sand, the definitive desert rock and avant experimentalists for a decade. In Eddie Vedder they have a writer with few peers and amongst their ranks some of the most innovative and capable musicians in America, particularly Mike McCready who worked with Staley and Barrett Martin from the Screaming Trees on the Mad Season side project, releasing the moody and experimental, *Above*, before joining up with Martin for the outstanding world-influenced side project

Tuatara (check out 1997's *Breaking The Ethers*) featuring R.E.M's Peter Buck.

Pearl Jam should have redefined post-grunge by now. They haven't. In fact, it was left to lesser lights, the Screaming Trees, to do so with 1996's *Dust*, a wonderful, spirited, fuzz of rock splashed by Hendrix-style electricity, chiming Byrds six and 12-strings, tablas and sitars, and Lanegan's unerring vocal performance. In the mist of *Dust*, the boundaries were obscured and grunge blown into the haze of its by now formulaic riffing. And 'In Sworn And Broken', the Trees produced the best song to come out of Washington since Cobain's 'Teen Spirit' and Vedder's 'Jeremy'.

If you're looking for a musical thread Michael admired look no further. We spent awhile in 1993 debating the merits of grunge and the way the heart had already been plucked from it by avaricious record labels. Michael admired Cobain and Nirvana, wondered whether Vedder would go all the way, found Courtney Love's Hole interesting, albeit not necessarily something he'd listen to on a pair of headphones on a long-distance bus journey. Most of all he just liked the attitude. He hoped it would last. But I think he doubted it would. I figured he also saw something of himself in the new breed and he recognised the wake-up call. But he also warned that it was po-faced, too down to be an upper.

"You have to get balance. It's like anything," he said. "Having a lot of people running round singing the world is a fucked place and doing nothing about it is just not helping. Strike out but don't just keep striking out until all you have left is despair. Cobain could be a genius but, in reality, he's only made two records (*Nevermind* and its independent predecessor, *Bleach*) that count. If he, any of them, go on with it then, do five, six, seven albums, they'll deserve all the hyperbole. And it's fucking tough to keep going year after year. But that's what marks the greats, man. Staying power and the ability to keep on writing great songs." We ended up talking about B.B. King and Ray Charles and John Lee Hooker.

The reason America turned away from INXS was quite simply grunge. They weren't cool any longer. Grunge was something new, distinctly American, and it would breed its own reaction from a chemistry with a short fuse. By 1996/97, grunge was officially dead – although unofficially it had been since '95 – but there was no universal panacea for record companies to latch onto and strange sounds were emerging from boltholes all over the US, wonderful, fascinating, musical hybrids: the post-rock of John McEntire's jazz-flecked instrumental Tortoise (their effortless *TNT* is one of 1998's most important records) and their Thrill Jockey counterparts Trans Am, Isotope, Eleventh Dream Day; the mixdown, cut and paste, looped and sampled pop of Beck (and Michael was quick to join in the critical acclaim reserved for this musical enigma) made him the most significant artist in the world according to both public and writer polls; the psychedelic nuances of Sky Cries Mary, Laika's brave and bedevilled electronic cosmos, Bowery Electric's post trip-hop soular etherealism, the extreme low-fi perfection of soundscapists Labradford, the poignant heartland atmospheres of Mazzy Star, Tarnation, Home; the dizzy pure pop of Ivy and Fountains Of Wayne; and the brilliant conceptualism of arguably the most important musical visionary in the world, dance/punk/ambient master Moby. There are hundreds more. And as the Nineties wore on they all made it harder and harder for INXS to find a footing in the US with anyone but the diehards. At least when millions buy your best record there were still plenty around.

The reason the now dance-fixated UK picked up on INXS was also quite simply grunge – INXS produced danceable records, the grunge class didn't – and the paparazzi. The British were dance, dance, dancing in the clubs to a turntable and sample driven tune that reduced music to bpms – beats per minute – and mindless, meaningless, endlessly repeated inanities uttered sensually over the top as a soundtrack to getting chemically obliterated. The Americans didn't get it and still haven't despite the efforts of the majors to sell "electronica" as the next musical revolution: the terribly clichéd and unimaginative Prodigy led the latest invasion in 1997 but the real class lay in the acts just below them, the Chemical Brothers, Underworld, Leftfield, Alpha, Morcheeba, jungle avant genius, Goldie, and the pioneers of the Bristol Sound, Massive Attack, and the inheritors to their throne, the dark, moody, spooked trip-hop, Portishead. Above them all spun, elfin and shimmering in her own unlimited imagination, Iceland's Bjork.

Michael loved dance music. Coming from different ends of the spectrum, INXS and Max Q proved that. But he looked way beyond the obvious limitations of techno. He understood its roots in the German electronic pioneers of the Seventies, Can, Neu, Kraftwerk and Faust, and saw the potential to create limitless sonic vistas that conformed to his own notion of song.

In that way Michael was very British and INXS were perfect for a Britain invaded by a musical formlessness that owed absolutely nothing to their most cherished heritage: harmony, melody, verse, chorus. INXS delivered all that consummately and with their own dance vibe attached. And there were hundreds of thousands of fans to whom a night clubbing was akin to six hours at the dentist. *Welcome To Wherever You Are*, the next INXS album, was the perfect soundtrack for the British and drew heavy support from both sides of beat street.

And if that wasn't enough, Michael's private life – which was now a constant source of headlines for the tabloid press – made him an English icon, almost one of their own.

Welcome To Wherever You Are is the third great INXS album but its impact in Australia was lessened by ordinary sales (after excellent reviews), a backlash against the band and the arrival of the best Australian rock band of the Nineties, the Baby Animals fronted by the rock steady dark-haired'n'gorgeous, Suze DeMarchi, a belter and seductress who could turn a lyric the way she could spin a heart. With sheer class. Their début would sell more than 350,000 copies and set an Australian record for first albums that would last until 1997/98 when Savage Garden savaged it. Their Eighties retro pop self-titled début soared on the back of five huge singles (including a couple of big and bigger ballads) past 700,000 copies in Australia alone, 10 times platinum, and then broke open the US charts where they eventually became the first Australian band since INXS, 11 years earlier, to have a No 1 single in 'Truly, Madly, Deeply'.

Not far behind the Baby Animals were the Newcastle-spawned Screaming Jets fronted by manic Dave Gleeson, the first genuine threat in a decade to Jimmy Barnes' throne as a natural born roar. With Hunters & Collectors entrenched as the quintessential Australian act – particularly live, The Church as its astral – if somewhat erratic – trailblazers, and Died Pretty finally breaking through with the all-time classic *Doughboy Hollow* album, and not forgetting Johnny Diesel, the by now legendary Midnight Oil, Yothu Yindi, Killing Time, Cruel Sea, Beasts Of Bourbon, Kim Salmon & The Surrealists, Dave Graney and the Coral Snakes, Tumbleweed, the ever-present, ever-great Ed Kuepper, Melbourne's essential Weddings Parties Anything and My Friend The Chocolate Cake, the first flaring of You Am I, and guitar jangle outfits such as The Clouds, Falling Joys and The Humming-birds, Australian music appeared to be booming and undergoing another of its watersheds.

It was in this environment that INXS entered Rhinoceros Studios in November 1991 – as co-producers – with Mark Opitz who had produced *Shabooh Shoobah* in '82 at the helm. Once again, a major break was out. Fired up by the latter part of the *Kick* tour, INXS were brimful of new sensations.

Kirk Pengilly told St John, " 'I think it's immediately obvious with this album that we've reached a whole new level . . . We're feeling very positive – and also very confident in our own abilities. This album hasn't been difficult at all – in fact we've had so many ideas it's just ridiculous. The motto for this album was 'we'll try any idea' – and believe me, we have. I really think this album is going to shock a lot of people."

It did – but by then INXS were embroiled in their first ever public controversy in Australia.

The Concert For Life was held on March 28, 1992, in Centennial Park, Sydney, to raise funds for St Vincent's Hospital organisations, the Victor Chang Cardiac Research Institute and AIDS Patient Services and Research. On paper, it should have been a triumphant return to Australia for INXS as headliners and a wonderful way to open up 1992 with a special one-off concert for the fans. Instead it became a nightmare which marks the official beginning of the backlash against INXS in their home country.

Sydney descended upon Centennial Park in droves: 65,000

strong at $21 a head, they came to see the cream of Australian music and its brash up-and-comers pound it out for charity. From the first notes of surfers of the mind, Def FX, who opened proceedings at 11.30am to a crowd of 50,000 and an estimated 1 million tuned into radio Triple J's live broadcast across the country, The Concert For Life sparked early and built through the day as Yothu Yindi, Jenny Morris, Deborah Conway, Ratcat, Johnny Diesel and Crowded House set the perfect stage for INXS.

They came on at 6pm to a deafening roar that seemed to shake the old park to its gnarled roots: you'd be excused for thinking that some deity intent on divinity had metamorphosed stage centre. It was Hutchence in a white suit.

The set was a mixed affair of classics such as 'New Sensation', 'Suicide Blonde', and 'Original Sin' interspersed with the first live airing of tracks from the forthcoming *Welcome To Wherever You Are* – the release of which was put back soon after to avoid the worst of the flack that followed. 'Taste It', 'Heaven Sent', 'Beautiful Girl' and 'Not Enough Time' sounded potent enough with the band both looser and more focused than the Calling All Nations shows. The encore was spectacular: 'Baby Don't Cry' and 'Never Tear Us Apart' performed with an orchestra. INXS were monumental for those few minutes and seemed almost imperious; Michael could have levitated and nobody would have been surprised. Australia's biggest band were just as they should be, a misty-eyed rain of emotion embracing and embraced. It was perfect.

Jon Casimir remembers that Crowded House blew them away that day and trying to work out why they had lights when the gig finished in the dimming glow of the day.

The excreta hit the blowout meter soon afterwards when it was revealed the concert raised $350,806 which with sponsor-ships and other donations came to $606,124 – about $900,000 short of the $1.5 million being touted by the publicity machine prior to the show. St Vincent's Hospital was happy enough with the outcome but the industry wasn't, and finger-pointing started, mostly in INXS' direction: the concert was the idea of the hospital, MMA and the band. The "indulgences" were exposed and listed. INXS were lambasted for what was judged as their over-indulgences: the orchestra, lighting and more.

Sian Powell and Casimir reported in *The Sydney Morning Herald* at the time that a total of $1,369,281 was taken in ticket sales and the operating costs amounted to $1,216,134 – leaving a profit on ticket sales of $153,147.

"The only benefit concert of comparable size, the 1990 Newcastle Appeal Concert, drew 42,000 people to the Newcastle International Sports Centre, cost $160,000, and raised $940,000 for the people of that city . . .

"The financial statement reveals:

"* A combined promotions and publicity cost of $215,634 (including the costs for the 2JJJ broadcast).

"* $85,235 spent on artist accommodation, catering and rehearsals (the artists were appearing free).

"* A $16,576 payment to the orchestra which appeared during the INXS encore and played during two songs.

"* $24,696 for the live broadcast on JJJ.

"* $3,097 for the lamination and string for concert passes.

"The concert has been criticised by sections of the music industry, including the manager of Crowded House, Mr Grant Thomas.

" 'On the strength of the ticket sales, the concert made very little,' he said. 'That's pathetic.' "

"Mr Michael Chugg, general manager of the Frontier Touring Company, one of the organisers of the Newcastle concert, said the financial statement was 'a disgrace' and that the interests of charity had been largely ignored.

" 'No expense has been spared,' he said yesterday. 'I could do you a budget for a commercial concert and bring it in for half of that cost, without a doubt.' "

"Mr Eric Robinson, owner of Jands Production Services, which provided the sound equipment for the concert at a cost of nearly $58,000, questioned the value of a $34,000 light show for a concert that finished at sunset.

"He said his company offered to do the production management of the show free but was not taken up on the offer.

"However, Mr Mathew Alderson, a representative of MMA Management and a director of the Concert for Life Pty Ltd, said every attempt had been made to contain costs. 'We had thousands of people working for us for one day.' "

"Mr Alderson said the Centennial Park costs – which totalled $300,000 – were all compulsory. He said they had not considered a cheaper venue."

It was a genuine pot-boiler and a slap in the face for a band who honestly believed it had done the right thing.

The media had a big month out and T-shirts appeared in Sydney featuring the mug of manager Murphy and the words Concert for Strife. Oh dear.

Worse was to follow as they were set upon by the local music and mainstream press who believed that the band was letting down its Australian fans by concentrating on overseas media in the lead-up to the release of *Welcome To Wherever You Are*. It began at the Concert For Life, where about 10 overseas journalists were given access to the band and the local contingent wasn't. Subsequently, as the early August release of the album drew closer, MMA issued an official line that there were no press interviews, only radio. Many observers took that as Murphy hitting back at publications involved in the post-Concert For Life free-for-all.

The logic wasn't hard to understand: if you don't talk to the local media, then you're ignoring the fans. The only problem was that the fans probably wouldn't have thought they were being ignored if the media hadn't convinced them they were. I never met any fans around that time who were card-carrying members of the I'm-pissed-off-because-INXS-are-ignoring-me union. Toby Cresswell, then at *Rolling Stone,* jumped all over the MMA decision in a *Stone* editorial and the debate nationwide. It was hardly the climate in which to release a new album.

Welcome To Wherever You Are went gold in the first week of release in Australia, but it didn't do much more. Eight months later it had made it to platinum – by INXS standards that's slow going, particularly in comparison to their previous three albums whose Australian sales figures by then ranged from 350,000 for *Kick* and 210,000 for *X* to 70,000 for the very ordinary *Live Baby Live*. Which all goes to show just how many sheep there are in Australia. *Welcome To Wherever You Are* pictured the band back on the creative edge, shedding the excesses of *X* and the live album and, again as they did with *Shabooh Shoobah*, pushing themselves in different directions, intent on realising the potential they'd discovered during the latter end of the *Kick* spin.

It's a brave album, a confident album, an album where a 65-piece orchestra washes 'Baby Don't Cry' and 'Men And Women' amidst a barrage of whiplash guitars, broad atmospheres, tight kicked out rhythms, some perfect pop that harked back to *Shabooh Shoobah* and *The Swing*, a worldliness engaged by Indian rhythms, European textures, and a sense of Australianness more pervasive than ever before.

And amidst a publicist's dream shower of great reviews, England's *Q* magazine helpfully continued the U2 thread while giving the album four stars: "The album has a far more engaging and heartfelt collection than anything the group has put out in recent memory. As a bold departure from a well-worn trail, *Welcome To Wherever You Are* stands in relation to the rest of INXS' portfolio at much the same point as *Achtung Baby* does to U2 and, indeed, both albums mark a similar stage in the development of their careers."

For once mostly everybody agreed. To an outsider, though, it looked like INXS were beginning to struggle, despite the album's No 1 in the UK and No 16 in the US. You had the feeling that despite all the grunt, machismo, wounded egos and bluster, the problem in Australia was quite deep and serious.

It was into such an environment that Murphy, who like the band had refused to comment on the fallout of the Concert For Life, arrived back in Australia and in an interview with Brett Thomas of *The Sun-Herald* (April 11, 1993) launched a broadside on the local media, claiming the band had fallen victim to the Australian tall poppy syndrome.

" 'Why I don't know,' he said. 'Should it be? No. Should it stop? Yes. What has INXS done? Nothing. What have they said? Nothing. What have they done to deserve it? Nothing.

" 'These six fellows have set a path for a lot of Australian bands. Every single band that has done anything outside this country has been advantaged by INXS. They've shown the international music industry you can make millions out of an Australian band. Up until *Kick* nobody took it seriously.

" 'At one stage I did think, "is this a tidal wave or a fart in a bottle?" but it's such a small percentage of people. The Australian public is not going to be fooled by a couple of fools in the Australian media.'

"On the Concert For Life, Murphy said he was happy he did not speak out as the allegations of overindulgence started to fly.

" 'I'm so glad I kept my silence and the band kept its silence,' he said. 'It didn't deserve comment. When it got past the super-moron stage I would've expected the credible people [in the media] to get behind INXS a lot better than they did. When we were approached we said yes and there wasn't a second thought. Some people said INXS was positioning themselves for the new album but we had to put the release off for seven months because of that show. If we were doing it to set up the album we would've had the record in the can ready to go before the show. At the end of the day the people in INXS have never done anything wrong.' "

The article then goes on to deal with INXS' apparent distancing itself from the Australian media and alleged arrogance regarding its home territory.

Even today that sounds like the worst kind of small-country-thinking. INXS made themselves superstars. Not Australia. Yes, they began and built their career in Australia but nobody from Australia suddenly gave them a million dollars and said 'now go overseas and make us proud'. By now you have a fair idea of how they got there. They worked themselves to death, put their normal lives on hold, asked huge sacrifices of themselves, their families and friends. INXS made INXS with a large helping hand from MMA and Murphy and Grant and their record companies and advisers along the way. They became super-stars because they were good enough to get to the highest level, because they were excellent musicians, because Andrew and Michael were great songwriters. Australia bathed in the reflected glory but it didn't own them nor did it have the right to appropriate them.

The same is true of nearly every band that makes it on whatever level they happen to succeed upon. This is a hard business in which the chances of success are minimal and the chances of getting to the top are rather like winning the lottery. In fact, you've probably got a better chance with the game. In 1997 about 25,000 records were released in the US alone, and of those only eight per cent at best attracted any real radio or media attention. It gets worse: of that eight per cent, the majority will be records by already established or on-their-way acts. The number of new acts to get any attention could be as low as one per cent or less. To survive is an achievement, to succeed is something else again.

By 1992/93 INXS were established players on the world stage. Why would anybody expect them to ignore it? Over the 20 years I've covered INXS as a music writer I've done about ten interviews with the band, split evenly I think five in the first decade and five in the second. That's not a reflection of a band ignoring its media. There were quiet times, sure, but so what? If 10 overseas journalists came down to Australia to see your band wouldn't you want to talk to them, give them an exclusive or two? As for complaining that INXS couldn't and didn't concentrate on Australia as much as they did earlier in their career: what were they supposed to do? Say, 'look, sorry, world, we'd really like to come over and play for several million people but we can't because our country won't let us'. As for the then common complaint that when interviews were available they weren't with Hutchence, here's his answer, nearly two years after the hue and cry as delivered to Katherine Tullich (*The Age*, January 16, 1994).

" 'I didn't really want to talk to anyone for a while but it was also an attempt to keep the whole band in the forefront – not just me. We did this all over the world but for some reason Australia got the impression that it was only here that I wasn't talking which just isn't true,' " he said.

" 'I think people misunderstood, just because I didn't play the *Hey Hey It's Saturday* (a high rating Australian light entertainment TV show) or *Woman's Weekly* game, but I'm not here to play every game. I'm basically still a songwriter and singer but there's a certain level that you reach especially in small population countries like Australia where you get worn on people's sleeves and it gets very tight and it gets very obvious when you are on or off the treadmill'. "

The biggest problem with the local media and music press is that some of its members think they are more important than the bands and acts they write about, more important than the music. That is crap. Australia represents about 1.5% of the world's CD sales. It's a minnow in the shallows of the music world. That is why each success engenders an outburst of nationalistic pride. It's charming, kind of *Happy Days* stuff, but when "fortunate smiles to sweet disdain" as Ron Peno so elegantly put it in Died Pretty's 'Doused' (from *Doughboy Hollow*) then you know something's horribly wrong.

Every Australian act and every act in the world who has gone out there with a dream and done it, whether they've made it or crashed and burned, has at least given it a go. What they reap is their own. What we have – and share – is the music. And I would have thought for that we should be grateful. Often it comes at an extraordinary cost. Like life.

"When the music's over, turn out the lights", Jim Morrison gently intoned in the Doors bewitched, revolutionary mantra, 'When The Music's Over'. Nothing is truer. But it seems we still need to break on through to the other side. To become part of the world you have to believe you are part of the world. To quote the 18th Century English poet, visionary, artist, William Blake, from *The Marriage Of Heaven And Hell,* "If the doors of perception were cleansed everything would appear to man as it is: infinite." From that sentence The Doors took their name and Aldous Huxley titled a book. Blake continued, "For man has closed himself up, till he sees all things thro' narrow chinks of his cavern."

Michael was a self-educated man, proud of it, who sometimes seemed to have swallowed a library. He was conversant with most of the great authors, happy to delve into the metaphysical thought on which he put his own unique, sometimes abstract, truth. In many ways he was looking for answers to the big questions and sometimes that search led him into dangerous territory. To the edge. The fine line between truth and insanity, the dark side of man which nearly every great philosopher and writer has entered and plumbed – at their own risk: Blake, Hesse, Fowles, Hansen, Burroughs, Kerouac, Pirsic, Mailer, Sartre, Easton Ellis and Capote. Michael considered *Siddhartha*

– the story of a soul's long quest in search of the ultimate answer to the enigma of a man's role on earth – a better book but recognised in us all the lonely hunter that is Hesse's *Steppenwolf*, the conflict between spirit and life and the struggle of the spirit against itself. "We all go there sometimes," he said in a whisper.

He had a passion for the writings of Sartre, Arthur Miller (*Nexus, Sexus, Plexus*), the Australian author Peter Carey whose work pushes the boundaries of reality and unreality until they are so blurred it's a mind play that creates a surrealistic state that could easily be as twisted a reality as Dante's *Inferno*, the Russian novelists Fyodor Dostoevsky and Alexsandr Solzhenitsyn and the great French poet Arthur Rimbaud.

Dostoevsky's *Crime and Punishment* was one of his favourite books and it's easy to understand why. In part 3, chapter 5, Dostoevsky wrote, "All people seem to be divided into 'ordinary' and 'extraordinary'. The ordinary people must lead a life of strict obedience and have no right to transgress the law because . . . they are ordinary. Whereas the extraordinary people have the right to commit any crime they like and transgress the law in any way just because they happen to be extraordinary."

But – and this is a guess – it was Rimbaud that spoke clearest to him. It is in the life and works of Rimbaud that the deepest – and ultimately most chilling – coincidences can be found. Jean Nicolas Arthur Rimbaud was born in Charleville, Ardennes, on October 20, 1854, the son of an army captain and a stern disciplinarian wife. When Rimbaud was six his father left for good – Rimbaud would never see him again – and his mother was left to raise Arthur and his older brother. He was richly talented and after a brilliant academic career ran away to Paris after publishing his first book of poems when he was just 16. But Rimbaud didn't last long in the capital, returning to Charleville where, as a 17-year-old, he lived an indolent life of leisure, drinking and bawdy storytelling. But his talent was extreme and couldn't be contained. In 1871 he published *Le Bateau Ivre* (The Drunken Boat), a prodigious mix of bold and striking imagery and almost fluorescent language. Soon after at the invitation of fellow poet Paul Verlaine – who also became a master poet developing a style of poetry which sacrificed everything for sound – he returned to Paris where they began a homosexual relationship that lasted until 1873 when Verlaine shot Rimbaud in the arm and was subsequently sentenced to two years jail for attempted murder. Rimbaud, however, appears not to have been exclusively homosexual. There are several examples amid his works of poems for women whom he loved or whose physique he admired.

A year earlier, in the summer of 1872 Rimbaud wrote many of his *Les Illuminations,* an astonishing collection of prose and verse poems that dealt through the use of childhood, mystical and dream images, with his dislike of the materialistic world and his yearning for the spiritual. A year later he would publish *Une Saison en Enfer* (A Season in Hell) which symbolises his struggle to break with his past – his 'enfer' his hell. The critics reacted with icy disdain and Rimbaud, just 19 years old, disgusted, burned all his manuscripts and turned his back on literature forever, becoming an adventurer, explorer, gunrunner, trader, soldier and gypsy. Over the next 18 years he would travel ceaselessly around Europe and to the Far East, eventually spending 10 years in Abyssinia until in February 1891 he developed a tumour on his right leg; in May the leg was amputated in the Hospital de la Conception, Marseilles. A few months later his condition worsened again and on December 10, 1891, Arthur Rimbaud died in that Marseilles hospital.

He was 37 years old. So was Michael.

Coincidence makes strange bedfellows, but this one goes further. Leap forward to '97 and *Elegantly Wasted,* the comeback INXS album after a three year break. There's little doubt its best track is 'Just A Man': a song Michael wrote about his past and family and delivered with a throaty huskiness that breathes pure emotion over stripped back pure rock rhythm'n'roll. In 'Just A Man', Hutch lays himself bare.

In July 1871, 126 years earlier, Arthur Rimbaud wrote *L'Homme Juste*... in English – *The Just Man.* Coincidence or reference? Decide for yourself. Rimbaud even wrote in one letter to a professor of his acquaintance that he was "paid for my trouble in beer and women". The trouble to which he refers is the words and deeds he served up to old school acquaintances so that he may live. You could spend a few years researching the Rimbaud connection and who knows what you'd find. I spent a few days and found enough to feel chilled right down to . . . lilies.

Michael and Paula Yates' beautiful daughter Heavenly Hiraani Tiger Lily – whom I've seen at arm's length just once – has extraordinary eyes, an extraordinary awareness. It could be that her name is born not only from Michael's love of Hong Kong but also his love of Rimbaud who celebrates the lily in several poems, most beautifully in *Ce Qu'on Dit Au Poete A Propos de Fleurs* (To the Poet on the Subject Of Flowers), wherein he describes lilies as "those pessaries of ecstasy!" and two verses later, "Lilies! Lilies! none to be seen! yet in your verse, like the sleeves of the soft-footed Women of Sin, always these white flowers shiver"; and in *Lily*, "A heavenly sweetness butters your stamens".

Perhaps these are just coincidences. Perhaps not. But Michael Hutchence wasn't the only or the first rock icon to be touched by Rimbaud. The legendary Patti Smith has acknowledged Rimbaud as her initial source of inspiration. Besotted and indebted to him, she wrote and published in Babel (1974), two poems about her object of obsession: *rimbaud dead* and *dream of rimbaud*. And Michael was certainly a fan of Patti's early work, particularly her début *Horses* album, one of the definitive records in rock'n'roll. That much I know because it came up during that April 11, 1993, interview by the Esplanade Hotel pool in Fremantle.

People don't look much more relaxed than Hutch did that day as he kicked his sandals off, stuck his feet up on a table and leant back in his chair. Mr Laidback. That brought a smile: "I haven't had to talk to any of you people for a few years," he grinned. "Only be persecuted across England and Europe. Isn't it peaceful here." It wasn't a question but a statement. Not a paparazzi in sight. As hotel guests – mostly kids and early teens – splashed in the pool, their parents leant back in lazyboys or gathered in gaggles around tables. Michael Hutchence would have been just another payer – apart from the giveaway tape recorder perched precariously on the edge of the table, next to his left leg. On the other side of the pool, Niki Turner, INXS' elegant publicist, kept an eye on proceedings from a suitably removed – but close enough – distance.

The night before INXS had kicked off their Get Out Of The

House tour – better remembered as the 'Back To The Pubs' tour – with a passionate, sexy, but slightly uncertain show. A few bum notes here, the odd dropped vocal there. "Yeah, it was good, wasn't it," he whispers. "What did you think?" He's genuinely interested. I tell him and ask him why. "We're like kids at the moment," he says. "It's hard to understand how different this can be for us and how much it can mean doing these kind of shows. I'm going to be kind of upset going back to the bigger venues and arenas. Maybe it will be good though." He didn't sound convinced.

"We did this to give ourselves a bit of a charge as well and it's certainly done that. We've gone the whole way with it, even down to starting the tour in Perth where we started in terms of writing songs and performing."

Broadway Tavern, Steve's, the North-West mining towns . . . he sits up. "Can you remember how bad were we then?" No worse than a lot of youngsters and a lot better than some. You corkscrewed a lot and bobbed up and down. "Yeah, that's because the stages were so small, you couldn't move. Actually, last night reminded me of all that. The stage at Metropolis [a club] is a good size but it's so small after all those arenas. I loved it. So intimate. Especially with the fans. I could see the girls' eyes." He chuckles, mischievously. If he'd looked closer it wouldn't have been all he'd seen.

This is all about perspective. And it's easier to lose than find. "Sure, it makes me realise what we've accomplished, why we did it in the first place, why we kept on doing it all over the year . . . 'cos we love it. Oh god, that sounds clichéd but there isn't any other answer. The only reason that any band loses its perspective is when it gets shackled to success and the products of it. You end up doing arenas, bigger places, T-shirts and the record company always wants the album, now, now, now. You have to realise that you have a choice about what you do at all times – that applies to all of this and it applies to life. You can do something else. This kind of tour isn't something we would've done a few years ago. We were running from this then."

Why? "See I left myself open there, I'm out of practice," he laughs. "Why, oh shit, why not? You know what happened after *Kick* and *X*, particularly all that Concert For Life stuff. How would you feel when your homeland pulls you down for doing the right thing, then puts the boot in? But that's not the whole reason. We had a lot to fit in the picture. It gets so big out there. You can't believe it until it happens to you. Then just when you think you've got it all worked out it changes on you. A lot like life."

So how far out did you get? "Not as far as people make out. Sure I did some stuff here and there. Some of it was excess but when the rush hits, well, it hits and it's hard not to get swept up in it. And there's a lot of pressure when you're so big and everybody is telling you how big you are and they want you to be even bigger and you start trying to live up to something you can't even really see for yourself. But the drugs were mostly recreational, man, metaphysical guides, and, sure, they kept me going for a while. But look at us. None of the band have ended up in a clinic – not even me. It's not like I'm a raving addict who's going to rush off in about five minutes time because I can't live without a fix. Where, when, how much, that's my business.

"This business can be so boring. Everybody knows that. Sometimes you just lose sight of why you are doing it, what life is about. For the past year or so that's something I've been really conscious of. It's extremely important to me to know I'm alive not just going through endlessly repeated motions. Okay, look it got a bit close for comfort of couple of times but that's part of learning too. You've been that close haven't you and you're still here as well. Look at history, I'm not using it as an excuse, but many of the greatest minds, writers, painters, musicians, were hopeless addicts or experimented heavily. Were they judged at the time? Maybe they would have been if there was tabloid press.

"I just think we take the whole thing way too seriously sometimes and that's something I've learnt to deal with, we've all learnt to deal with."

So you don't hope you die before you get old. Laughter, a lot of it. "Of course not. What worries me is that everybody else expects me to. I'd like to say I tried but I failed. Sorry. If I see Pete [Townshend] again I'll excuse myself. But even he failed; and so did the Stones and they really tried. A lot of this stuff is their fault because they kept on trying for so long. The only expectations I want to live up to are my own and those of the people I care about – and I think that's hard enough to do."

Which is how we got to philosophising about life and how we got to Rimbaud and how we got to Patti Smith and how eventually we ended up back on a small stage in a nightclub playing to 1500 people and talking about the rush, the adrenalin, the sexuality, the sheer rock'n'roll of it all. "I love it. I just love that feeling, I always have. But sometimes it's just a job and other . . . other times I don't even recognise myself. It's like I'm not there or it's a different me. But it is me, another part of me, the part that knows what it's doing and how to do it. That's weird and it takes getting used to. Try thinking too much about that and it gets very weird."

I ended up asking him if he was happy. He said that was a strange question because not a lot of people asked it. I asked him again. He smiled and said he was happier than he'd been in a long time and then asked me if I was happy. I replied that I was as happy as I could be. And at that he just nodded, smiled and shook my hand. And both of us knew that we were happy but we weren't.

Metropolis nightclub in the main drag of Fremantle was then the town's premier big night out and the venue for most tours by most major, mid-league and cult Australian and overseas acts who couldn't fill the Entertainment Centre in Perth or didn't want to take a chance on the acoustics of a large open space and a high ceiling, or preferred something a little more intimate. Most recently, Metropolis made headlines across the country when one of its bouncers, on patrol out the front, was seriously injured in a drive-by shooting, a form of violence and senseless act that in Australia is – thankfully – restricted to the odd isolated incident.

In 1993, Metropolis had been refurbished and grown steel wings with winding legs that reached above its stage and hung out over the floor and the mosh below. On April 11, the floor was unfriendly turf for even the most practised sardines and the balconies were lined two and three deep. Into this sauna the pigs, piglets and sows for passion sweated and drank. By the time INXS came on the big guzzle had revved up the anticipation and energy level to something approaching meltdown. Soaked to the skin before the gig began, it was the perfect prelude to a Bacchanalian blow-out.

INXS were staggering; gone was the reserve and uncertainty of the previous evening, to be replaced now with vengeance and grandeur, a band both that pulverised and then laid back, stroking their victims until they floored the unconvinced with swift, brutal arcs of razor-edged sound.

Down the front, the girls grew glassy-eyed with every move of Michael's pelvis. He was lost to it in the first few songs. They were lost to him. He became his most Michael, his most Morrison, his most Byron. He was primal sensuality to the land of the living dolls. On the balconies, they moaned for him, whispered about him, commented on the tightness of his leathers, craned dangerously forwards and outwards to get a better view. Dewy womanhood, lust incarnate, a breathless smog of perfume and sweat and beer only moved by the rhythm of the dancers. And by the bars their boyfriends waited, lecherous and content in the knowledge that in his gyrations Michael was doing them a favour from which they would almost certainly benefit before the night was finally over. Bad boys and good boys alike loved Michael Hutchence for precisely this reason. INXS might have been a bit soft and funky for the Swan and Emu brigade but who cared . . . that's rock'n'roll at its most primal too.

On the stage, Michael – drenched in sweat, shirt hanging loose – smacked into 'Suicide Blonde' to a scream that rent the haze; chances were it was going to rain if it got much steamier. Behind him were the best band in the world for those few hours, blowing free and reliving their glorious past, times when they just kicked out the jams free of expectations or preconception. 'Never Tear Us Apart' was unforgettable; even the boys with the plastic cups full of beer pressed close enough and sang along. It just needed somebody, anybody, to scream 'orgy' and it would have been on for young and old. 'The Loved One' was greeted with similar acclaim: around these parts it was always an anthem.

And the Loved One himself danced, twirled, splayed, curled, wrapped and wormed, reached out, laid back, crawled, rolled, jerked, thrust and blew his audience away . . . and the band played him into immortality.

About 1.15am, INXS arrived back at their hotel, obviously happy, obviously high, obviously thirsty. They gathered in a small group around the downstairs bar, a few friends drifting in here and there. That night INXS had found what they were looking for and even if didn't last, for those few hours they were new sensations again.

4

Men And Women

Michael and women. Bacon and eggs. Fish and chips. Snow White and the Seven Dwarfs. Fay Ray and King Kong. Sex, drugs, rock'n'roll. Some things are supposed to go together.

I never asked Michael about his relationships. I never asked any members of INXS about Michael's relationships. Occasionally in conversation somebody volunteered an impression; Michael even did once. No, twice. But I've always believed that unless you know somebody extremely well, then digging around in their relationships is definitely off the wall. I figure people are interested in people, in what makes them tick, in the music they make, why they make it, what it expresses, about what's going on inside their heads and what they're trying to say. That works, oh, 70 per cent of the time. Thirty per cent of musicians have absolutely nothing to say and are only doing interviews because the record company told them to and they're contractually obligated to do so. That's a waste of their time, yours and mine because you end up with the endless repetition of facts you'd probably find summed up with better precision on the CD slick.

When Michael died the local press went berserk and were stalking, amongst others, his father Kell. Just a couple of days after the tragedy one television reporter thrust a microphone in his face and asked, "How do you feel?" Well, how the hell do you think his father felt? His son had just taken his own life. What did they expect Kell to answer? It's so inane, tactless and thoughtless a question as to make any half sane onlooker or viewer wonder which tree the reporter fell out of that morning. No wonder people get sick of the media.

Michael, of course, had his own way of dealing with meddling reporters and photographers. He attacked one and verbally abused a few more. Who would blame him? Invasion of privacy? When you're a "star" it's conveniently overlooked.

We're all voyeurs. We love to see what happens in other people's lives; mostly, because it makes us feel better about our own – and enlivens them. We live vicariously – as a race – through other people's sins of admission and emission. More importantly, some of what you read is horribly distorted junk, exaggerated, blown out of context, and manipulated just the right side of legal. If you believe everything you read, hear or are told, then you are either extremely naive or a fool. Not much of this is ever about the truth, the whole truth and nothing but the truth. It's about getting some small piece of hand-me-down and beating it up to headline hogging status: then trying to prove it. Stick to top-line newspapers who present the simple unembellished facts if you want the closest approximation of truth. Ignore the rest.

Even in the real world, which is not the world in which Michael always lived, whenever a relationship ends badly friends will take sides, and gossip from rival factions will lead to conflicting stories. Friends will hear things they might not want to hear and opinions will be informed by misinformation inspired by hurt feelings. But at least the circulation of these stories will be restricted to friends, and friends of friends. In the unreal world, the world in which Michael sometimes lived, these stories will be circulated amongst millions of tabloid readers who will form opinions based upon versions of events exaggerated by editors to attract even wider circulation, often way beyond the truth of what may or may not have happened between Michael and his girlfriends.

All of which makes presenting the truth about Michael and his lovers an impossible task – as much as the tabloid press and a fat wad of weekly magazines might like you to think otherwise. To illustrate this, here are three reports about exactly the same event: the break-up of the relationship between Michael and Australian actress and model Virginia Hey.

On August 18, 1988, Wendy Squires reported in the *Mirror*, ". . . Citing logistics and the singer's lack of privacy as the major problems in the whirlwind affair, Hey says she will always have a soft spot for Hutchence.

" 'I'm terribly sad about the whole thing,' the stunning 35-year-old blonde said. 'We were very much in love but I want my career and he wants his career. I'd say it was the nature of his work that broke us up. It's just not conducive to an intimate, quiet, romantic relationship.' Hey admits the timing of the couple's steamy London affair also contributed to the break-up. 'Michael was right smack bang in the middle of the tour at the time,' she said. 'Perhaps, if he had been in between tours it would have been different. It was hard for us to be together constantly because I had to be in LA and he had to be in every major city of America and the world.' "

Hey said that Hutchence was coping with the pressure of international fame, but added it had its drawbacks. " 'The pressure on him to constantly perform affects his private life,' she said. 'That's just exactly what he doesn't have, a private life. I mean the tension is terrific – as in horrific.' "

Hey concludes by imagining that she and Michael will probably remain good friends because they became so close for a short time and that is something that will last forever.

On April 10, 1995, *Woman's Day* published a story by Karen Lateo, with the eye-catching headline: *Aussie lover tells/Paula's fatal obsession for Michael.* By this time Michael had, of course, been involved with both Kylie Minogue and Helena Christensen and had only recently become involved with Paula. That's all the background you need to know.

This second story reads as follows: "Paula Yates is a selfish woman who will stop at nothing to get what she wants. Even worse, she has no respect for that golden rule: never steal your friend's boyfriend.

"To actress and model Virginia Hey, that's the most damning thing anyone could say about a woman. And she has no reservations in condemning Paula. Eight years ago, she was the first victim of this determined woman's desperate pursuit of INXS rocker Michael Hutchence.

"Virginia is not the only gorgeous victim of a Hutchence romance – he has split with Kylie Minogue and now Helena Christensen. Virginia has formed her own theories about what went wrong – and one theory points the finger at Paula.

" 'She broke up my relationship with Michael, now he's broken his relationship with Helena,' " Virginia says matter-of-factly.

"Michael is the greatest love of Virginia's life. She still sings his praises as a sensitive, intelligent, charismatic and romantic man. Their affair, in 1988, was passionate and intense and they'd spoken of marriage.

" 'When I first met him I was bowled over. I looked into his eyes and melted,' she says. Yet in the interests of fairness, Virginia wants the world to know the blame should fall both ways. Sure, Paula wanted Michael. But Michael welcomed the attention to distract him from his biggest fear – commitment.

" 'We talked about commitment. We joked about the "M" word. But I think it terrified him really,' she admits. 'It is very difficult for him to commit to one woman. Some guys are naturally commitment-phobic. Unfortunately for me, and for Helena and Kylie and possibly Paula, he is that kind of person. It seems that every time he reaches a point in a relationship where he's expected to make some kind of commitment – I don't mean marriage, I just mean monogamy and fidelity – he turns, just turns his back and runs away.

" 'Paula walked into his life in New York at the perfect time for him.'

"The fateful New York interview was set for 9am. Virginia slept in, but awoke at 3pm to find herself still alone. Immediately she was suspicious and phoned Paula's room, two floors below.

" 'When I rang Paula sounded sleepy – the phone dropped off the hook. I heard all this rustling of sheets and soft, sleepy mumbling. I knew even before I phoned. I just said, "put Michael on".

" 'He was nervous and distracted. He instantly made excuses – but I hadn't even asked him what he was doing.'

"Virginia told Michael to get back to their room, and about 20 minutes later he arrived, looking an absolute fright.

" 'He was flushed and dishevelled, covered in lipstick and his buttons done up the wrong way. His cowboy boots were outside his pants.

" 'The whole image was of someone who had just made love or was about to, or someone who had just been wrestling a giant gorilla with lipstick on!

" 'He went straight to the bathroom and had a shower and brushed his teeth. He protested his innocence, but I knew.'

"Virginia packed her bags and left. She has not spoken to Paula since that day.

" 'Privately I was bitter. I was really hurt and disappointed. I don't get aggressive very often. I threw a few things at the wall, not at him.

" 'If it was an innocent situation I'm sure I would have heard from Paula by now. She'd have to be deaf, dumb and blind not to know Michael and I split up that day – that she caused the end of my relationship with Michael.

" 'She seems to have little regard for other people's feelings. She seems selfish and disrespectful – she doesn't see any other situation except her own. She wants what pleases her, and that's Michael. Obviously, he does too. They've both thrown away a lot to end up together.' "

The story concludes with Virginia saying, " 'I think he's finally found the soul mate he's been searching for. He found her and then kept going back to her.

" 'I think the sparks started flying when they first met. She's as irresistible to men as he is to women. They are like star-crossed lovers.' "

This story also appeared in the *News Of The World* which is where Paula Yates saw it. In her book *Paula Yates: The Autobiography* (Harper Collins Publishers, 1995), Yates recounts her meeting with Michael that day in 1988. She says he was 20 minutes late for the appointment and when she called him he responded that he was "just feeling up Virginia" and he'd be "down in a minute".

At the end of the interview, Paula concludes that by the light of a neon sign flashing outside the window "he looked a real heartbreaker". It is during this interview Paula records what was to become Michael's better known comments: " 'I'd like a baby, but not just one woman,' he paused, reflectively. 'Maybe five women. I guess you'd have to have some kind of arrangement.' 'It'll never work,' I muttered darkly."

A page further on, Paula writes, "Years later, when Michael and I were together, the girlfriend he'd been with in New York sold her story to the *News Of The World*. Virginia claimed that Michael and I had been in bed all day. She said I was perfect for him because I was a sex toy. The truth was that Michael and I had been shopping for an egg poacher, some baby clothes and a Chanel dress before going back to church. When Michael went back to his room, Virginia was sitting in the dark holding a pair of scissors. She then threatened to kill him, me and herself, and probably Sue (a friend who travelled with her to New York to visit 'the land of her ancestors') as well, because she was in bed with me at the time. Michael and Virginia split up that night, but the whole incident sounded like a scene from Fatal Attraction."

Remarkably, there is more. It gets serious out there in gossip land. *The Daily Telegraph-Mirror* reported on March 27, 1995, 'The English press – who started the latest paparazzi frenzy to catch Yates and Hutchence in the act – have been sparing nothing in the chase for the story.

"*News Of The World* did an exclusive interview with Hey in Sydney, but did not count on the cunning of rival Fleet St paper, the *Sunday Mirror*.

"Hey was woken at her Bondi home at 4am on Saturday morning by a caller from England who claimed to be *News Of The World*'s lawyer wanting to check a few quotes.

"Before a groggy Hey got wise to what was happening and slammed down the phone, she gave enough to the 'lawyer' to ensure the *Sunday Mirror* had a taste of the story."

Such shenanigans are, apparently, commonplace.

And what did Michael have to say about all this. Not a lot. In *Woman's Day* (August 16, 1988), he's quoted in a story by Steve Dougherty and Todd Gold: ". . . Hutchence says that his longest relationship lasted several years, but his most recent, with actress Virginia Hayes (their spelling at the time), less than a year. 'Basically,' he said, 'music destroyed it. You get so good at saying goodbye, you might as well not be together.' "

So who do you believe? Which story is the most accurate? Where lies the truth? Who had the most to gain, the biggest agenda? Most of all, does it really matter? Reduced to this level of analysis, it's just a soap opera. Emotions, whether they are those of the rich'n'famous or those of the everyday man and woman, don't deserve cheapening. The spotlight doesn't beam a licence that says "you have the perfect right to screw me over". If somebody wants to bare all, hand over their life to public analysis that's their decision but wait for the invitation. More often than not it won't come.

So let's try and do this with some dignity. If that's possible.

According to a mixture of women's mags and tabloid reports, Michael's first love was a girl called Holly whom he met when he was 10 and living in Hong Kong. "Holly gave him a book about dogs, but the flirtation didn't last. Michael caught her kissing another boy, and the seeds of sexual jealousy were sown," reported *Woman's Day* of July 27, 1992, in a story by John Smallwood, headlined Michael Hutchence: Life and Love IN-XS.

Their story continues, "He didn't have much better luck when, by now living in Hollywood with his newly divorced mother, the future film star Nastassja Kinski came to the Hutchence residence for dinner with friends.

"'She was about 12 years old and very gorgeous,' Michael reveals. 'I tried to play doctors and nurses with her, but I didn't get very far! Nastassja was extremely intelligent and didn't want to waste her time on boys.'

"For seven years he had a steady girlfriend, model Michelle Bennett, in Australia. But she refused to meet him at concerts after nearly being trampled in the crush at one of his gigs, and grew to hate the rock'n'roll business."

On November 22, 1997, Michelle Bennett was one of the last people Michael called – unsuccessfully – before he died. They had stayed close friends.

Extraordinary as it may seem, Michael was like most other youngsters of his age – keen to get it on. There is a well-documented story of an affair with a 17-year-old girl who was 'given' to him at a party on a dog collar and chain.

Woman's Day quotes him on this one in a story by Serge Simonaert titled Sex, Drugs & Kylie Minogue as saying, "'We got on really well. She was smart. When I was 19 – in the punk era – we used sex to shock in a real way, not the way the media uses it today. We'd run around with her on a chain . . . It was hilarious. You had all these real men who thought they'd seen it all and we sorted them out.'

"Michael has spent many of his 33 years sorting people out. His anger is directed at those he considers hypocrites – the British upper classes, stick-in-the-mud Australian politicians, music business bosses – but he is also able to recognise his own internal demons.

"He talks openly about past dalliances with drugs, including heroin, about his life on the road. In the early days the band fancied itself by selling marijuana from the back of a car covered in Christian stickers to foil the police.

" 'You get offered things when you are on the road and you take them,' he says. 'And if you're a person like myself who wants to get as much as possible out of life, you keep on taking.

" 'It's a bit of self-fulfilling prophecy: sex attracts sex, like money makes money.

" 'The first years INXS toured America I slept with a lot of women . . . I was in a hotel room with someone, and the bedhead was making so much noise on the wall, so I put a pillow behind it. Then the girl left and another girl came in and asked, "What's that pillow for?" and I thought, "You'll find out in a second".' "

What seems more interesting than Michael happily bonking his way around America is the attitudes he expresses in the three *Woman's Day* pieces and how they shift over the five years.

In the August 16, 1988 Dougherty/Gold article he says, " 'I don't really get chased by girls . . . [Well] maybe leaving or entering a place.' And what sort of women does he meet on the road? 'They lose their minds, and by Monday, they're going "Oh my God, why'd I do that?" ' "

"Really? 'I mean,' he said, perhaps a tad defensively. 'I've met lots of people. They're not all bimbos.' "

By July 27, 1992, Michael's getting blunter. He tells John Smallwood, " 'I've led a much more decadent life than I've ever admitted,' he says with remarkable candour. 'I used to be Mr Fun Time, drinking and all the rest, but self-destruction is pointless. At one stage I started sniffing heroin out of curiosity. I didn't inject it, and I'm not the sort of person to get hooked on something but it was easy to see how persuasive heroin can be. The problem is that, while a lot of so-called heroes use heroin, people will continue to take it because they think they can be heroes, too. It's really pathetic.' "

A year later, June 7, 1993, and he's talking to Simonaert about his relationship with Christensen. " 'I remember Bono of U2 saying, "Rock stars know what it's like to be beautiful women". He's right. We're stared at all the time. Women come up to us like men walk up to gorgeous women. We can be lazy in bed because the women are eager to please the star, just as beautiful women don't have to lift a finger, because the male is eager to please.' "

Later, the story continues, ". . . Success turned him [Michael] into the typical sex, drugs and rock'n'roll star, but now he says he has calmed down, mellowed.

" 'I'm not quite the gypsy I used to be,' he says. ' I used to see how far I could push the barriers. Now, however corny it sounds, I treasure the value of a good relationship, and I realise that experimentation and wandering cause pain.' "

The Divinyls enchanted pop rock smash, 'Pleasure And Pain', contains the lines: *"It's a fine line between pleasure and pain, you've done it once you can do it again, whatever you've done don't try to explain, it's a fine, fine, line between pleasure and pain."*

Michael and Kylie Minogue crossed that line after 16 months. These days Kylie is so strong, so poised, so smart, so warm, so much woman. So damned gorgeous. It wasn't always that way. Kylie grew up in public: the hardest way there is.

When Kylie burst onto the local scene in 1987 with her smash teen bop reworking of Little Eva's early Sixties classic, 'The Locomotion', she was just 18 going on 19, and innocent. She became Australia's darling, the star of the *Neighbours* soap series with equally young, equally attractive Jason Donovan. They were the hottest couple in the land – or they weren't a couple, depending on who you read. *Neighbours* made Kylie the hottest thing on television and prolific hit producers Stock, Aitken and Waterman ensured she did the same to the charts. On July 16, 1988, her début album *Kylie* arrived, hit the British charts, took a firm grip on the No 1 spot, and spent 67 weeks in the top 50; in October 1989, the follow-up, *Enjoy Yourself*, also went to No 1 and enjoyed a 33-week run. Seven singles in a row went top 10. In Australia, Kylie became a gay icon, in part because the 'Kylie can't sing etc' backlash had already started, and the gay fraternity's love of and identification with the underdog is well-documented.

What's consistently startling about the music industry mob who put the boots into all the Kylies and Jasons over the years is that they miss the point, and it's the big point, the big reality: without them, without the Spice Girls, Bay City Rollers, Take That, Hanson, without teen pop sensations, without the cloying and oh-so-safe-and-dull adult contemporary/soft soul-pop-dance blockbusters from the likes of Michael Bolton, Mariah Carey, Celine Dion, Whitney Houston, there wouldn't be a music industry. It's economics. Without such mega-sellers and massive commercial success stories, the big six majors would struggle to exist, yet alone sign anything off the wall or alternative. The whole indie industry would also fall apart – as it did post-punk in the late '70s. Overseas many of the big "indies" now have majors as partners. In fact, the whole question of what is indie and what isn't is a can of wrigglers that constantly reproduces itself.

So there we were in Australia in 1988/89 with Kylie in England and INXS in America: Australia ruled the world in a peculiar way. How fitting that Kylie and Michael should become Kylie *and* Michael.

Around the same time Michael and celebrated supermodel/ actress Elle Macpherson had enjoyed a brief fling after meeting in Sydney's Oxford St. Apparently, it was lust at first sight (the press of the time has them "instantly mesmerised"). The sole evidence remaining today is a close-up of an unshaven Mike and sun-glassed Elle locking lips somewhere, sometime.

Kylie came as a surprise. And it put Michael into a spotlight from which he would never escape. " 'This is all new to me and it's something I've always tried to avoid,' " he told Katherine Tullich in *The Sun-Herald* magazine (March 25, 1990), " 'but I guess I've just been thrown into it.

" 'I know all's fair in love and war but when you go off and try to be yourself and it ends up on the front page of the press it's frightening, knowing your life is under such scrutiny.' "

Their romance was perfectly public. Kylie on Michael's Harley remains one of the first and most memorable pictures of the time. It was here in Sydney that they were photographed strolling hand-in-hand for the first time and straddling the hog. In January 1990, the rumour mill announced they were engaged.

In June, the paparazzi snapped them smiling happily after four days on the Orient Express from Venice to London. A few months later, they apparently bought a $500,000 (Australian) "secret hideaway" in the south of France.

And on the other hand . . . the tabloids happily spilled rumours of Michael and other women. In May 1990, the *News Of the World* alleged that Kylie had dumped Michael after a row about his womanising ways. The report alleged he had been "romancing" three other women: Hollywood model, Rosanna Klitzner, 23, whom Michael had apparently been seeing for eight months before he began dating Kylie; Justine Clarke, 22, actress in yet another Australian soap, *Home And Away*; and an "old flame", Cathy Lee.

Whatever, Kylie and Michael were over by early 1991. Short it may have been, it changed both of them. Kylie emerged from it as a young woman who was beginning to understand exactly what that meant: mini-skirts that hugged her butt, eyes that smoked and talked much louder than words in photos, a way of walking that spoke of an awakening – and a thorough enjoyment of it. Somewhere in time she said memorably, "when I found out what I was missing I wanted it all, and then more." Or so the legend goes.

Michael in turn was mellowed by Minogue: he smiled a lot – even at photographers, took up yoga, became a vegetarian and seemed more settled. He told John Smallwood, "The first time I met Kylie was backstage at one of her shows . . . I remember seeing this diminutive person surrounded by five huge record company guys, like she was their golden egg and they had to protect her.

"I thought 'God, how terrible' and I think I said something quite rude to them, and something quite rude to her probably, and then staggered off into the night. But the thing about Kylie is that she's just a really good person. I wish everybody could meet her so they would know."

Two years earlier in March 1990 when the couple were still happily doing what couples do in the early daze of their relationship, Michael explained to Katherine Tullich, " 'We come from totally different situations. And obviously all this affects me because I don't have that sort of image. For me to have that relationship with her, people are saying "What the hell are you two doing together?" '

"But Hutchence readily praises the much-maligned Minogue. 'Because she's copped so much criticism she's a really strong person,' he said. 'I can't handle it.' "

And, finally, in 1993 to Serge Simonaert, "Kylie's no Barbie doll . . . She's a really bright, really nice person. And I didn't corrupt her. If anything, our relationship made her more independent."

And he's right about that too. In the past four years, Kylie has shrugged off the *Neighbours*/soapie tag, tossed aside the disco queen image, and earned the begrudging respect of some of her harshest critics for her self-titled set of 1995 and the recent *Impossible Princess* (title simply *Kylie* in the UK). Not that either is perfect, but both show a woman determined to grow into her music to open it out and ignore commercial expectations. 'Confide In Me' from the '95 album stands as her best ever song and performance, a huge ballad wrapped in strings which instead of folding into goo, hits at the heart.

In 1996, she took off, recording the swampy duet 'Where The Wild Roses Grow' with Nick Cave: that alone not only quadrupled her indie cred points but it made most of the music media sit up in shock. St Nick with Kylie . . . strange things were afoot in the world. It wasn't as strange as it looked: Nick and Michael had become close friends over the years and Cave admitted to wanting to work with her. Perhaps, the most unlikely live scene of '97 was seeing Nick and Kylie sharing the stage as she guested on his Australian tour. Even more unlikely – all the Bad Seeds in the audience loved her. All these kids who one moment were mouthing lyrics about red right hands and masturbating in some confessional rite and wouldn't have a bar of Kylie, suddenly roaring at her prescence as she oozed over their hero.

Kylie is bonkers about Nick. A few weeks before Michael died in the Ritz Carlton hotel (just a block away), I sat in a small, intimate press conference in the comfortable roominess of a plush suite in the Sir Stamford Hotel in Double Bay, an inner city haven for the successful. Big boats and expensive cars and smart hotels for the smart set. Everything is shiny in Double Bay, even the clothes glitter.

Yet this Kylie is and isn't Double Bay. It happens to be the venue but it doesn't need to be. The room is full of mostly young writers chaffing at the bit just to talk to her, to feel her magic. For once, I got to sit back and just watch.

I wrote afterwards: "She laughs a lot this Kylie, smiles in little secret ways to herself, gestures often with her hands and body. Breathtakingly beautiful, she doesn't need to try and be a woman anymore; she knows she is one. It's in the toss of the head, the moisture on her lips, the eyes that meet rather than avoid, the just see-through black top and the firm, ripeness of the pale skin that shimmers through the inch-perfect cloth, the hair that hangs just right over the nape of the neck, a soft flood from a bob on the back of her head. It's an unbeatable story full of all the pitfalls and chasms that come with the kind of teen stardom reserved for a very few, of a past that damned a future, of acceptance and iconism in gay circles when a hetero world was sniggering, of a desperate and barely disguised eventual struggle to escape, of big worldly men who came and plucked the wild rose and planted her in an earth of potential, and her taking root in a world of renewed determination and self-confidence.

"Nick Cave is the godfather of the final stanza in the poetry of her awareness. She uncurls one leg, lets it float towards whatever destination it finds and says, 'I wasn't nervous when I first met Nick because I hate to admit that I was really naive and I didn't know about this *god* that was Nick Cave, the icon. I didn't know. That's probably part of the reason he'd been wanting to do something with me for a while; I'm so far removed from where he comes from that in a strange way it makes our meeting in the middle much more harmonious because if I was here and he was there (the distance is the small space between her outstretched hands) it's 'okay, so . . .' when you meet, but to come from the Birthday Party (she devours the title) and me trying to speed read his autobiography and learning about urination at various gigs and whacking the people over the heads with microphones . . . this guy and the girl that had the hair coming out of that gorgeous hat – a real fashion statement (and she laughs, a gentle trill at her fashion none-sense) – and those sunglasses!!!, for them to meet when you've got all that space between them, for them to overcome, to get to that point,

I just think it's gorgeous and it constantly thrills me. I just adore him.' "

About Michael she says nothing but a few years earlier during a phone call from Singapore she told me, "I laugh when I think back to how we must have looked. Me the naive little girl next to this big worldly rock star. And I wonder what it was he saw in me in the first place. I learned a lot from him and maybe he did from me. It was special."

The song that stands out on *Impossible Princess* is the Eastern-influenced 'Cowboy Style', a kind of Jah Wobble meets the Indigo Girls fluctuating atmosphere that pulses on some heavy percussion work. The lyrics make interesting reading. It isn't hard to make a strong case for 'Cowboy Style' being inspired by and about her relationship with Michael. Whether it is . . . well, I never asked her. I forgot. Honestly.

True to form, Michael's next relationship seems to have begun before the previous one had ended. Photographer Herb Ritts introduced him to Helena Christensen, then Denmark's top model; these days she's dubbed by some 'the most beautiful woman in the world'.

Outside of Paula, there's little doubt that Helena was the woman most likely to claim Michael for the term of his natural life. Their relationship ran four years, becoming so established and accepted that even the paparazzi seemed to back off: new sensations were required. Instead they became, in the public eye, another couple in the ocean of beautiful couples, an ocean Michael dismissed once as ". . . Yes lists and No lists and all that crap".

Helena encouraged the rebel spirit in Michael. They seemed to share a common dislike of pretence and artifice, despite their combined wealth and status. In *The Daily Telegraph-Mirror* of April 24, 1993, in an interview by Kathy McCabe, Michael says, " 'I think there is a certain sensibility to someone you are attracted to and when it rubs off, that's good,' he said.

" ' You have never met anybody like this, anybody that truly doesn't give a shit about being a star, who really doesn't care in an enormous way. To her detriment and mine, too, at times. It's really funny – we get in the most hilarious situations. If someone's on the big star trip, it's like a red rag to a bull.

" 'But we always end up being really good friends with those people because they need somebody around to do that to them sometimes. With the cameras and things going on, she finds that amusing because that's her life and she can just stand there and look great. I'm the guy standing next to her looking like . . . well, you know.' "

After Michael's death there was a school of opinion that the head injuries he received in a traffic accident (he was riding a bicycle home from a nightclub) in Copenhagen in September 1992 – at the time it was rumoured to be a deliberate attempt to run him down – contributed to the depression for which he was being treated. Michael suffered major concussion and a fractured skull which affected his senses of taste and smell. Again, depending on who you listen to, he either recovered fully or regained only his sense of smell. Without wanting to put too fine a point on it, the loss of the sense of smell robbed him of some scents he treasured, or so that theory went.

It can be best traced back to an article in *Details* magazine at the end of '93 in which he commented that one in four people with similar injuries lost their sense of smell and, by extension, of lust. Helena was said to have nursed him back to full health at the time.

Now it seems that those injuries may have had a long-term and possibly devastating effect. Robert Milliken wrote in a feature in *The Independent* (March 1998), "His friends are convinced that the accident was a turning point that led to increasing bouts of depression and reliance on Prozac.

" 'Ever since the accident, he was on a slow decline,' says [Richard] Lowenstein. 'I'd never seen any evidence of depression, erratic behaviour or violent temper before it. I saw all those things after it. One night in Melbourne, he broke down and sobbed in my arms. He said, "I can't even taste my girlfriend any more." His girlfriend then was Helena. For someone who was such a sensual being, this loss of primary senses affected his notion of place in the world and, I believe, damaged his psyche.'

"Hutchence grew increasingly sensitive to criticism and conflict. The tabloid dramas of his life with Paula affected him deeply. So did public put-downs such as that by Noel Gallagher of Oasis, who called him a 'has-been' at the 1996 Brit awards. 'He was a lost soul, to tell you the truth,' says [Greg] Perano [formerly of Hunters & Collectors, and one of his closest friends in Australia]."

By contrast, the picture that emerged of Michael and Helena over 1993 and 1994 was of a comfortable, loving, well-grounded couple. Happy and settled, living – when schedules permitted – in his villa in the south of France. There are two snapshots that stand out.

The first appeared in *The Australian* of March 5, 1994, under the headline Reflections of a coy-boy. Amruta Slee wrote: "It's 8pm in New Orleans and INXS fans are pushing their way into the band's dressing room for a 'meet and greet' arranged by a local radio station. Michael Hutchence, a straw cowboy hat on his head and a look of blank resignation on his face, signs autographs and makes small talk. At one point his girlfriend, Helena Christensen, statuesque in a long maroon skirt and belly-button skimming sweater, floats through the crowd. A girl called Leslie digs the watching reporter in the ribs.

" 'Who is that woman,' she asks.

" 'That's Helena Christensen.'

" 'Is she a model?'

" 'She's a supermodel.'

"Leslie is very excited. 'Wait till I tell my friends,' she squeaks, 'that I saw a supermodel at the show.'

"Another man might balk at being upstaged at his own gig but, at 33, after 15 years in the spotlight, Michael Hutchence understands the vagaries of fame better than most. 'Somewhere between farce and boredom,' is how he sums up public life. He says this with a genial grin: after all, there are compensations. If INXS chose to retire tomorrow they would do so as very wealthy men . . ."

Later, Slee continues, ". . . Through all the ups and downs, Hutchence has remained a compelling figure. Though he takes a Four Musketeers approach towards being singled out – 'One for all and all for one' – he has clearly landed the role of D'Artagnan. In a world of fanzines he is still young enough and attractive enough to sell product. His ability to send himself up makes him a refreshing interview prospect. He could branch out in interesting directions . . .

"Michael and Helena are staying in a cottage in the French quarter of New Orleans in a lodging so discreet there is no doorbell. Luckily a waiter carrying a tray of cocktails arrives to jiggle with the code. Leading the way the waiter says, 'Are you sure they know you're coming? I don't think they're ready to do an interview.' Taken in conjunction with Hutchence's alleged love of a good time this remark conjures visions of indescribable decadence. But when the door opens the scene is domestic; the couple are watching television and the only sign of pop star excess is the selection of drinks – Bailey's, beers and Bloody Marys – two of which Hutchence gulps down in quick succession. He does not overlook the impression this must make. 'You're going to paint me as drunk, I know it,' he says affably. 'It's so politically incorrect to drink these days.' "

Later still Michael muses about Helena, " 'She's got a really good ear. A great record collection. Helena is a very real person. Very real. This cliché, the model and the rock star, we laugh our heads off but it's cruel and it's embarrassing. We didn't meet as the press imagine. "Hello, I'm a rock star, you're a model, let's get to know each other." ' "

Just as compelling is the picture David Cavanagh painted of their life in the south of France, in a 1994 interview which was printed in several major Australian papers in November '94.

His introduction is a lovely piece of writing and quite fitting: "There's a wonderful story, possibly apocryphal, that people tell about one-time soccer superstar George Best. At some point in the Seventies – the fleet-footed No 11 having long since given up any pretense of an ascetic lifestyle – a room-service waiter brings him breakfast in a hotel. Entering the room, discreetly, the waiter's gaze is met by a bomb site, sheer dishabille chaos: empty liquor bottles, rolled-up 20 pound notes, suspicious-looking residues on compact-case mirrors, strewn pantyhose and, finally, Best himself, sprawled comatose across a voluminous bed, his limbs interlocked with those of two of the top stewardesses of the day.

" 'George, George, George . . .' tuts the waiter sadly. 'Where did it all go wrong?'

"As we sit on the verandah of Michael Hutchence's old stone villa in the south of France, looking out over 2ha of rolling green landscape, with its 25m pine trees, its cute little lawns and the host's 1964 Aston Martin in the garage – not to mention the swimming pool next to which Hutchence's girlfriend, the jewel-eyed supermodel, Helena Christensen, is making last-minute preparations for an *al fresco* luncheon – there is only one question to ask. Michael, Michael, Michael . . . where did it all go wrong?

" 'I don't know, mate,' he says gravely.

"The wine: Macon Villages, a petulant white. The cigars: Havana. The climate: intensely pleasant. Hutchence's parents are house guests, as are Helena's parents and her grandparents, who at the ages of 78 and 71, have finally sallied forth from native Denmark armed with only three English expressions: 'You are my lucky star', 'Old man, young boy' and 'More beer'. They are lovely people.

"Hutchence monitors the pre-prandial fuss good naturedly, chomping on his cigar. Secluded and happy in this Eden, he has no trouble from paparazzi. They expect him and Helena to be sunbathing down on the beach at Nice. Instead, he is a good half-hour away tucked into the heel of the Alpes Maritimes. Only after several wrong turnings does one get within 200m of the place. A sign on the gate warns of a CHIEN MECHANT. What one actually finds is a small, stripy cat."

Heaven sent . . . and Helena.

"Helena Christensen, wearing a gossamer pink summer dress, is by the pool. But not only that. She's on the coffee table. She's on an advertising hoarding at Warren Street station. She's got an entire issue of *Elle TopModel* to herself, which Hutchence, without a word, turns face down as he walks past to get another drink from the kitchen.

"Inside the gloss of *TopModel*, Helena speaks wistfully of Michael ('J'ai craque pour son cote sexy' – I flipped for his sexy side: she speaks six languages which is five more than he does) and speculates about additions to the villa's *dramatis personae*. In 10 years, she calculates, they will have four kids – two of their own, plus two adopted Peruvians. This is clearly news to Hutchence. He tops his glass up.

"Outlandish reports about him and Helena filter back to the villa, usually to their amusement. The couple were recently married (they learned from a German newspaper). Hutchence didn't mind that so much. He just wondered what Rod Stewart, whom he doesn't know, was doing on the guest list."

It would be nice if this book could reach a perfect conclusion right here. The couple, holding hands, her head on his shoulder, last seen watching the sun set, a passionate French kiss on the horizon.

Three months later all this would end . . . in the arms of Paula Yates.

5

Girl On Fire

Gerry Humphreys of The Loved Ones is singing in that head-in-a-bowl echo and throaty roar that only Gerry can. Gerry's voice was a natural boombox. He didn't need technology. He was . . . raw. Live At Blueberry Hill, 21 years after the *Blueberry Hill* EP (1966). A reunion. The same year as INXS are playing to arenas, 70,000 full, The Loved Ones play Australian pubs to a couple of hundred curious, devoted or nostalgic. Gerry sounds like Eric Burdon doing 'Ring Of Fire' submerged in a metre of water; he sounds like his throat is peeling off layer by layer; he makes Joe Cocker sound like a soprano. Stomp, swamp, blues and strut. The Loved One is five tracks in, the audience ends up bellowing it. But there's much more to it than that. Gerry Humphreys was the Michael Hutchence of the Sixties (albeit briefly), and the swing and loin fire of The Loved Ones is the same open-ended sexual innuendo that INXS delivered effortlessly a decade later. R'n'b and urban blues had transmutated to funk rock but the intent was the same: dangerous bedfellows, seduction. They churn through a filthy version of the Willie Dixon standard, 'I'm Your Hoochie Coochie Man', before Gerry intros 'Sad Dark Eyes', one of The Loved Ones' earliest sheet wrinklers. The lyrics are sly, lethal, lust.

A chapter about Michael, Paula and Bob should read like this:

In 1977, a scrawny punk rocker, Bob Geldof, met Paula Yates, a blonde nymphet with a penchant (then) for wearing nighties to parties and gigs who had several years earlier been photographed relaxing naked on a billiards table for *Penthouse* magazine. She didn't give him the blow job in the back of the limo everybody thinks she did on their first or second or something date. They moved in together. Ten years later they married. They had an open-ended relationship. Apparently. In

95

other words, they probably screwed around a bit without any long term intent or collateral damage. Bob organised Live Aid, was knighted in 1986, nominated for the 1987 Nobel Peace Prize and became a national hero. Paula co-presented a score of TV shows, most famously *The Tube* (a British rock show) and *The Big Breakfast,* on which she interviewed her mostly famous to very famous guests on or in a bed, wrote books on mother-hood (mostly well-received) and gossip/music columns for newspapers and magazines (not so well received), advocated breastfeeding for as long as possible (up to three years), and was an enthralling – if slightly misunderstood – siren to the Brit public (in particular).

In due course the couple parented three girls – Fifi, Peaches and Pixie. They spent 18 years together. Then, in 1995, Paula left Bob for Michael whom she first met in 1983 (while present-ing *The Tube*), may have slept with in 1988 (see chapter 4), wasn't a Sir but was one of the few great rebel rock stars left on the planet. Thereafter Sir Bob was dignified and quiet and fought for his rights as a father. Paula and Michael lived in a paparazzi-filled nightmare yet still created not only a seemingly deep and loving relationship but also the beautiful Heavenly Hiraani Tiger Lily. Paula wrote an autobiography which made Bob seem – in order of appearance of Bobs – not a Byron, not a stud, but grotty, grimy, grumpy, very smart, very literate, very charming, heroic, triumphant, "the missing link, He-Man, She-Ra", and upset, and delivered Michael as just left of God's gift to women, and hung (which nearly everybody knew anyway). A combination of stud and sensitive, shy, emotional guy (which nearly everybody else knew anyway). She also had her boobs done (bigger) and loved Michael more than all the great loves of the world put together and truly (and maybe domineer-ingly). Michael made more music with his band INXS who weren't as big as they used to be but could still cut it and then some (although some of the press foolishly didn't think so), was worn down by life (in every possible way) and tragically took his own life, leaving the woman he loved (and he did, per-haps addictively, certainly to the extreme) and the daughter he adored and half the world to wonder why.

That should be it. That tells you everything. That tells you about the birds and the bees and the Pees and the Cees (the English language is particularly uncomfortable when it comes to plurals of letters: you may make your own assumptions as to what the letter P and the letter C stand for, as long as they are sexual) and even Cupid and a bunch of arrows and, eventually, tragedy.

I don't actually feel like giving you anymore than that but that would be unfair to Paula and Michael. They deserve better. Most of all they deserved to be left alone.

It is a peculiar obsession of white people (particularly British, Australians, Americans and some Europeans) that whenever a relationship involving anybody vaguely famous for more than five minutes breaks up with somebody who is also famous or not famous or famous by association that they (the white people, nearly all of whom don't know them) have to pan fry them (lightly sauteed) or scramble them, or poach them, or toast them (spread lightly with a sticky substance of your own taste) and serve them up for breakfast where their transgressions, emissions, decisions and vicissitudes are swallowed whole with cereal, bread, muffins, bagels and a cocktail of vitamins, supplements, hormone stimulants, pain-killers, booze, and fruit. With cream. Or jam, honey, treacle, all the "mites" (brown extract spreads that taste bitter and are adored), and pasties. With coffee, tea, natural this water and that water, fruit juices, herbal tonics, and white-label remedies.

I never saw Michael and Paula together in the flesh. Although I wish I had. I'd have liked to see what passed between them, how they looked at each other, how they walked and talked and swayed and touched and embodied each other. I'd have liked to have seen it, because I'd like to be able to write: these people were soul mates. As it is I think they were. I hope they were. People close to them tell me they were.

So it's crucial to understand that there are no baddies. Or there shouldn't be. On a worldwide vote (one to three, lowest score gets to play the angel), Paula is always, of course, cast as a baddie. That is because Sir Bob is . . . Sir Bob. Therefore he can't be bad. And Michael can't be bad, firstly, because he's the hero – or is it anti-hero – of this book, and, secondly, because he's a rock superstar, and rock superstars are supposed to be slightly unclean and covered with juices of mortal sin and panties ripped in lascivious abandon.

Michael told Susan Chenery (*The Sydney Morning Herald, Good Weekend* magazine, October 18, 1997) what he thought of Sir Bob in response to her comment that she'd interviewed the former Boomtown Rat who didn't like Mondays, and found him highly intelligent: "'Satan,' he responds. 'If people knew the truth . . . You know he said he would never support a family, and he never has, not one cent. He has completely manipulated everybody, including the press.'"

This is the one of only two recorded comments about Sir Bob in the whole affair up to Michael's death. It's also the only time since Live Aid that Sir Bob's sainthood has been in question. Judith Whelan reports in a story from London (*The Age*, October 21, 1996) that Paula – who found herself TV show-less and column-less after the then recent alleged dis-covery of opium in the couple's London house – "revealed she was debt-laden and virtually broke, complaining that Geldof provided only $600 a week for groceries". This, unfortunately, doesn't quite sit with Mike's "no support" comment. You also have to wonder just how expensive groceries are in the UK. The rents and taxes are high in Australia but you can feed a family of six on half that.

The other comment was an interview in Australian *Vogue* in which Michael says, "If people actually knew the truth about what happened . . . and why somebody has left somebody, they'd lower their heads in shame." So Sir Bob, even if he is the entire *Omen* trilogy compacted and edited into one scraggy body, appears to have escaped lightly.

The same cannot be said about Paula and Michael. She got it worse than he did because she had the unmitigated gall to leave a living saint! Phew! Michael, meanwhile, was presumed to have had a massive lapse in taste: how else could you explain leav-ing one of the world's most fabulously gorgeous supermodels for a short, mouthy, loud, platinum blonde of a certain age (that no-one seems quite sure about). Surely, this was an error in judgement from which he would shortly recover, ran the general tenor of thought.

The earth-shattering news that Paula Yates and Michael

Hutchence were lovers was revealed first by the *News Of The World* in February 1995. *Who Weekly* (February 27, 1995) pictured the drama that followed so perfectly in a story by Michael Sheather and Paul Pottinger.

"On the chilly evening of February 11 in London, the cynical staff of tabloid terror the *News Of the World* were, for once, dumbfounded. Creeping millimetre by millimetre from a fax in their office was a barely legible handwritten note from rock and roll humanitarian Sir Bob Geldof announcing, in a profoundly public manner, the break-up of his 18-year relationship – the last eight in marriage – to British TV personality Paula Yates.

"Geldof, 40, who helped raise more than $100 million worldwide with Live Aid in 1985 for the victims of Ethiopia's famine and was nominated for the 1987 Nobel Peace Prize, had caved in to the newspaper's demands for confirmation of his separation from Yates, 35. This was after a week of cloak-and-dagger antics during which reporters stalked Yates to a $1,000-a-night hotel where she allegedly stayed three nights with INXS lead singer Michael Hutchence. Geldof's hastily scrawled message read: 'After 18 years of happiness together, Bob and Paula decided to have a break from being in each other's faces all the time. Or, to put it in what Bob calls the "repulsive parlance" of the day, they are "giving each other some space".'

"Quite a lot of space, it turns out. Yates moved out of the couple's $1.5 million Chelsea, London, home on February 8, two days after being tracked to 35-year-old Hutchence's room at the Halkin Hotel, in Belgravia. With her three daughters to Geldof – Fifi Trixibelle, 11, Peaches Honeyblossom, 6, and Little Pixie, 4 – Yates moved into an apartment in London's posh Regent's Park district. Hutchence, who is rumoured to have broken off his engagement [see chapter 7] to Danish model Helena Christensen, 26, apparently renewed his friendship with Yates when he appeared last month on the British cult morning programme, *The Big Breakfast,* during which Yates hosts a celebrity interview segment titled On The Bed With Paula.

"It's not the first time Yates – who posed nude at 16 for *Penthouse* and wrote two well publicised books about parenting, *The Fun Starts Here* and *The Fun Don't Stop* – has been linked with other men. Shortly after her marriage to Geldof in Las Vegas in 1986, she allegedly had a fling with singer Terence Trent D'Arby while her husband was in Africa, and later was involved with pop stars Ben Volpiliere-Pierrot, of Curiosity Killed The Cat, and Spandau Ballet's Martin Kemp."

In her book *Paula Yates: The Autobiography* (Harper Collins Publishers, 1995), she writes of the alleged Trent D'Arby liaison: ". . . Marsha [a friend] woke me with the news that one of the Sunday papers was running a long article about me and Terence Trent D'Arby, which included plenty of details about us both snorting coke in front of some woman I'd never even heard of. I'd never done coke in my life, and Terence treats his body like a temple – he never puts anything noxious into it, not even Mexican food. I jumped out of bed, really frightened. That's the trouble with really horrible stories about you – the fear. Everyone says you just have to get used to it, and that it doesn't matter, as though you have no feelings. But I don't know anyone who's got used to it – not even really brave people like Elton John. These stories don't only hurt you, they hurt the people that love you as well . . .

"In the end, I was linked to just about everyone I spoke to. I once sat on a beach in Barbados with my godfather's son's best friend who, I believe, was some kind of market gardener. The papers ran a photo of us saying we'd had sex while Fifi built a sand castle nearby, which was one of the most stupid stories ever. As we didn't sue the papers, it became a free-for-all. Another paper said I'd been out drinking gin slings all night in London. As I was the leading light of the temperance society, this was also pretty unlikely."

A plea for sympathy or the truth?

Paula has, of course, always used the press, as well. She ain't no saint and there's a simple argument in Britain that she's got what she deserves as far as the paparazzi goes. "If you can't stand the heat, then stay out of the kitchen," – as the saying goes – but opening a hotel room door to find a drunk and naked journo proffering his dubious manhood is way beyond just desserts. It is plain pathetic. She should have pulled his chain and flushed him but she didn't.

Soon after Paula moved out, Sir Bob arranged some time away for the family in an effort to try and work things out. They went first to Ireland and stayed in a folly at the bottom of Bono's garden.

Yates writes of this time, "As we walked into the kitchen, Bono's wife Ali was trying to unstick a picture of Michael from their fridge and hide it before Bob saw it... The week in Ireland was like *Cape Fear.* It rained all the time, the sea crashed outside our window in huge, foaming waves, and Bob was incapable of sleeping because he was so troubled. So was I. It was hard for me to believe I was determined to leave.

"Bono calmly and patiently listened to Bob up at the house for hours. He was patient and understanding, and neither he nor Ali took sides. It was hard for him because he was the only person who knew everyone involved in the story, yet he remained friends with all of us. Bono is totally non-judgemental and Ali is a beautiful, fragrant orchid of a girl. Bono defended Michael always, saying that he was a 'good person', and tried to create some serenity in the maelstrom of passions."

Michael and Paula's romance became 'official', according to *Woman's Day*, (the couple must have been relieved) two months later. On April 24, 1995, Karen Lateo wrote, "Michael Hutchence wraps his arms around Paula Yates in a protective clinch that tells the world: 'Yes, she's mine and we're in love.'

"After months of speculation, midnight trysts in strange hotels, attacks on snooping paparazzi and desperate attempts at marriage mending, the romance between Aussie rocker Michael, 35, and beautiful blonde Paula, 34, is now official.

"At a star-studded $50,000 bash thrown by Janet Jackson at London's trendy Brown's nightclub – attended by Prince, Dannii Minogue, Mica Paris and U2 – the love-struck pair barely noticed other guests as they kissed, cuddled and gazed into each other's eyes like obsessed teenagers. Insiders say they commandeered a sofa and only broke off from their smooching to whisper sweet nothings.

". . . Paula, looking a real sight in a tiny green mini dress, tattoos and smudged lipstick, chose that night to speak out about her feelings for her INXS lover.

" 'Michael and I are very much in love,' she says. 'We're really happy. It's a serious thing between us. Hopefully we can get on with our lives now.'

"A subdued Michael posed for photos with no complaints, smiling and shyly burying his head in her hair.

" 'We're just glad it's in the open,' he says."

There should be a very large space right here . . . to breathe in fresh air, a sniff of which (and just about the only sniff) came a few months later. Amid the usual crop of neo-mortic whisperings and jean-creamings was a piece in *The Daily Telegraph-Mirror* (October 9, 1995) by Malcolm Holland in London, which bore a headline which wouldn't have been out of place as the title of a Woody Allen movie: Is Paula Yates making an *utter fool* of herself or is she, *quite simply*, a woman in love?

Holland did something quite extraordinary: he went into bat on a sticky wicket for Yates and Hutchence, and popped a couple of those sacred condoms that had been hanging around for months.

"She's a short woman with straggly thin hair, chubby upper arms and she has given one almighty 'up yours' to the world. Paula Yates should have won the hearts of almost all by winning the attentions of one man; Michael Hutchence . . . She did it through force of personality, not the length of her legs.

"Instead, Yates has been pilloried in a way that would shatter lesser souls, and it's all Bob Geldof's fault.

"If he wasn't the man behind Band Aid, his estranged wife would not have suffered half as much as she has.

"As it is, she ditched a saint for a sinner, at least in many people's minds, and is paying the price.

"Poor Bob, they say, he gave us so much hope with his vision of help for Africa. Poor Bob, he deserves a happy life, seeing as he made us feel better about ourselves, at least for a week in 1985.

"But not only is Yates cast as the super slag betraying a shining knight, she has also usurped two icons of our age.

"Yates has dared to challenge the supremacy of the supermodel and our preoccupation with youth.

"Hutchence's ex, Helena Christensen, at 26 is 10 years younger than Yates. Christensen is high priestess of the cult of the body. A beautiful body means a beautiful life, according to books which fill a wall of your local bookshop and whole rack at the video store.

"All happiness and the man of your dreams, so say *Cosmo* and *Cleo*, will come to you if you have a butt of steel. Wrong – not when there are women as strong as Paula Yates around.

"One of the countless style-driven magazines – *GQ* – couldn't let this dangerous tilt at the natural order of things go unchallenged.

"*GQ* put a semi-naked photograph of Christensen on the cover of last month's [September 1995] issue, next to the question, 'Seriously, would you trade her in for Paula Yates?'

"Even Christensen was upset by the callous question. 'It was such a horrible thing to write. I was hurt by the thought of how Paula would feel when she saw the headline, so I called her up to give my support,' she said.

"Hutchence traded up because Yates is her own woman. She does not trudge behind a famous partner, as the wives of Hollywood actors do, a metre or two after their spouses, at every movie premiere or Oscars night.

"She demands equal billing . . .

"She learnt independence after her parents' marriage ended when she was five years old. Her father, then the presenter of a Sunday evening television programme, had an affair with a woman 50 years younger. [Recently, Paula has found out that this man was not her biological father.]

"Her mother left to live in the south of France. She was sent away to boarding school and has said she never saw enough of them. [The parental split mirrors that of Michael's parents.]

"Paula Yates is also a woman who makes men feel good. In many ways. She is an expert in that special style of canoodling that takes place when girls ride limousines with rock stars . . .

"Of Hutchence she said: 'He's the most honourable man I've ever met and certainly the strongest.

" 'I'm trying to keep this relationship the way I always dreamed a relationship should be – as happy and as easy as possible.

"I've always thought it would be wonderful to be with someone who was your best friend at the same time as being God's gift to women. Michael is certainly that.' "

Holland also points out that the Paula-Bob marriage was in trouble before Michael came along: nobody else did.

British journalist Louette Harding, who had known Paula for several years, then contributed an even keel and thoughtful interview with Yates to *You* magazine that was reprinted in *The Australian* (December 23, 1995) with the headline, The Education of Paula.

"Paula Yates, in 1995, polarised public opinion as few women before her have done. The Duchess of York springs to mind; the same ability to imitate, the same breathless self-justification.

"I first met Yates years ago, and found her fine, if rather tediously absorbed with her own fine image . . . This time we met the day after she had recorded the edition of the television show *Have I Got News For You* in which *Private Eye* editor Ian Hislop savaged her. Yates was a different person; subdued, more thoughtful. The fund of juvenile hyperbole had, thankfully, dried up. I thought her a much more sympathetic character.

"Afterwards, I caught a video of another interview in which she batted what looked like Barbara Cartland's cast off eyelashes at the interviewer in winsome fashion. Then she appeared, yet again and seeming hard done by, in *Hello!* magazine, the British gossip sheet which week after week allows the stars to wallow in their own view of themselves. It was difficult to remember, after this predictable and unlikeable Yates, the usual media Yates, the person I had met.

"Let us try to be objective. Some of the criticism is valid – she complained to me that interviewers kept rabbiting on about her breast enhancement operation, which was more than a bit rich when she herself had written about it in her book and been pictured in British *Vogue* displaying a cleavage as deep as a gorge. But some of the fault-finding is spurious and resembles barbaric sport . . .

"Hutchence, who comes downstairs in the middle of the morning and joins the interview, a man with a Middlemarch haircut and leather trousers, wolfing baked beans, is sweet about what he did see in Paula. 'I love her ability to give, her strength and courage. It has overwhelmed me; having not really been around much of that myself, now that I think about it. And we have very similar ideas,' he says. The circumstances of their affair – 'We had four days together before tabloid hell started' – intensified it.

The centrepiece of Harding's interview, though, is a brief observation and reply: "She [Paula] had made two statements about Michael which are extremely illuminating about her marriage. One was that Michael was the first man she had slept with who was also her friend, which means that her 18-year-old relationship with Geldof was not founded on that easy familiarity.

" 'I never put the two together. I hadn't thought of Bob being my friend. He was Bob. Does that sound really mean? I don't intend it to. I had my friendship with my friends.' Michael calls from the kitchen. 'Very difficult [to grasp] I know. She had a split life.' And the second comment was that Michael was the first person to whom she told the untarnished truth.

" 'Yes, I don't ever tell Michael fibs. I don't have to because he doesn't get cross with me,' she adds, pathetically. 'I don't have these things I keep quiet about.' "

Take it a small step further. Susan Chenery quotes Michael in her on-the-road-with-INXS interview: "The death of Diana, Princess Of Wales, was says Hutchence, 'a wake-up call for everyone. Everyone has to realise that it is a different world now, obviously.

" 'And there by the grace of God go many other people. I knew Dodi from my time in Paris, he as an old-fashioned womaniser.' And then he is leaning against me, almost tearful, confiding. He is talking about his friend Gianni Versace.

" 'When things were really bad, when Paula and I were living in hell because of the press, when you've got no friends left, there would be Gianni on the phone [with heavy Italian accent], "You must come and stay." Everything would be paid for.

" 'I went to his house in Miami, it was over the top. If I had $50 million, well, I wouldn't spend it like that.'

"Oh yes, Michael Hutchence knows the deadly price you can pay for fame in these voracious days, as the millennium hurtles to a close.

"Paula Yates recently told me that when she left Bob Geldof, there were six different news teams permanently on her tail. 'It is so distorted and weird,' she said. 'They case the kids and push them around. When it first happens, it is really great because it is such a novelty and it is really glamorous. It is shallow but thrilling.

" 'Then they start to pull you down and it ceases to be fun. You find yourself becoming what they expect of you because you are so antagonised. You really start to feel contaminated and poisoned by it.

" 'It has been an incredible feat of will on Michael's part to see it all through. It has been very much directed at me and so nasty. I have been very distressed. I haven't really coped that brilliantly and he has been incredibly strong and so kind . . .'

" 'There is a logic that escapes us, but I suppose it goes that when a marriage breaks up, someone has to be wrong,' Hutchence says grimly, 'and they have to pay. They must be bad. It has got very out of hand when you get front-page headlines after an altercation with Bob and the police were called. It was a violent situation, shall we say. One of the papers ran a headline "Who wants to line up to slap her again?" This is a mother of children. She doesn't want it. She says, "I am just a mummy." She doesn't get it. But she is so brazen, she just says, "F . . . you." ' "

I flick the remote at the CD player and Gerry starts singing 'Sad Dark Eyes' and 'The Loved One' . . . over and over and over again.

They were just two big kids from broken homes who found strength in each other, that's all. And I can't help remembering some comments Michael made in an interview with Sharon Krum in New York a few months before he died.

When asked how he kept sane, Michael replied, "I am barely doing it . . . You see the destruction of the person you love in front of your eyes . . . and to fight it is to be violated all over again. Where are the human beings in all this? The stuff that has happened to us, it could make you lose your faith in human nature."

"Then Hutchence backtracks. He wants to talk more about society and celebrity worship. Diana's death, he says, forced everyone to sit up and ask hard questions, ones with which he has been grappling since his own life imploded. When does the torture stop? Why does it even have to start?

" 'See it's against the law to destroy Jews, blacks, people for religious causes,' he continues.

" 'The law and Parliament have stopped discrimination like

that. All we have left is celebrity, and every society has to kick a dog, it's a fact. Someone to raise and someone to burn. It's human nature. Celebrities are the last bastion, and it's not against the law.'

"Hutchence, who is friends with the distinguished human rights lawyer Geoffrey Robertson, agrees with Robertson's theory that at its core, a public figure's right to privacy is a human rights issue. Celebrities, he says, do not enter into a contract with the public that entitles them to share in, pass judgement on and castigate their private lives.

" 'They say you asked for it. That's bullshit . . . I am not a cynical manipulator of the media, I never have been. I think there should be limits. The average Joe Blow is living vicariously through MTV and Planet Hollywood and what does it say about us?

" 'It says we don't trust each other anymore, we have lost faith with each other. Do we not care about people on the street, only about images that can be constructed for us?

" 'People have forgotten that celebrities are human beings.

" 'That is why the Diana episode has made everybody take a breath,' Hutchence says.

" 'I remember once she pulled up in the car and pulled Paula in and said, "Between you and me, I'm so happy when you're on the cover – it gives me a day off." ' "

The Princess' death, says Hutchence, " 'knocked us for six . . . This has to be a wake up call for people.

" 'Your appetite for celebrity has led to this. Your vicarious pleasure for 25p has cost the life of magic.' "

It's a long way from the Jefferson Airplane's rallying call of "feed your head". Or maybe Axl Rose was right: it's an appetite for destruction.

6

Elegantly Wasted

January 1997 was one of those 'isn't summer lovely if you're partial to jungle fever' months. It humided – a word that isn't in any dictionary but should be. Humided should – and will – one day stand for living in a state of constant dampness in which the temperature fluctuates a whole seven degrees or less a day and the air is so still at night that mosquitoes doze off on the buzz and need amphetamines just to get that old blood sucking instinct flowing. Large vampire-looking bats fly around; leathery creatures on secret missions that return to a secret base as dawn approaches, the truth of their night forever shrouded. Daylight is not worth talking about. It is simply bright. And soggy warm to hot. Rather like the temperature at the core of that disgusting porridge your mum used to serve when you were five years old. Australians – and misguided immigrants intent on 'Aussifying' themselves – love it. After all, this is the culture of sun, surf and sand . . . and skin cancer. Australia is a world leader in skin cancer, with more of it per square inch of bronzed Aussie skin than nearly anywhere else on the globe. Fake tanning lotion is safer if you must. But that really won't do. Cultural tradition says 'down the beach with you and expose that skin'. But why crisp it and char it then let it dry out, why have the look and texture of the chunks of steak traditionally overcooked to frisbee status at barbecues? No, the dark is safer. Moon tans are rarely threatening – except during periods of witch hunting.

It is into this rarified atmosphere that the summer tour is launched. Overseas bands intent on avoiding winters back home flock in from England, Europe and the US for 10-day to two-week jaunts around the coastal big five (Perth, Adelaide, Melbourne, Sydney, Brisbane) with perhaps a few provinicials thrown in. Smaller, less fussy, bands also play a bunch of unis and all the outposts. On big years there can be as many as 10 or 12 overseas outfits circulating the country over a two-week period. This makes Australian bands extremely happy – if they can get a support. Then there are the festivals, the most famous of which was The Big Day Out, a three-stage and tents spectacular that embraced the country and New Zealand. Here a couple of dozen local outfits got to swap drugs, alcohol, tall stories and crowd-baiting techniques while occasionally performing to vast seas of young flesh ripened in the sun.

Thousands and thousands of Australians will tell you The Big Day Out was a fab, fun-filled, 12 hours of moshing, flirting, drugging and getting pissed to an enervating soundtrack. Well, it started out that way. The enervating bit. There were certainly some splendid moments and performances in the early days. The first year – 1992 – boasted Nirvana, the Violent Femmes (almost an Australian institution by then), the Hard-Ons with Henry Rollins guesting, Yothu Yindi, the chart-topping teen faves Ratcat who flopped disastrously in England and never recovered their momentum or spirit, Falling Joys, The Clouds, Died Pretty and You Am I. A Sydney-only event, its success inspired the drum roll for the all-national big gig the following year.

The line-up was staggering, probably the best rock-solid aggregation of anger and attitude ever to assemble in the name of the unholy ghost: Nick Cave and The Bad Seeds, Iggy Pop, Sonic Youth, Mudhoney, The Beasts Of Bourbon, Helmet, The Disposable Heroes of Hiphoprisy, Carter: The Unstoppable Sex Machine and You Am I, plus locals in each state.

Iggy was still a Stooge in his own head; a magnificent leather-clad (his skin) reminder of rock's warrior soul: a metallic k.o. merged with a lust for life. Saint Nick was lighters at sunset as the masses sang the 'Ship Song': darkness never had a better introduction. Magnificent, really. And Sonic Youth – without them where would the boys and girls of grunge have discovered their soul. Sonic Youth are the forerunners of just about everything that musically matters within a certain conduit of rock and the avant, and they were thoroughly waspish that year. Michael Franti's Disposable Heroes of Hiphoprisy lived up to their reputation as a revolutionary fusion force drawing in hip-

hop, rap, rock and electronics as a bed to Franti's streaming image-laden lyricism. Of course, Franti and the Disposable
Heroes appealed to Hutch, although a lot of rap, particularly
the racist, sexist, hardcore, derivative, annoyed him, mostly
because they were throwing away the only new form in music in
20 years and the chance to articulate their cause in a ghetto of
bad-mouthing and soundalike scratch and sampling.

After that The Big Day Out seemed to lose focus. It still had
its moments. Ministry's war of sound, Bjork's vocal gymnas-
tics – Bjork is the future of music in many ways; listen to
1997's *Homogenic* and understand how advanced is her vision – a
great performance from The Cruel Sea, and another from the
Screaming Trees who were close to perfect, even if half the
piss-ants in the crowd didn't get it. Other than that the best
opening 15 minutes of a set belongs to Primal Scream: then the
drugs set in.

But it was the endless, unrelenting, passage of countless
soundalike grunge bands that eventually made Big Day Out the
boring day out. Even the mighty Smashing Pumpkins came and
failed in a heat-induced lather, admitting backstage it was one
of the lesser moments of their career – as did Belly who were
diabolically bad, Teenage Fanclub who spent more time kicking
soccer balls around than playing, The Cult (close to the end)
sounding like it shouldn't have got that far, Soundgarden who
just weren't, Offspring who got the crowd off but should have
been forced to wear labels saying "derivative" or maybe that
should be "dull".

The 1997 Big Day Out was the last and featured an all star
line-up of re-runs plus Patti Smith – who was supreme, untouch-
able, magical, uncompromising and punk at the Enmore
Theatre a few days later. It didn't matter that BDO was going,
going, gone. It had more than done its job. By now there were
plenty of other festivals trying their hand.

INXS never played the Big Day Out, it was supposed to be the
preserve of alternatives even though it became precisely the
opposite, and an invitation was probably never likely.

The more observant will have noticed that a small part of
history has been skipped: that surrounding INXS' 1993 set *Full
Moon, Dirty Hearts*. I listened about 12-15 times and just never

connected. I honestly thought they should go away and take a long break. Working out how a band could be so brilliant on stage and so lacking on record in the same year was a black hole best left unresolved. There's a thin line between being a fan and being obsessive and blind to the truth – which is that no band, not the Stones, not U2, not The Beatles, The Who, The Doors, Pearl Jam, is going to endlessly create works of great impact, art and significance, year after year after year. Artists, writers, actors, directors, they're the same. Bursts of greatness surrounded, sometimes, by lengthy ordinariness, even mediocrity. INXS had definitely reached some inbuilt used-by date in 1993 and the near three-year break that ensued was marked only by the three-ring circus that was Paula, Bob and Mike and his/their endless paparazzi-induced profile. INXS were written off by the pundits as being completely out of time and place – and I guess if you were 10 to 20 years old and thought rock music began with Hanson or Nirvana then they were.

Michael had flagged the break much earlier, commenting to Shaun Carney of *The Age* (April 22, 1993), " 'I think I'd like to edge my priorities a little more after this album. I would like to be a fascist for a while and do whatever the hell . . . whether it's sitting around and having kids or acting or writing something or music. I don't know. But there's lots of other things to do in this world. I mean, this is just singing on stage; it's just a pop group. People tend to forget. As my friend Chris Bailey (of The Saints) says: "At the end of the day, Michael, it's just a pop group." ' "

Carney continues, "Michael Hutchence gives the impression of a man coming out of a fog. Something, or some things, have caused him to question himself. When told there's little ever written about his interests outside music, he feigns dismay and says: 'Probably people haven't heard much about what I do because there's nothing there. I must admit that I've lived and breathed this band for a good while. I haven't seen much distinction, at least until lately, between a gig and after a gig; an interview and after an interview.

" 'It's all just a lifestyle to me. In the meantime, I do read. I don't watch television. I'm self-educated and I think I've done

111

a pretty good job. I've learned a lot on the way. I live an exploratory lifestyle, I suppose. My favourite thing to do is to have a few friends for dinner and have conversations that are, hopefully, meaningful.' "

Earlier in the article, he says, " '. . . Obviously, I must be – and I have to admit this to myself, and I've been trying to do this recently – a very ambitious person. I must have an extraordinary amount of willpower, ambition and ego, somewhere in me – although I do find I have to go to the ego shop occasionally – and I'm emotionally worked into this on all kinds of levels.

" 'So, yeah, I'll be stupid and say, "Yeah, I want girls and money" and I'll also say whether or not we sell another record tomorrow, we'd be worth nothing if we weren't still doing it for the music.'

"Ultimately," Carney writes, "he is convinced that he keeps doing it because he likes to sit in a room (or a house in the south of France, where the band recently spent two weeks rehearsing) and make up rock songs. 'I have no other answer. I don't know why we are still together. It's not for money. Don't need money. Don't need any more money. Don't need things. Don't need that shit.' "

INXS re-emerged from wherever they were in September 1996 in time to be the star attraction at the 10th Annual Australian Record Industry Awards, for which I was scriptwriter. Not only would INXS unveil and perform for the first time their comeback single, 'Searching', but Michael would present a couple of awards with Neneh Cherry.

The ARIAs are a book in themselves. There is nothing like being involved in putting together a live show with associated television broadcast. The fact that such awards shows actually happen on the night is one of the unrecognised wonders of the world. I love working on them: chaos and madness perfectly dovetailed into a show that always runs over time, looks good, sounds good and leaves you utterly wasted. For three months it gathers speed then in the last two weeks flicks gears several times, goes beyond overdrive and bursts out of the limitations of all its composite parts to take on a life of its own.

Michael and Neneh Cherry were perfect together. Professional as all hell. Hutch looked all dark and mysterious yet affable – as he always does; Neneh sparkled next to him and the chemistry was tight and right. Yet here was a man whose personal life was under seige with the news only a few days earlier that a Smarties tube allegedly containing opium and some pornographic pictures of him and his partner Paula indulging themselves in their favourite variations on the horizontal fandango had been discovered by a nanny looking after the children (excepting Hiranni Heavenly Tiger Lily who was with mum and dad in Sydney and meeting her grandparents for the first time since her birth seven weeks earlier) in their absence.

Because of the uproar in the UK, Michael came and went briefly those days. We passed just once. He stopped and we shook hands, exchanged a couple of pleasantries. I asked him how it really was. "Fucked," he replied. His face wore a three-day growth easily, the eyes were bagged but he didn't seem completely overwhelmed. Then again, as anybody will tell you, Michael was always good at hiding what he really felt when he had to. He smiled, began walking away and then turned back and said, "It'll all turn out okay, you know." I nodded. He waved a hand. And disappeared.

At rehearsal I heard 'Searching' for the first time. A slow but fat ballad with a funky/soul feel, I thought it was one of the blandest INXS songs I'd ever heard. Watching this great band playing this soporific by-numbers slice of AOR soul, it was hard not to wonder whether they shouldn't have stayed away. It remains one of the least invigorating moments of *Elegantly Wasted*, its only distinction being it precedes 'Just A Man' and makes that track sound even better. On Awards night it flopped. There'd been a lot of talk going on in the weeks leading up to the show about INXS' return: the bottom line was they needed a killer re-entry. Anything less and the past-the-used-by-date mumblings would start all over again. They did. The talk post-show was not about how good the band sounded – the on-the-night performance was about 200 per cent up on rehearsals – but on how sludge-like the song was and why on earth had they gone with it. Even INXS fans – and they do have many ardent supporters in the industry – were scratching their heads and trying to find excuses such as "Well, maybe it's a grower, you know, needs a few listens." Or "Well, they wouldn't unveil the best material this early; it's just a market tester, an introduction." Never a good sign.

When Mercury Records sent word through a few months later that their new album would be called *Elegantly Wasted*, there was no great outburst of press enthusiasm. It was a wait-and-see vibe.

So it was that in mid-January the invitation came to a special industry-only "secret" gig to preview the new album in one of the old Australian Broadcasting Commission (ABC) television studios in Gore Hill.

January 29, 1997, was terminally foul. When it wasn't raining it was pretending that the very next second a storm of such severity would suddenly be unleashed that Sydney would be driven into the Harbour or absorbed by a tidal wave of rising water: either way a modern-day Atlantis. About 6pm we hailed a cab – and got lost. Gore Hill is somewhere north of the city and for the virgin Chinese cab driver it was not only a word he hadn't encountered before but also a near impossible target at which to aim. Still, we found the complex and a couple of dozen other lost looking souls and route marched round to a roll-a-door which remained implaccably closed no matter how hard we all stared. It was the wrong door. It started to rain. The omens were not good.

Eventually we were rescued by a security guard and shown a perfectly normal driveway leading to perfectly normal stairs, a perfectly normal door with a handle on it that was jammed ajar, more stairs, another door manned by Mercury staff with lists – tick, tick – more stairs, another door, a corridor, a door, a bend, then finally . . . humanity. Well nearly – industry, which shares some key points in common with humanity.

Pointed in the direction of a big room with . . . a lot of space and everybody doing their best Mr and Miss/Mrs/Ms Mix-a-lot bit. Amid this bunch of predictables stand – like those flying insect zappers they have in the outback – commercial radio MDs, programmers and jocks who RCPs have to smile at and be positively sweetness, light and sucky-up to because they need their discs on the dial (while backstabbing them to anybody who'll care to listen outside of such events) – not that it makes

much difference. The majority of commercial radio is pro-
grammed by a bunch of tasteless, talentless egomaniacs with
little initiative or imagination: ditto the management. Radio is
so staid and so boring in Australia that getting a playlist 'ad'
(addition) is usually cause for celebration at most record companies: getting two or three in a week is almost unheard of.

Word finally filtered through: it was time for the show. A
short corridor, another door and . . .

In an elongated room with low ceilings, dim lights, a blaze of
candles running along the back wall, INXS were captured in
the centre, surrounded by a semi-circle of "industry". It's so
bloody intimate that when Hutch gets worked up later his sweat
splatters and splashes the faces of the front row.

In this any-mistake-is-going-to-be-so-obvious environment INXS
chose to preview their 10th studio album *Elegantly Wasted*, a
different yet familiar, loose-limbed and aggressively unpredictable
set. A record that is better than many gave it credit for and
marked a change in emphasis and a shift in thinking. Certainly,
Elegantly Wasted was far from perfect but it offered potential and
freshness and the embryo of new adventure.

But this . . . this was a big brave call.

It started quietly with Hutchence, shades on, singing – with
raw feeling; so much better than he has in recent years –
perched on a stool.

Yet in that very calm there is a precision and a fire that's been
missing for a while. They want it. They want it back, all they've
achieved. They all look so serious. There's a grit and determination going down that's palpable and slowly but surely they turn
it up and slip gears working through the new material, loosen-
ing it up, feeling its heart.

And Michael is sliding, unwinding, off the stool stalking and
walking, his eyes shut, his hands beginning to cut the thick air.
And all of a sudden he is gone, back to the great rock vocalist
he always was at his best. The glasses are tossed aside, the dark
jacket chucked on the floor, the buttons on the shirt are almost
ripped open and he's tribal, feral, swaggering, pouting, minc-
ing, Michael Hutchence, and the band kicks it down under
him, a thunderous machine that's taking chances, doing crazy
things to the middle of 'Devil Inside', mixing up the textures,

playing with atmospheres, slipping from funk to rock to pop to that peculiar meld that's all INXS. It's loud and louder but crystal clear and primal.

Wendy Matthews is bopping her butt off on some scaffolding running along the wall; Richard Clapton is stomping, beer in one hand, conducting with the other; the Baby Animals' guitarist Dave Leslie has a big fat grin on his face; some normally stuffed industry shirts are getting sweaty and singing choruses. The new material mixes with the old, already forming partnerships for the live set, most of it works, some of it – like the pivotal core of *Elegantly Wasted*: 'Just A Man', 'Girl On Fire' and 'We Are Thrown Together' – is just damn good. For 90 minutes INXS are better than I can remember; maybe the '93 pub tour, but this is greatness. This is the stuff of story, the belly of legend.

'Original Sin', 'Bitter Tears', 'The Loved One' (oh yes, 'The Loved One'), 'Suicide Blonde', 'Kiss The Dirt', 'Don't Change' . . . by the end there wasn't a dry shirt in the place. Hutch was a sweat-soaked rag with a grin amid the soaked curls pasted to his white face. He looked exhausted. He looked happy.

During the encore, Clapton wanders over, cups a hand, yells in the ear, "Fucking great, fu-ck-ing great".

Tim Farriss laughs, "You thought that was good. We got better after that. That was really a warm up for the Aspen, Colorado, show for VH1, the new MTV in the US; MTV isn't music TV anymore, really. VH1 is what MTV used to be. We blew ourselves right away. We also had some backing vocalists we rehearsed the day before and it just clicked. The VH1 people were freaking.

"Since then 'Elegantly Wasted' (the single) has been on high rotation and it kicked us into the whole thing," he says. "We can feel we're on a roll. It reminds us of why we're still together. These songs. The whole reaction to the single. Actually, it got us by surprise.

"We're not so big in our own heads that we thought we could just come back after a break and pick up where we left off but the reaction is just amazing. To be honest we were nervous about the single. Really nervous."

Some three months later he's talking about a single that was among the top 5 most added in the US, UK and Australia at the time. Written off by a solid slab of the biz, INXS had made a joke of their critics. So far. And as for the press . . . Tim had something to get off his chest – precisely two minutes into the interview.

"There's one thing I want to stipulate and say: There are always rumours about us breaking up. That shits us because we're not a rumour band. We'll tell people if we're breaking up."

This is the rest of the interview as it went to press in early May.

Tim Farriss doesn't mince his words as he mulls over the general perception of INXS' extended break that wasn't so extended when you look at it in the cold light of day – three years isn't so long in the life of a rock'n'roll band these days, particularly one as long-serving and all-achieving as the 20-million-records-sold INXS. So there are things that need putting in perspective as a new chapter to a 20-year-old epic begins.

"We can take most things but the constant rumourmongering is just really trying," the 39-year-old guitarist continues. "One day we're reading how it's all over for us, the next thing we're reading the things we're fascinated by, and there's so much rubbish written about Michael it's laughable.

"We've been living in the UK for a few months now, based in London, doing a lot of press. I've been watching how the music press operates compared to the tabloids and while the music press gets booted a lot compared with the tabloids they aren't so bad.

"Michael never talks to the tabloids so they make most of it up. He says he's damned if he's going to have some paparazzi schmuck destroying his life."

Farriss says that, simply, there comes a time in a band's life for a break, for sorting things out, for getting space. That's really what happened after *Full Moon, Dirty Hearts*. There's a lot of factors that come into play if a band is to survive. Life, space, management, kids, family, working your head out, are a few of them. And it was time they all got taken care of.

"The only time we've ever thought about not doing any more is after a two-year stint on the road at the end of which you're totally exhausted," Farriss says. "That's natural. Every band gets to that point where it's enough planes, buses, late nights, early mornings, hotel rooms.

"Next to AC/DC there's probably no other band in the world that was as hard at it for so long as us. And there comes a point when you have to decide that it's time to do something for yourself. All those years cut heavily into our family and love lives. They also made us somewhat numb to the industry. It's like being on a big exercise wheel in a mouse cage. We had to get off the whole thing, get our lives back.

"The past three years we've been through life and death. The family INXS. And it is a family. This is our family. There's been three babies (to Hutchence, Andrew Farriss and Garry Beers) and we (the Farriss brothers, Tim, Andrew, Jon) lost our mum (the album slick carries a simple dedication of the record to Jill Farriss).

"There's now 12 kids – including the three of Bob's (Geldof). My eldest son – who's in his teens – is a reborn punk who's forming bands all the time while my youngest, Jake (going on 10), is into Pink Floyd and, umm, INXS. It's a funny feeling watching them grow up. I took them to the Smashing Pumpkins and then backstage. During the show the Pumpkins threw in parts of 'Don't Change' and 'Need You Tonight' and it was like they gained a sudden respect for what we'd achieved. For the rest of the show I watched the eldest floating across the top of the moshpit now and then. I thought, 'yep'.

"You know, that stuff may sound tame but it's what allows you to get wound up again. You need the time and space to work out what you're doing. A lot of success makes you wonder what you're trying to perpetuate. Do we want to maintain that level of success? Repeat that level of stardom?"

Simply, it's about the kick inside, that excitement, drive, need to create, just do it.

Brother Andrew, who co-produced *Elegantly Wasted* and co-wrote it with Hutchence, sums it up nicely on the band's last bio: "There's a lot that's different about the new record and the way we approached the making of it. We used to record every year, year and a half. We felt we were prolific, but maybe we weren't, even though we were putting out more product. So prior to the making of this record, we found it difficult to place ourselves. We had to ask 'Who is INXS?' because, in the past, we had been too busy being INXS to really know. Or to enjoy it. And making a record, first and foremost should be enjoyable. Exciting. That's when our music is most exciting. When it's exciting to us."

So they did it differently, treating every demo, every moment of music as a potential final take, recording – instead of on four-track, TASCAMS, portables – on proper tape and microphones. What you hear on more than half of *Elegantly Wasted* is first takes. In some cases even the original demo. What they got surprised them.

Farriss comments, enthusiastically, "For ourselves, that's half the trick. We wanted to sound like INXS again. Having a big break meant we could throw everything off, do what essentially INXS just is. We didn't need to reinvent ourselves but by the same token we did want to sound fresh, like we'd just rolled off the tip of a song. So, as Andrew says, we kept it very live, and I think that's what you hear in *Elegantly Wasted* and that's something you haven't heard on an INXS record in a while."

And from Hutchence they got a vintage performance. He sings, really sings. Listen to 'Just A Man', to the cadence of his voice, the delivery, the way he works his way around the song. "That's my favourite, that's just a great song," Farriss cuts in. He pauses, maybe there's something else that needs saying.

"Michael's really cleaned up his act. He's a really straight guy now. He's looking after himself. When we play or perform, you just know you've never heard him sing like this before. We feel like, 'Hey, Mike's back'. Around *Full Moon, Dirty Hearts* he was going through a dark period. We needed to leave him alone for a while, get away from him and let him work it out. Michael gets like that sometimes. We knew he would work it out and he did."

While Tim was talking it up, *Wasted* was going down.

Elegantly Wasted was precisely that in the end. A goodish record wasted by cool press and radio. If Michael had ever needed an excuse to take an axe to Australia's radio stations then surely it's reaction to *Elegantly Wasted* would have offered one on a plate. As a declaration of his love to Paula, he'd turned in his most personal set of lyrics ever; songs about his family, the

119

birth of his first child, fatherhood, his place in the world, his woman and her man. Not a lot of people seemed to care.

Overseas things were better. The tour kicked off in the US on April 17 for five dates, then some more press, resuming in South Africa in late May and early June, before moving to Europe where it opened in Glasgow on June 9 and ended in Copenhagen on July 5. The first leg of the North American tour ran from July 11 to July 22, the second including Canada from August 22 to a finale in Pittsburgh at the Star Lake Amphitheatre on September 27. It was the last show INXS would play with Michael Hutchence. And of all the tours of the last 10 years the one comment that's uniform from anybody who knew him, met him in these months, shared a drink or time is that this was the tour that he enjoyed more than any other.

Despite acceptance problems in the major markets, *Elegantly Wasted* still sold close to a million worldwide and the tour – while not the grand tour of old – sold out scores of smaller arenas and theatres from 8,000 to 45,000. Perhaps the most noticeable difference could be seen in England where INXS had triumphed at Wembley Stadium on the *Kick* tour in front of 70,000. They played Wembley again – but this time in the adjoining Arena to 10,000. You couldn't help thinking . . .

In the US, *Elegantly Wasted* failed to make the top 40 and is slowly crawling even now towards the 200,000 mark – a decade after *Kick* sold six million, in England – where *Kick* spent 103 weeks in the top 100 – sales were even worse after a top 20 opening, while in Australia a promising début at 14 was matched by a rapid slide out of the top 50. But Europe (Top 30 in Denmark, France, Germany – where the band headlined a couple of summer festivals – and Italy, and top 20 in Switzerland and Norway), South America and South Africa all bought up big, particularly the South Africans who took the title track to No 1 as did those avid and funky Argentinians.

The US reaction, which saw good crowds and a sell-out West Coast tour matched by relatively poor sales, can perhaps best be explained by MTV's cooler attitude. INXS – the band who dominated MTV in the late Eighties and the early Nineties – failed to get a video in MTV's top 20 when the channel screened its Top 500 videos in May 1997. While the band scored six placings behind Nirvana's grunge anthem 'Smells Like Teen Spirit', only one made the Top 100 – 'Need You Tonight'/'Mediate' at 29. After that came 'New Sensation' at 150, 'Devil Inside' (184), 'What You Need' (225), 'Never Tear Us Apart' (240) and 'The One Thing' (333). INXS had become a much-loved live memory who would be endlessly revisited whenever they took it on stage, but the audience that once bought their records by the sackful had aged and didn't now buy as many records, and these fans had not really been replaced by new ones with the disposable income to buy INXS' recent records.

But when writer Susan Chenery of *The Sydney Morning Herald* went on the road with them she found Six Mad Funky Boys as the paper's *Good Weekend* entitled her feature length report on October 18.

Chenery is one of nature's small gifts to journalism and writing, a short, compact, highly-strung, emotional time bomb who can be absurdly brilliant and stultifyingly self-indulgent – in one week. Her book, *Talking Dirty*, in which she chronicles a six month on-the-road binge interviewing luminaries as sweeping in character and cultural extremes as Salman Rushdie, Tim Robbins, Traci Lords, Dominick Dunne, J.P. Dunleavy, E.L. Doctorow, James Brown, Marianne Faithfull, and, yes, Paula Yates, reaches its high point in the exchanges with Keith Richards and Hunter S. Thompson. Not only does she have the guts and gammon to get in there but she has a fatal need to pull them on and suffer whatever consequences may arise.

Her opening is lovely: "Norfolk, Virginia, USA: 'Ah, the f . . . ing glamour,' shouts Michael Hutchence, shoving on a shoe and slamming on his shades as Garry Beers shimmies past in leering lime-green and platform boots. Jon Farriss is knocking himself out in violent viridian and Andrew Farriss is confiding that they used to keep a margarita machine behind the stage, back when they were fast and loose rock stars: 'We just had time to mix the drinks between songs.'

"Two blonde back-up singers glisten tinsel silver in the same suggestion of a dress that Liz Hurley wore in the film *Austin Powers*, rounded off with silver wedge-heeled boots. 'It wasn't our choice,' mutters one, with a thin smile. 'Never,' laughs

Kirk Pengilly, 'let the the band choose the back-up singers' outfits.'

"I am quietly hoping that no-one lights a match here in the dressing room, what with all this flammable synthetic fibre. And I'm wondering what's happned to the Michael Hutchence we used to know – the truculent rock star. You know, the one who has glared sullenly out of front pages all over the world, resolutely recalcitrant in the intensity of his gaze. The other party in a divorce scandal that assumed Everest proportions.

"If there is a single image identified with Michael Hutchence, it is the photograph of him, teeth bared, eyes bulging in anger, fist clenched as he lunges at the flock of Fleet Street photographers who had booked out the entire country-house hotel where he was – hold the front page – romancing Mrs Bob Geldof. No, make that Lady Geldof. Strumpet. Paula Yates, whose men seem to start out as rock musicians and then turn into something else . . . Flash, flash, click, click.

"In that lurid moment, Michael Hutchence moved into another sphere of fame. His band may have sold 20 million records but, from that point on, his musical achievement would be forever eclipsed by the newsworthiness of his sex life . . .

"Earlier tonight, Michael Hutchence was certainly entertaining himself, ladies and gentlemen. He was going right off, out there in Norfolk, Virginia. In full rock-star mode. Prowling across the stage. Feline. Salacious. Articles of clothing peeling away. Theatrical. Down to a singlet. Sinew. Down on the ground. Really! Girls reaching for his crotch as he leant out over them. God, it was hot in there. Feverish in raspberry smoke and white noise.

"Unfortunately, the British press have been taking him apart for this kind of behaviour lately. 'Desperate hysterics,' sniffed *The Independent* in July. 'The long last fart of the '80s,' pronounced *The Guardian* in a total demolition job . . .

"Times have changed. We're now in an era, says Hutchence, of 'premenstrual angst music' and not strident funk-rock anthems, INXS' stock-in-trade."

There's that old equation we've discussed before: how do you get old gracefully and keep your cool? Somebody solve it, please. It's an endless source of discontent and grief for "middle-aged" rock acts worldwide. Seriously though, there's not much anybody can do about it but then why worry when your place in history is as absolutely guaranteed as that of INXS.

What they hadn't quite worked out was that they could do anything they liked now, they were free to challenge themselves musically – and anybody who wanted to listen. And there would always be a million or two of those. This wasn't a band that was fading away, it was band that was learning to be older, to reconsider its position. That takes time. Sadly, so sadly though, time had nearly run out.

7

Building Bridges

Drive straight down William Street from the heart of Sydney city towards the skyline dominating, flashing, neon-lit Coke sign at the top of the hill a few kilometres distant, past the park, the hock shops, Frontier Touring Agency on your right, the office forecourt where the hookers and transvestites hang out each night hoping for a trick from the passing traffic, up the incline where car showrooms mix with the local betting shops, delis, natural food shops, odd little cameos of restaurants and cafes, to the final lights and left into Darlinghurst Road.

Welcome to Kings Cross, the historic heart of Sydney sleaze, vice, drug-peddling and organised crime; 400 metres of strip shows, bars and grills, takeaway – where everything is on the menu.

Kings Cross used to be bigger, badder, tougher. In the Sixties it was damn near life threatening at times. Today, it's a tourist trap with a grimy underbelly. Caught between a police sweep to clean it up and the constant redevelopment of its surrounding streets by eager property investors who can see a killing with the 2000 Olympics not so distant, the Cross is becoming a pussy pimple on a hard, tanned, aerobically flattered butt.

It remains, however, a genuine microcosm of life. The rich'n'famous rub shoulders with so-stoned-they-can-hardly-stand prostitutes, their skin a pale blancmange of no future and fear; inquisitive middle-aged and pensioner parties pass by dealers trying not to look like dealers; back-packers – always in pairs or trios – with their burned bark skin and shiny faces search for cheap meals and safe lodging while, everywhere, Chinese, Japanese, Malaysians, Indonesians, in gaggles and straggles of chatter, take endless pictures with instamatic cameras. If you could turn the traffic down all you'd hear in Kings Cross would be click, click, click, click, click . . .

The Cross stinks as well. Sometimes it smells of vomit and booze and urine and stale food and rotting vegetables; they wash down those 400 metres regularly. The used syringes float off with the refuse of all tomorrow's parties down the gutters, out of sight and mind. Not so, really. Every street for a couple of kilometres around, especially the alleys and stairs and lanes has a needle sharp reminder of how low life can get.

Tucked a side street away from the main drag is the Hotel New Hampshire, touring home to a litany of low to medium level acts over the years. The Hampshire has a wonderful history of sex, drugs and rock'n'roll. Nick Cave and his road manager cleaned me out to the tune of $100 late one night playing pool and couldn't remember doing so the next day. But when you stay at the New Hampshire memory loss is a clear and defined hazard. Pop Will Eat Itself, Tool, Tex Perkins, Deadstar, The Badloves, The Screaming Jets, Truth, Hunters & Collectors, the list of interviews in its comfortable-sized rooms or cosy restaurant (great coffee!) counts out time; and if it isn't the Hampshire then it must be the Sebel Townhouse, a couple of blocks away, where the bigger players stay. The Sebel is rock solid and rock famous. There are pictures and gold discs in the foyer announcing its heritage. From Phil Collins, John Farnham and Bon Jovi to Steeleye Span, Status Quo and The Angels, the Sebel has seen them all – and every year the only post-Australian Record Industry Awards (ARIA) party that counts and traditionally ends about 11am next day. A wrecking ball for the majors in the majors. And there are plenty more hotels within a square kilometre with stories to tell.

Funniest thing about the Cross though is that it ends just as quickly as it begins. Round the corner that ends Darlinghurst Road by the infamous El Alamein Fountain and Macleay Street begins. Exactly where is hard to tell but it does. Travel 100 metres and seedy gives way to seeded with money. Plush designer cafes and restaurants mix with apartment blocks – both old and charming and new and bland – and even more hotels. Even the air is different. Rollers, stretch limos, sporty coupes, lush bra-less women in clothes they shouldn't wear and men with expensive suits and bad taste in ties flash credit cards and mobiles at one another in a mating ritual that begins with pose and strut and ends with pissed and ragged – just like the blokes and women in the Kings Cross bars 400 metres away: only down this end of the street you get to pretend it's cool. Amongst them the local gay community hugs and holds hands and laughs, seemingly impervious to the stares from matrons and portly gentlemen who have either forgotten about lust as a factor in love or just still can't deal with blatant homosexuality. In some parts of the Cross, the spill from the gay-dominated Paddington (the next suburb up the road) is so great that heterosexuals are in a minority. And even more backpackers wander by looking at menus they just can't afford. It's a rich vein of life this neighbourhood and I wouldn't live anywhere else. Reality is always just around the corner.

Talking of corners, that's where you'll find Morans the finest coffee shop and mid-price eatery (with 'posh' restaurant next door) in Potts Pt which is what the Cross has become by the time you get three-quarters of the way down Macleay Street. Here you can sit at a sidewalk table and watch the schmooze go down. Morans has lots of semi-famous persons drop by: actors, producers, TV stars and starlets, musos . . . and lots of characters, the best and most enthralling side of the Cross and its surrounds. Like the man with the piercing eyes, thick moustache and ground length dreadlocks and his blonde, European girlfriend; they always seem so deep together. Odd couples, the balding 55-year-old, fat, cigar-smoking, loud bloke with the 30-something, slim, well-detailed and finessed woman – who obviously loves him. Or is it his wallet. And Steve, the only waiter who supplies his and his husband's world and techno music for comment while you eat.

On a perfect Sydney November morning, a few weeks before INXS' *Elegantly Wasted* tour of Australia is due to kick off, Kirk Pengilly sits just inside the coffee shop, not so far from his Sydney home. Recently shaved and dressed low key and unobtrusive, Kirk's a warm, thoughtful, intelligent man. On stage he flips between guitar and saxophone with deceptive ease, prances notably when the riffs come charging like a sledgehammer out of the foldback and his fingers are dancing the fretboard waltz and blows – time honoured saxophonist manner – a ducking, weaving solo that brasses with the best. As a guitar player he is horribly underestimated. Pengilly plays the odd angles, cavorts with the ordinary, does subtle smart things that are there but aren't unless you're really listening.

Kirk's also an observer, an avid keeper of diaries that date back to the earliest days of the band. While I usually frown on question and answer, in this case it makes sense. So for the next hour, here's a life of INXS through Kirk's eyes. And one of the very last band interviews before Michael passed away.

MG: *Elegantly Wasted* must have gone better than you expected, I suspect?

KP: Well, yes and no, we felt very positive about the album and getting back together again after a couple of years off. It was all very positive, all like a gang kind of thing.

MG: I thought when you did the intimate session at the ABC studios in Sydney in February '97 that things looked good.

KP: It was loud! I think that the band is playing better than it's ever played at the moment which is one of the reasons why we really wanted to tour Australia and leave it to last because we so often started here. This time we thought let's do Australia when we've got it exactly right and also because five of us live here it was a good way of getting all the gear back home.

The strangest thing is that no matter how we go saleswise with a record we tend to sell out shows. I think that's because we must have a good track record live. The same applied to the UK – when we first started we went to America first then back to Australia then Europe and the UK – and England was always that old English/Australia thing but always we sold out shows way bigger than our sales and it seems that it's still that way.

MG: And you did well this time round despite some poor reviews.

KP: Some of the reviews were really good, the shows went really well, but probably the backlash of the Michael/Paula thing had some effect. You can never say what the reason is but the UK is not vibing as much as it has in the past. On the other hand the UK has slowed down overall when it comes to sales.

MG: Yet America which had been slow for a while seemed to be very good.

KP: Yes, and as you say the whole tour was a bit surprising to us. We were still headlining festivals in Europe and they just went nuts. The same in America. Going out on this tour we just didn't know what to expect as far as what size venues, what size crowds we'd pull, what age groups, all those sorts of things. So the whole thing was exciting for that fact. It was like the unknown. It wasn't like 'oh here we go again'.

MG: I think the band surprised people by coming back, as well. And coming back so strongly.

KP: Yes, I do too. I think most of us try not to think too much about it all, to think 'yeah, we're just a band', but the bottom line is we have to be happy with what we're doing and the records we make and we won't tour unless we're enjoying it. These days the bottom line is 'as long as we break even' – which is pretty hard for anyone.

The whole industry is struggling now. The difference between now and the Eighties – which is probably the first decade when bands actually made money – is phenomenal. Before that everyone else made it. But now a band or an artist is competing against computer games, computers, videos, and people only have so much to spend. Kids have less to spend, people on a whole have less when it comes to the disposable dollar, and far more choice. In music itself there's so much new stuff going round.

MG: 26,000 new records in America last year. I guess that reflects the current record company adage of signing a lot of acts and throw 'em at the wall and see what sticks.

KP: It's a lot isn't it. I agree and I think the record companies need to look at the way they're developing young acts. When we started they signed an act for four or five albums and nurtured them. Now you get signed up, do an album and if it stiffs you're dropped from the label. It's all about marketing now and facts and figures and graphs.

So we try and ignore all that and almost try to live in a bubble so that we're not affected by it and we're still making the music we love playing. It's really quite corny in a way but we've never tried to be anything we're not, we've never tried to jump on the bandwagon of whatever is the 'in' sound.

MG: But a lot has changed hasn't it since you and I grew up. The fan has been lost, at least in the way they were looked after. You know, you grew up collecting all the coloured vinyl and different pressings . . .

INXS in 1984. Left to right: Kirk Pengilly, Gary Beers, Michael Hutchence, Andrew Farris, Tim Farris and John Farris. *(Rex)*

Above: Michael on stage with INXS, at the Jag Club on Long Island, New York, July 1984. *(LF.*

Below: Michael with fellow Australian rock stars Greedy Smith, Kate Ceberano and Jimmy Barnes, in 1986. *(LFI)*

chael with Kylie Minogue (top) and brother Rhett (below). *(LFI)*

Michael with Helena Christensen in 1992 (top) and 1994. *(LFI, Rex)*

...ael with Paula. *(Rex)*

...w left: Michael with Paula and daughter Heavenly Hiraani Tiger Lily. *(LFI)*
...w right: Paula Yates with Tiger Lily at the funeral. *(Rex)*

Michael Hutchence, the rock star, in his prime. *(LFI)*

KP: And you went to every gig and knew everything about your bands. That doesn't happen these days.

MG: I think people forget a lot these days. Like with *Kick*, they forget that for several years you were the biggest band in the world.

KP: Yeah, we were and it was pretty frightening in a way for us. We were kind of luckier than a lot of other bands though in that it was a gradual climb so we were able to absorb some of the punches along the way. But when it actually hit in America just after *Kick* was released – because they're so much in awe of stars and entertainers – it got tough, really tough, particularly everyone wanting a piece of your time. It got to a point where we just had to stop.

MG: You also had a lead singer who was a focal point for the press. Michael, no matter what he does, has always been a magnet.

KP: Yeah, he's one of a handful of true rock star singers which has good and bad things about it. For him, maybe more bad, because he just can't do anything. He's Michael Hutchence rock star and they're (the press) always watching him wherever he is, wherever he goes.

MG: Like the piece in the paper the other week about Michael going to marry Paula after the tour in Bora Bora or something.

KP: That was really funny – if it was true, he hadn't told any of us about it. What was even funnier was I went to a thing that Peter Morrissey (the fashion designer) had in Bennalong. I didn't know the girl who wrote the piece for whatever paper it was. Anyway she came up to me and asked me if there was any truth to it and I'd only just started hearing from people about the article. So I said, "You can't believe anything you read in the papers. It's all bullshit." And I'm carrying on, you know, bagging the gossip press, not realising who she was. So then she put something in a few days later about my fiancee and I, that we consulted an oracle about getting married and it was just like . . .

MG: Congratulations on the engagement.

KP: Thanks mate, we're still umming and aahing about whether we're going to do a big thing or a small thing.

MG: Joining the ranks of the married boys. Again.

KP: Yeah, I was married to Deni (Hines, the Australian soul/pop singer now-based in London) as well. But that's all over, of course. Michael's the only one who hasn't been married yet.

MG: He's been engaged enough according to the press

KP: Well, even that I don't think is actually true. I don't think he's ever been actually engaged. I think long-term de-facto relationships is the correct description.

MG: One of the more interesting things since you've all been back is that you are still very much news in your own right. There was the Michael marriage rumour, the pictures of all of you at the show jumping competition, then a story about how you were seen at the bar at Blur. It hasn't gone away despite the absence.

KP: Yeah, which is obviously healthy. Actually, it's amazing after 20 years now when you think about it. I sometimes forget we're supposed to be stars and I'm not supposed to be normal and I'm like in the supermarket or something doing the shopping and I'll ring home on the mobile and go "Have we got any ketchup or tomato sauce?" and Louise, especially when we first started going out, would think it was hilarious because like this is meant to be a rock star and here he is in the middle of a supermarket.

MG: You've all been pretty normal and accessible through the years though.

KP: Yeah, I think there were times when on a media level we were not. But you can chat till the cows come home can't you. Chris Murphy, our divorced manager, was fantastic on that level of keeping us protected but in other ways not, for the simple reason of keeping us down to earth. Keeping our feet on the ground. It's a fine balance thing and he did it very well. I would never say a bad word about him.

MG: It was a long, enduring classic relationship between a band and a manager.

KP: Totally, it was a marriage. He built up his empire until he didn't have any time for anything and then he made some decisions, one of which was to divorce us. Even if it looks now that his empire is crumbling, it isn't, it's just him winding it down. There's always a method to his madness and there's always a motive to what occurs. He's a very calculating person. He's without a doubt one of Australia's best managers ever as far as being able to take a band from the pubs and do what he did.

MG: I put him and Grant Thomas (Crowded House, the Finns) together as long-term type managers who are capable of doing anything but both, I think, are particularly good at envisaging the world picture without losing the smaller picture at the same time.

KP: That's quite right. That was one of his main things he worked on. He always had the picture in mind, right from the point of ... I remember sitting in one of his first offices in North Sydney in 1981 or '82 and he said "What do you guys want to do? What do you want to be?" and we just nutted it out. Basically it was a question of "Do you want to be an international band or do you just want to be Australian?" And we all just said "international" not knowing really what it meant. And he said "okay" and from that day on that was the plan and he just locked it all in place and we went and toured and toured and toured.

MG: I would guess that with AC/DC you've toured more than anybody.

KP: I'm not sure of the facts but it wouldn't surprise me. We just kept going and going and I'll always remember Murphy's motto was "You can sleep when you get older".

MG: Basically, at one stage, you were on the road, in the studio, out with the record, on the road in the studio ...

KP: Yep, it was 10 years of that. We sort of pulled in the reins after the *Kick* tour and said, "That's enough, it's time for a real break". And then when we started doing the *X* album it basically didn't stop until *Greatest Hits* so it got up to another six years. I would say it's been ... extraordinary and extraordinary ... they say you only get out of it what you put into it. And we certainly put into it.

Oddly, I don't think we ever really lost the pace despite all the shit that went on here and over the last two years, all the stuff that's been surrounding Michael. We've always been able to see through that and keep it together as a band. I mean the great thing about it is that we're all still such great mates. I think that's what helps bind it, helps stick it together.

MG: Talking to Tim at the time the album came out, he was saying that in '94 and later Michael was going through one of his dark phases and you all as a band said, 'Michael go away for a while and we'll all get back together when you're through it.'

KP: Yeah, that's true. One of the more important things – even though we've always been together, a sort of unending bucks party – is you've still got to have time out and we've always catered for that and always made sure that if anybody wants to do anything solo there's time to do that, because if not there's going to be a build-up.

MG: You haven't done a lot of solo stuff between all of you over the years though?

KP: No, not highly publicised stuff. In down time we've always been doing stuff working with other musicians whether in pre-production or playing on albums or writing with other people, whatever. But it's never been stuff that's "look what I'm doing".

MG: And you never got to the point where there was the Kirk, Michael, Tim, Andrew, Jon, Garry solo album thing. That's often an indicator that things are going seriously wrong in a band.

KP: Yeah, that's true. But it's a difficult situation for us any-way. Michael has obviously been in the position where he can go and do anything he wants solo and he'll have the media atten-tion straight away, where as for the rest of us it has to be more, invariably is more, subtle. We don't have the profile. But I always remember what we did in the first decade and a bit, which was to experiment with the b-sides of singles where every-body did their own thing. That was great fun. While all the stuff was going on in the studio, one of us would be off working on a b-side, then some of the guys would come in, play something and add in their two bits worth. That was always something very inspiring as just a freeform thing, particularly in contrast to the box that is the band where you are kind of restricted in some ways.

MG: I think one of the most exciting things I heard at the ABC show was the new sense of experimentation and inter-pretation you put on some of the old songs, like the funky wah-wah thing you added to 'Devil Inside'.

KP: Yeah, yeah. We've always tried to keep things pretty true to the record but this time – on quite a few of the songs – we've just been stuffing round with them so we're not bored with it. And we've been doing some older material on this tour, some songs of which we haven't played for over 10 years. We've been trying to do one or two songs from *Shabooh Shoobah* forwards. I don't think we'll do anything off the first two albums though.

MG: I always believed your version of 'The Loved One' was really true to the original and it deserved to be heard again by another generation and immortalised.

KP: It's a great song as are so many of the songs that were written both then and in the era we recorded it – the mid-Eighties. I still love the song we did with Jimmy (Barnes) – 'Good Times'.

MG: Great rock'n'roll.

KP: That was the beauty of so many of those Australian bands from the Seventies and Eighties. There's always been the strength that comes from the whole Australian pub scene, great rock'n'roll like AC/DC.

MG: Isn't it weird that here we are in late '97 and you're back here and The Angels are out on the Barbed Wire Ball tour, Cold Chisel are back and are working on a new album, Midnight Oil are up and firing again. It says so much about that pub scene and how its loss has hit the current scene so hard: we just don't have the bands coming through now because the circuit isn't there to support them or for them to gain experience on.

KP: That's really worrying. It's important for the music scene anywhere in the world to have young bands coming through. I think it's great Chisel are back. I think they'll come out with a killer album. People are sort of saying 'Well what are they doing that for?' and it's like 'Well why not!'.

MG: It's also the attitude of this country which needs to understand there's nothing wrong with people being over 40 and still playing rock . . .

KP: Or being successful.

MG: Look overseas at the Stones in America now, they're killing it.

KP: Probably them, U2, and Elton John and Billy Joel are the only three or four acts that can play the entire States now whereas 10 years ago . . .

MG: It's like this great odd belief worldwide that rock'n'rollers should drop dead at 30 whereas blues guys . . . they're not even recognised until they're 50.

KP: That's absolutely true. I also think a lot of it is the unknown. People said rock would be dead in five years and it kept going and kept going. But there's still a lot of people who would still like to see it dead.

MG: I think *Elegantly Wasted* is a kind of sleeper album that's grown on people the longer it's been around. A strong collection of songs that needed some time with them.

KP: That's how we felt when we finished it. We were so positive about it, so in some ways it's quite valid to ask 'did it do better or not as good as we thought'. The way we went about recording it and putting it together, it felt really strong. Actually, we've only been doing about half the album live for some reason. We just got it to that point where at the start of the tour we said 'okay let's do these songs' and we never sort of added any more.

MG: 'Just A Man' is classic, probably the stand out track on the record.

KP: I think so too. In fact, it's very difficult when you're going to choose singles first off and you listen to the record company and you listen to the management and other people, then read the initial reviews of the record. 'Just A Man' was one where half the band was always saying "It's gotta be a single" and it's now the current single in Canada where it's doing really well. Yet they never picked up on it in America or Europe which is strange to me because I think it's the best song on the album.

MG: 'Girl On Fire' is strong too.

KP: That was one song America always wanted but it's just really difficult with someone saying this song or that song.

MG: It strikes me that *Elegantly Wasted* is a really interesting album in terms of development. There are lots of ways you can go off this album. I think it'll be really interesting to see where you guys go next.

KP: Me too. I think this album is really bland in a way. I think the next one will be very experimental and more open. Interestingly, we've worked harder this year than we have in a long time. We did the biggest promotional tour we've ever done in our lives at the start of the year. It was like three months. And all of us were doing press rather than just Michael, Tim and I. We just paired off and flew out all round Europe.

MG: Which would have given people a much broader picture of the band.

KP: Yes, and that was important. You know, sometimes I do interviews and you can feel with the journalist that they've asked for Michael and they've got me, but you just end up going different roads and they find they've got a different point of view. In some ways we offer a different reality and perception to say that which people are accustomed to from Michael.

MG: Spinning off that then . . . you sit at home and there's this huge history of INXS, two decades, what are the highlights for you?

KP: Always the first is Wembley Stadium. It was by no means the biggest gig we've done. But Wembley Stadium has a sort of stigma about it like Madison Square Garden. So for that reason and that we headlined it and sold it out, it was kind of like finally we've cracked the UK. Kicked some butt.

I think the US Festival in California in '83 because there was reputedly about half a million people there. That was the end of our first tour of America. We were the second band on after The Divinyls actually, and I remember looking out in the audience and the audience disappeared into the smog. It suddenly occurred to me on stage that the people in the smog that we can't see can't see us. But we got an encore and it was like 'wow'. It was really awesome. I guess the year we cleaned up the American MTV Awards was pretty cool.

MG: The first No 1 single – that must have been a buzz.

KP: Yeah, I can't really remember the first time I heard one of our records on the radio. I think it was in Melbourne when 'Simple Simon' was released. I vaguely remember driving home in one car as you did in those days and hearing it on the radio and all of us were screaming or whatever.

MG: I think I've still got a copy of that on vinyl.

KP: Hey, especially in America where you meet the real fans, they pay anything up to like $500 for that. I've probably got half-a-dozen sitting in my lock-up and it's like hmmmm (laughter).

It's amazing though how the recording industry here has come of age though. Even for us. We were completely naive and ignorant when we did our first album, although I think it sounds better than our second album. Then the only producers that really existed in Australia were Vanda and Young. It was pretty limited going in and now it's like there's no studios but there's all these great producers.

MG: And no hotels, and no touring circuit, and pretty soon in Sydney there's going to be no middle size venue because the Hordern is going to close.

KP: Yeah, I heard that because it's owned now by the corporation which are developing the old Showgrounds into film studios. That's a real tragedy because for people like me and you it holds so many memories. I saw Thorpe and Lobby Lloyd and everyone there. I used to go and see all the great Seventies bands like Daddy Cool, Spectrum, Madder Lake – they were fantastic, fucking amazing . . .

MG: '10lb Toothbrush', what a song.

KP: That was great, and what about the original La De Das, Band Of Light . . .

MG: Magic days for Australian music.

KP: I'm 39, but for Tim and I, we met in secondary high school, and every weekend we used to go a lot to the Hordern or a lot of those surf hops as they used to call them and see Hush and all those bands and they were like our biggest influence, bigger than Deep Purple records and all that stuff.

MG: I was living in Melbourne at the time and I can remember every second Sunday, I think, they used to have an all-day show at South Melbourne football ground as it was then. One Christmas show there was Sherbert headlining: they arrived in stretch limos dressed as Santa Claus. Skyhooks were the second band on the bill, Daddy Cool had folded and become Mighty Kong. Spectrum.

KP: Spectrum were great. Remember Indelible Murtceps.

MG: At another show Thorpie (Billy Thorpe) came on and he had this endless bank of speakers stretching from one end of the stage to the other and he was so loud I thought my ears were going to bleed.

KP: I'll never forget the Sunbury (legendary Australian

outdoor festival – one year in a bog, the next in a desert) he played and Deep Purple played. They were reportedly the loudest band in the world and after they'd been on he came on and the whole audience moved like 500 metres back. He was so loud, he blew them off stage.

MG: True. I was there. Not that I can necessarily remember all of it. But that's part of the Billy Thorpe and The Aztecs legend.

KP: I see him quite a lot. I always run into him in LA.

MG: He's a lovely bloke.

KP: Oh, he's great. I had a fantastic conversation with him a few months back because I got buried in his book and couldn't put it down and I don't read a lot (the book dealt with rock'n'roll and the culture of Kings Cross in the early Sixties). I told him I thought it was fucking fantastic. I found it really intriguing to find out what it was like back then, particularly as I live in this area and it's based around here. He's now writing his next book which basically takes it through The Aztecs' era which is going to be great because that's when I picked up on him.

You know the first two songs Tim and I ever played together in second year high school – when we used to muck around on guitar together before we got a band going there – were 'Gonna See My Baby Tonight' and Thorpie's 'Kind Of Lip'. Really funny. That shows where Tim and my initial influences were. Very much Australian.

I can remember some hilarious times, especially in the early days. We used to stay at Macey's in Melbourne and there used to be us, The Reels, Mental As Anything and three or four other bands all staying in the one building. And the partying . . . it was hilarious.

MG: I can vaguely remember a party after the Australia Made tour that was pretty lethal. I think there was you guys, The Models, maybe The Divinyls, Barnesy . . .

KP: I can remember with Barnesy that always when there was a party it was a challenge to see who could drink the bar. If only he wrote a book. God, could you imagine. He defied nature the way he could drink then. He's such a great guy though and he's got the biggest heart. And he's had such a great career as well.

MG: Talking about The Divinyls, they did better in the US than most people are aware of.

KP: And that was always the way with us. I think we always did way better overseas than the average Australian was aware of. Probably because we were always trying to play it down a bit for fear of the tall poppy.

MG: It's ridiculous this syndrome . . .

KP: It's the English heritage, the English are very much like that too. They're very much into that tearing success down. It's weird you know, America's the complete opposite.

MG: It's a funny time isn't it? This year is Mushroom's 25th Anniversary and I hope, finally, Australians are going to get some sort of vibe about Australian music and what it's all about.

KP: Australian music needs that, it needs that local support. It's only a relatively small industry because of the population and it needs that support to keep it going and keep it moving forward.

I just remembered what I was going to say before is that in that era, the late Seventies/early Eighties Australian bands, a lot of them suffered from going as far as they could in Australia and the going "oh shit, what are we going to do now". Which is what happened to Cold Chisel. They had a few tours in Europe but one of the things we learned from others' mistakes was we started touring around the world before we were even success-ful here, so that everything was building gradually everywhere, instead of going zoom here then going overseas and starting building from the bottom.

MG: Where you guys triumphed though was that you developed a cosmopolitan sound whereas with Chisel they were a pure Australian rock band and somewhat limited by that.

KP: I remember touring the first two times in America and often thinking about – because you are very aware of how you sound and of how you fit in to what's going on – timing and what's going on and how easily your progress can be killed by someone cutting a song from a playlist or releasing the wrong sounding song for that time. I think the same thing happened to Diesel: he's brilliant, but in America there are hundreds of him – the Stevie Ray Vaughans and so on – whereas here he is unique.

Sometimes you can't understand why such immense talents just don't get picked up on, but I guess that's just the way it is. It's so easy to get lost – completely, and it's so much a matter of timing – and all that can be a fluke anyway. All the cards have got to be right. You've got to have a full house and that's why often you buy an album and it's bloody amazing and you think 'why didn't this happen' and you end up realising it's any number of reasons.

MG: Why do you think the Americans took to you so well?

KP: I have no idea. I think probably because – like we did everywhere – we built up a ground base from playing live. We got a name as a great live band and I think in America we also just came in at the right time with something really different. In those days nobody was mixing up – you were a this or a heavy metal band or a MOR band – and we came in right at the start of MTV which was a real big thing because the 'One Thing' video was like nothing they'd ever seen. They jumped on it and before we knew it – on our first tour – we were walking around college towns and getting recognised which was astounding. That was all through MTV. That had a lot to do with it. And we were doing something really different. We were mixing funk with rock.

MG: I think the funk element was really vital.

KP: Yep, but our biggest problem then and there was that they couldn't label us. They'd really gotten by that point in time into marketing and labelling everything. They always have. Everything has to be compared to something else and they couldn't do that with us and I think that's what a lot of the young kids found really cool about us. That's why we had so many weird chart things going on in America. Like we had No 1s on the r'n'b and soul charts where you find that you are six white Australian guys and just about everything else on the chart was black. That helped because we crossed over into all the different formats, as they call them.

MG: Have you got a favourite INXS record.

KP: Hmm, *Elegantly Wasted* is definitely in there, but I think probably *Welcome*. I still think in some ways it was the greatest thing we made and it was just so much fun doing it, as well. We really went in there with not necessarily no idea – but no idea.

And the criteria for that album was try anything and everything. Just really experiment as a band. And also there were a lot of things going on internally. One of the guys was getting married, so he had his head around wedding plans; Tim was really ill, so he wasn't there for most of the album; there was all sorts of stuff going on around Michael. There were just all sorts of emotions going on, so there was a large emotional tag in making that album. And it was the last one we made in Rhinoceros which we were partners in. It was a real shame but that was the end result of trying to do something world class but the industry just wasn't large enough to support it. A lot of stuff was changing technologically then. There was midi on computers and there just wasn't the need for big studios for whole bands to play in at the same time.

Funnily enough with *Elegantly Wasted* we backed right off the technical and got back to really organic and doing virtually first takes. Lots of pressure and really human. I've always been Mr Effects man but this time I was plugged straight into my amplifier. It was 'do it as raw as possible'. And it sounds so much clearer for it. I can remember with Chris Thomas playing a part or guitar solo and having to do it like 50 times before he was happy with it! But in hindsight you'd get so angry and aggro that sometimes it would take on new forms. However, for say Jon when he's up to his 20th take, he just loses it and doesn't know what's good or where to start. There's definitely something to be said about trying to get things straight off. Sometimes I imagine the old days where bands went into a studio and everything was recorded with one mike. I don't know whether any band could do that these days.

MG: It's like a big circle, these 20 years, in some ways.

KP: In some ways.

Kirk paid for the coffee. I wandered off thinking that of all the INXS interviews I'd done this was the best. The history, the emotion, the obvious commitment and love of the band for what they do. The setting the record straight. The honest appraisal of Michael's conundrum. The spirit. Without spirit any form of expression is meaningless. That's what separates the greats – whether they sell 1000 or 1,000,000 million records

– from the rest. It takes something unfathomable to survive 20 years at any level.

To borrow a much-used line for AC/DC: It's along way to the top if you wanna rock'n'roll.

And it's a damn sight further to fall.

Madonna has expressed amazement at INXS frontman Michael Hutchence's decision to commit suicide so soon after the birth of his first daughter.

Madonna – who gave birth to her first child about the same time Hutchence became a father – said she could not attempt to contemplate how "dark life became" for the Australian to kill himself . . .

"I can't imagine getting to that place," she said in an interview.

"It is like trying to imagine what death is: you can't.

"If you have a child I would think, no matter what, you could try and hang on for them. But I don't know; I wasn't in his shoes."

Madonna, whose daughter Lourdes, is 14 months old, said she could understand how people in the spotlight often found themselves deeply depressed.

"I'm the queen of despair. Read the lyrics to my songs.

"I've felt despair many times in my life, but I have very good survival mechanisms.

"No matter how bad it gets, there's something that stops me seeing life as completely hopeless . . ."

– The Sunday Telegraph, February 8, 1998

8

Death

Fame is vapour
Popularity is an accident
And the only earthly certainty is oblivion

– Mark Twain

When Vincent Crane of Atomic Rooster sang "Death walks behind you" he didn't know how right he was or how close it was. On February 20, 1989, suffering from recurring depression, Crane committed suicide, a largely forgotten lead singer of an early Seventies spook rock trio that had two hits, 'The Devil's Answer' and 'Tomorrow Night', and three reasonable albums and actually lasted into the Eighties on the back of numerous line-up changes with Crane the only constant. But they were lean, uncelebrated years and nothing Vincent did would bring him close to the original Rooster, not even the presence of Pink Floyd's Dave Gilmour on their final *Headline News*. He ended up guesting with Dexy's Midnight Runners in 1985 and writing some songs for Kim Wilde before taking his final bow. Vincent wasn't wrong – death does walk behind you. And just like love, death is all around you. Death accumulates, never goes away. Learning to live with death is a lesson in life itself.

Saturday, November 22, 1997, was another warm Sydney day in a series of warm days that seemed to have begun the summer before the calendar gave it the official nod. But it was a day that hadn't felt right since the moment of waking at about 11am. Some days are like that: they are out of balance, crotchety, edgy, wrong – they say hello with a twitch and a nagging and a gut sense of wonk. Wendy (girlfriend, writer, bookworm, sometimes photographer) and I spoke of it over what constitutes breakfast on our world time clock. The answer to wonk is – more often than not – go out and spend money, especially money you can't afford to spend.

Phantom Records in Pitt Street is part of Sydney and, indeed, Australian music history. In 1980 Phantom Records was born on the back of its owners' desire to release music they liked: that it became a major independent force they never considered. Today, it still seems to work that same simple philosophy. The store is small, snuffly, full of smatterings of taste and obscurity. Nosing, I found three or four CDs that would start the hunt perfectly. Peculiarly, when I went to buy them, the disc for one was in a locked drawer. This meant finding a key which turned out to be with the manager (I think) who was upstairs. And took several minutes to come downstairs.

The drawer was unlocked, the disc located, when the man with the key suddenly spread his arms, looked at us and said, "You heard it first at Phantom. Michael Hutchence is dead." A lot of stuff can pass through the mind in an instant: I just felt dizzy and hot and tried to look cool. "The stupid bastard comes back to Australia just to fucking kill himself on some bad . . ." I missed the last word completely. "It was on the radio just now. They've taken a body from the Ritz Carlton Hotel and while it hasn't been officially identified, it's him. He's dead. How fucking stupid." I picked up the CDs, I can't even remember what they were now, negotiated the door and steps and attempted to walk straight. You don't expect to be standing in a record store idly wasting money and contemplating wasting even more, only to be assaulted with the news that somebody you have known in a small-but-big way and were expecting to see in concert a few days later is dead.

There are several very good secondhand stores further down Pitt Street where collectors trawl the vinyl and CDs, the smell of the possessed upon them and a certain madness in their eyes. Wendy discovered me in one of them about 40 minutes later. She began speaking and I cut her short, "Michael's dead." "What? Who?" "Michael Hutchence is dead, maybe a drug over-dose." "No, oh no." She nearly burst into tears. Didn't. Picked her way through M,N,O and P without seeing one cover and said she needed coffee.

By 4pm we were in a taxi heading home. The radio news confirmed – almost immediately – that Michael Hutchence was dead, and there was a hint of suicide. Michael, suicide? It didn't make much sense at the time. Michael had never seemed suicidal. Of all the 'rock' people I'd met Michael seemed one of the least likely to commit suicide. His beliefs, the books he eschewed, the philosophies he'd turn to, none of them were those of a potential suicide. In 1994 he'd said, "There's a lot of seriousness that I think is totally unwarranted ... people killing themselves – literally [the reference was to Cobain] over stuff they shouldn't. That's sad. Pop eats its young, that's for sure."

Exactly two months short of his 38th birthday, Michael let something devour him. Or perhaps it had been devouring him for a while, so maybe it was just finishing him off. Yet, in retrospect, the signs were there that something was wrong, seriously wrong, in his life. But we are always wiser with time.

Michael flew into Sydney's Mascot airport at 11pm on Tuesday, November 18, 1997. He was home. He'd been talking about coming home for a while. He wanted to bring the family to Australia and settle here: he also realised that Sir Bob wouldn't agree to that and that a solution needed to be found.

His last few years had been demanding, erratic, exciting, testing. He had found his soulmate, become a father, seemingly survived the worst the paparazzi could throw at him and particularly Paula. Professionally, INXS were back and while not embraced with the kind of fervour of a decade earlier, at least with a warmth that was satisfying; they had survived a separation that had no return date pencilled in when they drifted apart in late '94, the loss of their manager for 15 years, C M Murphy, and personal dramas within the brotherhood including the break up of Kirk's 17-month-old marriage with Deni Hines, the daughter of Australian music legend Marcia Hines. And Michael had been working on and off on his début solo album [news of which at the time in 1995 was seen by some as a sign that maybe INXS would never pencil in a return date].

On Friday, June 9, 1995, somebody within the closed shop that was MMA leaked the news that Murphy was giving his svengali role away. It was over. One of the longest and most successful rock'n'roll marriages ended with a cheap leak to Sydney's street press that enraged the always emotional Murphy who had intended keeping it secret for several months hence.

On paper it was potentially devastating. Murphy was the ram-rod that pushed INXS into unheard-of zones for an Australian rock band. By using his business brilliance, Murphy built a platform beneath the sextet that meant they didn't have to look over their shoulders, worry about whether their business was being conducted efficiently or whether – as has happened so often to performers in the past – their assets were being drained by incompetence and sheer greed. Secure, INXS could concentrate on what they did best: making records and playing live.

If INXS were shocked by C M's resignation they didn't seem it and the issue of 'what-would-happen-next?' drifted out of the media as Murphy set about restructuring his business interests, having decided that now was the time for his family to come first.

Like everything else it seemed to point to the end of old ways. If INXS were to come back it would definitely be afresh. With *Elegantly Wasted* they had begun the process of reshaping. A close friend of Michael said that he was relieved to be back in Sydney and positive about the future – despite the perpetual stream of INXS as iconic has-beens stories that seemed to surface regularly, not to mention an oft-quoted [in the days after his death] comment that Michael didn't know where INXS fitted in any longer, which concerned him, as did the possibility of his own obscurity.

His arrival at Sydney airport was marked by a short and playful banter with the press who seemed surprised that he actually stopped to talk to them before heading off to the Ritz Carlton Hotel in Double Bay where he checked in as 'Murray River', a reasonably straight pseudonym as they go, and moved into the smallboat harbour-facing room 524.

The Ritz is a high-class elegant mix of old-fashioned furnishings and luxury with plenty of shiny, polished wood and metal and a guest list that would keep celebrity spotters happy for weeks on end. In the past I've shared the lift with former Australian Prime Minister Bob Hawke and his wife Blanche, talked acid daze and halcyon ways in the beautifully appointed lounge with Ray Manzarek of The Doors and their biographer Danny Sugerman, spent three hours dissecting the local music and radio industries over a very long lunch with Richard Clapton who couldn't afford to be there but was, sat in the gym with teen-dream dance/pop sensation Peter Andre who's done so well in recent times in England and Europe, spent half-an-hour by the pool with the gorgeous Heather Nova who has the kind of eyes you really want to fall into, and wandered by the suite in which both Axl Rose of Guns'N'Roses and George Bush, then US President, had both slept – separately, of course.

The next day Michael took it easy, made some phone calls and allegedly caught up with a couple of old friends. On the Thursday he had breakfast with his father Kell, rehearsed with INXS at the ABC Studios in Gore Hill, and managed to sleep through the entire evening, missing a fundraiser for former girlfriend Kym Wilson's theatre company. Michael was also believed to have had several prescriptions filled, including one for Prozac, the anti-depressant medication.

On the Friday he was back at the ABC studios where Channel 9 got the exclusive inside story and film of the band rehearsing. It showed a band honed and shiny, intent and intense. Michael even commented at the end of one song how perfect it was, then muttered 'perhaps too perfect'. He and they seemed happy, looking forward to the 13-date Australian tour. Maybe not. There was one unforgettable shot on that strip of film. It was taken when Michael wasn't aware he was on camera. Slumped on a stool, he looked utterly drained and exhausted . . . and haunted.

Then again it had been a long year on the record and the road and Yates' custody battle with Sir Bob had become a hard-edged war. Sir Bob wasn't giving an inch, then again as a father and wounded ex-spouse it is hard to see why he would. That is human nature. But for Michael it was more. If you read the hundreds of thousands, perhaps millions of words that have been written about Michael before and after his death, and you sift through all the theories and you try to gauge the truth behind all the hot air, hyperbole and standard responses, there emerges a gut-wrenchingly sad snapshot of a man uncertain about his future, perhaps about his band, certainly about himself, who seemed in the end desperately lonely without his woman and child. Michael said many years ago that he had his mid-life crisis at 24; perhaps, and perhaps not. If this wasn't such a time of crisis in his life, it was a time of change and a depth of feeling that defied words and explanation. It was easy to see what Michael needed most when he arrived back in Australia: Paula, Tiger Lily and the girls.

He would explain how much pressure he felt to his father that night when they met for dinner at the Flavour Of India restaurant in Edgecliff, a few kilometres up the road from Double Bay. Later Kell would tell *The Daily Telegraph* (UK, February 3, 1998) " 'He was in great form: joking, mimicking friends, big smiles . . . He'd just been in LA, screen-testing for a new Tarantino movie. He was elated – he'd won the part.'

"But Kell also knew that his son was taking Prozac and had been depressed. 'I grabbed his hand and said: "Look, Mike, tell me. What's this all about?" Michael said he was distressed about the legal battle raging between Paula and himself, and Bob Geldof.' This centred on Paula's plan to bring two of her three daughters by her former husband – Peaches and Pixie – to Australia for a three month holiday. Not unreasonably, Geldof had objected because of the amount of schooling the girls would miss. That day, Michael and Paula's lawyers had been arguing their case in the High Court in London.

"According to Kell, his son was 'furious' with Geldof who, in his view, 'would not let go of Paula.' After dinner, the two men went back to the Ritz Carlton. 'We said fond farewells outside the hotel. It was the last time I saw him,' says Kell, his voice breaking."

Fifteen days later, *The Daily Telegraph* (Sydney) quoted an interview with Kell that appeared in the British magazine *Hello!* In the interview Kell said "his son spoke of a 'vendetta' against him the night before he died.

"Mr Hutchence said he thought Michael's death was due to disappointment over his lover being prevented from bringing her children to Australia, to the pressures of the INXS tour and to 'booze, Prozac and other substances'.

" 'Michael was absolutely fed up with the situation over Paula's children', he said.

" 'He told me "Dad, I feel there's a vendetta against me and it doesn't matter what plans Paula and I make, something always happens to destroy them".'

"Mr Hutchence said there was no indication that Michael had planned to commit suicide when they dined together the night before he was found hanged in his hotel room in Double Bay.

" 'But I feel in my heart it was suicide,' he said."

Kell was also quoted earlier in *New Idea* magazine as saying, "I had never seen him so bubbly. Michael was so full of fun that night – mimicking [an old party trick] and carrying on. I remember saying, 'This is vintage Michael.' "

Kell also said that as a result of the screen tests Michael was wanted in LA straight away but had concluded "I can't walk off the tour."

In mid-December Kell appeared on television in an extensively quoted interview during which he took a swing at Sir Bob. Both *The Sun* and *New Musical Express* reported that Kell said, "He [Sir Bob] made their lives miserable. It's like he was on a vendetta – to get them. And that's really the truth of it. He created extraordinary situations and I think contributed very much to what happened . . .

"Those kids, Pixie and Peaches, loved Michael so much. And he wasn't trying to take the children away from their father."

Back at the Indian restaurant, reports of that final dinner are much the same. Superficially, they don't depict a man considering suicide. But as Kell noted in the press he felt that beneath the surface and the frivolity was a tangled mess of emotion. Michael and Kell drank beer and wine and chose four main courses at which Michael picked throughout the night.

At 10.30pm, Kell dropped Michael off at the hotel where he went straight to his room and stayed for about half an hour. *The Daily Telegraph* (December 13, 1997), in an extensive feature of Michael's final days by Marcus Casey, reported that it had interviewed "a Southern Highlands woman – named 'Karen' – who had known Hutchence for more than 15 years, and believes she met Hutchence in his room at this time.

"The woman, nervous and distressed that her name entered the final loop of Hutchence's life, did not have a sexual relationship with the singer.

"She would not elaborate on what went on in the room, but displayed intimate knowledge of prescription medicines and said Hutchence was taking many.

"Adamant that no hard drugs were present when she was in the room, the woman said Hutchence told her he'd been on a variety of medicines for a full month.

"One was Keflex, considered the strongest antibiotic available over the counter.

"Karen would not elaborate on the others.

" 'His body was saturated with them that's all I know,' she told *The Daily Telegraph* after being interviewed by police investigating the death.

"Michael was so up when I saw him, but looking back, he was like a volcano waiting to explode with the amount of pharmaceuticals in him."

Exactly why "Karen" visited Michael's room has never been disclosed.

About 11pm, dressed in black jacket and pants and alone, he left room 524 and entered the elevator which he shared with two sisters, Zinta Reindel and Tamara Brachmanis, and according to Liz Hannan of *The Sun-Herald* (November 23) ended their plans for a late-night dip in the hotel swimming pool. " 'I think it's closed girls,' Hutchence told the sisters and their friend, Tanya Turnbull."

Ms Reindel also said, " 'He looked like he was a bit high on something but stars are always on something . . . But he was happy'."

Michael left the lift and entered the hotel's piano bar where, according to several witnesses, he spoke to two women, applauded the woman who was singing, had a drink and seemed a "happy guy".

In fact, happy seems to have been the key word for the evening so far. And it got happier when Kym Wilson arrived with her boyfriend, Andrew Rayment, a solicitor and son of leading Sydney silk Brian Rayment.

What happened next is best told in Kym's own words.

Kym Wilson was to become the victim of one of the worst pieces of rumour-mongering to erupt in the wake of Michael's death: that she'd committed copycat suicide herself, unable to deal with the guilt she felt for what had gone on with Michael that night or, according to who you listened to, she had hanged herself in a police cell after being charged with manslaughter over Michael's death and that her death had been covered up.

I turned up for work at *The Sydney Morning Herald* about 5pm on November 28 to find the rumour the hottest topic of the day. Journalists were seriously investigating it and at least three people asked me if I knew whether it was true. A few phone calls and I knew it wasn't. It appeared to have started as a sick joke in the Goodbar nightclub in Sydney's inner city Darlinghurst, close to the renowned Oxford St strip, the social home to many of the city's gay community. From there it spread with alarming rapidity. Several people told me starting such rumours was a game and the rumour surrounding Wilson wasn't the first.

On December 3 a picture of a very much alive Kym Wilson and a story about her theatre company appeared on the front page of *The Daily Telegraph*. But it wasn't enough and Wilson was forced to surface and tell her story in an effort to reclaim her life: she had been forced to move out of her home at Scotland Island, an hour north of Sydney, where the world's media were camped out on her front lawn, and had spent hours convincing friends that she wasn't dead.

Woman's Day (December 15, 1997) carried the exclusive interview [for an alleged fee of $150,000 which Wilson donated to a Trust fund set up for Heavenly Hiraani Tiger Lily] by Leigh Reinhold. The British tabloids had shown her no mercy. The article records for posterity headlines such as "The Woman Michael Had Sex With That Night" and "The Woman Paula Didn't Want At The Funeral". Compassion? What compassion? Fact? What fact?

Kym Wilson, pretty, strong-willed, independent and in some ways, according to those who know her best, quite shy and old-fashioned, was probably the last person to see Michael alive.

" 'Because Michael was a rock star, people want to believe scandalous clichés over what happened,' she says. 'But the night I spent with him, which was followed, five hours after I left by his death, was a night with a friend, of catching up with a man who predominantly was very in love with his life at that time and so in love with his family.

" 'He told me over and over again that night that he loved Paula and Tiger Lily, who was his pride and joy, and he also felt Paula's three other daughters were part of his family too. It was one of his greatest moments of pride in his life that all the girls called him Daddy.' "

Wilson says they had gone up to Michael's room rather than stay in the bar where they had met him because he wanted to be close to the phone in case some news of the custody battle Paula was fighting with Sir Bob came through from London.

" 'He was concerned about the custody hearing but I wouldn't say he was depressed,' she says. 'His attitude was that he believed he was right that he and Paula should get custody of the children and if they didn't have luck this time, they would keep fighting on. I never for one instant think he thought that would be the end, that he would give up if the case didn't go their way. He spoke with such excitement of his future – I had really never seen him with so much to look forward to.

" 'Michael talked about how he desperately wanted the girls to be with him and he thought that was what they wanted too. Michael wasn't very fond of Bob Geldof, he didn't paint a good picture of him at all.'

"While waiting for the phone call, the trio ordered strawberry daiquiris and Michael talked about the exciting ways his life was changing and evolving.

" 'He was very excited about his solo career. He had a CD demo of one of his songs which he was desperate to play, but there was no CD player,' she says. 'While we were there, he also had a phone call about a film Quentin Tarantino was very interested in him doing.

" 'He'd been working up to that for a long time and he was very excited about the fact – he put his arm around me and said, "Kym, I'm an actor now too!" '

"Michael was anxious to know whether Paula, Tiger Lily and the other girls would be able to join him for the 20th anniversary tour of INXS. Kym told him they would wait until the phone call came through.

" 'He took a phone call while we were there, saying that they still hadn't got a judge for the case. By this point, it was about 4.30am. My poor darling boy was falling asleep lying at the foot

152

of the bed. Michael just looked at him and looked at me trying to keep up the conversation and said, 'Oh look, you two go home.' "

Further on in the story Wilson talks about the reaction after the story broke and the rumours that began to emerge.

" 'People have wanted to imply that there was a sex and drug-crazed orgy happening in Michael's room that night,' she says. 'Nothing could be further from the truth. It was a night of catching up with a close friend trying to find out the result of a court case about his family.

" 'Of course we had a drink. But in the six hours we were there, we would have only had between six and eight drinks and we were hardly drunk. There were definitely no drugs in the room when I was there and there wasn't any sex either.

" 'The police have been very public about the fact that Prozac was found in Michael's room and I'm very dubious about that drug. I don't understand enough about it to analyse what potential it had in the situation, but from what I've heard, Prozac may well have been one of a number of things that culminated in Michael's death.

" 'Paula, and I thank her, has said she places absolutely no responsibility on me and she knows there was no sexual activity and attributes no blame for the situation to me at all. She understands even in the enormity of her grief, that I was just a friend of Michael's who happened to be with him at the time.

" 'I'm sure she knows from the relationship she had with Michael that none of the rumours are true and the police are in no doubt that there was no sexual activity in the room that night. Nor have I been charged with manslaughter, nor am I dead after hanging myself in a cell after I was charged. It's not true.

" 'The insinuation that there was sexual activity in the room was more hurtful than anything because I have a very strong relationship, a monogamous relationship, and Paula and Michael loved each other so desperately. How dare the press insinuate something that didn't happen, especially about someone who can't respond.'

"Kym is quick to defend the friend she met when she was 17, at the birthday party of her best friend Mouche Phillips . . .

" 'I remember the night we met vividly, he wore a blue feather boa and there were feathers left wherever we went for a whole week . . .

" 'Michael and I had a romance, but it was a very long time ago and it was very brief,' she explains. 'It started a wonderful friendship that would last for many years.'

" '. . . I think that it was a beautiful way for us to get to know each other to become friends. Most of the time we spent together was as friends.' "

The oddest fact in Kym's story though comes at the end. Earlier she has said how she and her boyfriend had left their telephone numbers on a page in Michael's diary and told him to ring if he needed someone.

The last two paragraphs of the story read: "Kym says she knows that Michael appreciated their final hours together because of two words written in his diary where she had left her telephone number.

" 'He had written "Thank you" in between my boyfriend's and my name which was not only a wonderful little message from him but it also made it a lot easier for me to cope,' she explains. 'When you're the last person to be involved in that kind of tragedy, the questions that you ask yourself are endless. But I know that I tried to give him as much support as I could that night and there was no way that I could have foretold what was going to happen. I think he wrote that thank you for a reason.' "

Left unanswered is a question: if Michael Hutchence had intended to live, why would he leave a message for Kym Wilson? Obviously, he could thank her in person or by the phone and just as obviously she wouldn't be likely to see those pages in his diary again. So why the message . . .

In the last five hours of his life, Michael was hardly ever off the phone. He is reported to have made about 10 calls out in that time and received several more. One call was from Paula Yates who rang about an hour after Wilson and Rayment left with the news that the custody hearing had been adjourned until December 17 and she couldn't come out immediately with the children.

This was the first of several crucial calls that some, including current INXS manager Martha Troup, believe caused him to snap. Troup had spoken to Michael about 1am when Wilson and Rayment were with him. On December 5, she told internet e-zine *Addicted To Noise* [http://www.addict.com] senior writer Gil Kaufman that a nervous breakdown in the early hours of the morning had caused Michael to take his life.

"He snapped," said Troup. "He felt pressures and it was snap . . . he snapped for that momentary time. I think [it was] pressures about his child Tiger and Bob Geldof and all the escapades that went on in the last year . . . It just reached a climax. It was the culmination of everything, how he [Geldof] treated Paula and how he was making his [Hutchence's] life miserable."

Troup also confirmed that Michael was indeed happy during that last call. "He was in a brilliant mood when I spoke to him," she said. "He was talking about film things, and he'd read a script. Just the second I got on the phone he was 'Martha I love you,' just lovable, lovable, lovable. And he was very excited that day from rehearsal and he felt it was going really well. He was happy. He loved Australia, he loved it."

After Paula's call an angry Michael then phoned Sir Bob about 5.30am on November 22 and according to Sir Bob begged him to allow the children to come to Australia. In the room next door Gail Coward stated that she heard a loud male voice swearing at that time. Sir Bob confirmed the nature of Michael's call. He later said, "We didn't have a row – it takes two people to have an argument. He called up late and I just couldn't understand a word he said. I just put down the phone. Michael had been bombarding me with calls for the past few months. It was impossible to talk to him because he was always off his head."

About three hours passed before Michael made his next call: to his former lover, Michelle Bennett, who lives not far away from the hotel. He left a message saying, "I think it's seven o'clock. I need to talk to you." It was 9am. Ms Bennett told the NSW State Coroner, Mr Derek Hand, that Michael sounded "drunk". During the next hour, he rang Martha Troup at 9.38am – at the New York-based office of Entertainment Consulting Company and at home. He left a message: "Marth, Michael here. I f . . . ing had enough"; a second call followed 12 minutes later. On both occasions Ms Troup was unable to get to the phone. According to *The Daily Telegraph* he also rang INXS members and other friends and associates, although they have subsequently never been identified. He found more answering machines.

Finally, he called Michelle Bennett again at 9.54am and began crying. Concerned about him she rushed to the hotel, arriving about 10.30am. She got no answer when she called his room from the hotel lobby and no response when she knocked on the door of his room. She wrote a note and left it at reception. Michelle Bennett had arrived too late. Michael Hutchence was probably already dead . . . on the other side of the door.

Michael Kelland Frank Hutchence died between 10am and 11am on Saturday, November 22, 1998, when he tied a leather belt around the self-closing device on his hotel door, put the other end around his neck and – naked – hung himself.

He was found about 11.55am by a maid.

Love will tear us apart.

"I don't know whether I'm angry or guilty . . . You always think if it's a mate that there was something you could have done.

"I still find it hard to figure it all out because I had a conversation with him not that long ago where we talked about something like this and we both agreed how dumb and selfish it would be, and Hutch was not all that selfish. . . .

"He was very light, whereas I don't think I'm the easiest person in the world, so we balanced each other out. But I hadn't seen him for a while, because we were both off doing our thing. I'm finding the whole thing very hard to understand. . . ."

– Bono of U2 in *Q* magazine talking about Michael's death and
how they had once discussed suicide.

9

Last Rites

For three weeks we lived death. Michael's death ruled the Australian, British and European media. The frenzy was as eerie and scary as it was sad to watch. As Paula Yates flew to Australia with Tiger Lily so did the British media. The death of Princess Diana may have turned public opinion against the paparazzi but it was only a brief refrain. When Michael died the vultures returned, seemingly hungrier than ever for sensation.

Every rumour became a fact until the facts and rumours were hard to distinguish. In the first week seven people came up to me and told me they knew – or a friend knew – a policeman/detective/ambulance officer/hotel worker who had been in the room, had seen the body, who knew the 'truth'.

And the 'truth' was – variously:

*There was semen on the sheets, drugs scattered over the floor/table/furnishings and the police statements were a fabrication designed to protect the family's feelings and prevent the media and the world from knowing the gruesome details.

*That Michael had slept with Kym Wilson then killed himself besieged by guilt; that Kym, Michael and Andrew had a wild ménage à trois (Michael somewhere in the totally distant, forgotten past had said he had once kissed a man!).

*That Michael had sex with both the women he had met at the bar, then met Kym and Andrew, the latter of whom had gone home soon afterwards leaving Michael and Kym alone whereupon they debunked to his bedroom and messed up the sheets. In fact, if you added all the rumours up, Michael would have slept with up to seven women that night (in the most bizarre rumour he slept with Martha Troup who was in America!) in the space of about 11 hours, this after he'd swallowed copious quantities of alcohol, prescribed drugs, cocaine and Prozac. His declining physical state would, of course, render this impossible; and where he fitted in

158

talking to anybody, making phone calls . . . it's doubtful if he'd have had the strength left to do anything but sleep.

Which leads us to the 'biggest truth' of all:

*Michael didn't commit suicide. His was death by misadventure; sexual misadventure – auto-erotic asphyxiation gone wrong. This is a practice where you reduce your oxygen intake dramatically by putting something tight around your neck/throat so you are to all intents and purposes slowly dying of strangulation. Why? Because oxygen deprivation greatly increases orgasm intensity. The trick is to orgasm before you pass out . . . and, maybe, die.

Its proponents pointed to the fact that Michael was naked. Why would he want to commit suicide naked? That's a good question, in fact. A noted Australian music and crime writer told me a while later about a conversation he'd had with a friend who was also a crime writer and who believed that very few people who commit suicide do so naked, probably because they are either ashamed of themselves, of what they were about to do, or ashamed of their body, and thus prefer to be clothed. A quick flip through research on suicide doesn't support that in full but it does indicate there's some strong credence to the proposition. Not that it really proves anything. Michael was a guy who did things differently: naked we come into this world, naked we depart.

In a vain attempt to kill off media speculation the police were quick to announce they didn't suspect foul play, had found no evidence of sexual activity and that it was suicide. But that didn't necessarily make great headlines. Well, not long-lasting headlines.

Truth be told, between November 22 and November 27 when Michael was to be buried there was little genuine news. Much column space was devoted to the opinions and eulogies of anybody who had ever known Michael. Even those who didn't like INXS and had actively knocked the band in the past were to be found paying tribute on TV and radio stations. Shawn Deacon and her staff at Big Media Pty Ltd, the band's publicists, tried to maintain some sanity in the face of the growing storm of insanity, producing an endless flow of official statements.

They were simple and to the point. We put them straight

online in our e-zine, THE iZINE (http://www.thei.aust.com), where the fans could read the facts along with tributes, earlier interviews and other related material. Details of the funeral, the family's wishes – they all went online. How loved was Michael Hutchence? In the first two weeks after his death more than 28,000 people hit these pages. Now five months later, there are more than 60 pages online and they still register more than 500 individual visitors a week. And they are only a small part of a giant web of INXS and Michael sites – many of them beautifully designed, all of them genuinely emotional. (See the addendum for more on the internet experience.)

The first two statements were from the band and Michael's parents. They read:

ON BEHALF OF INXS

The band members of INXS are all in extreme shock at the loss of their dear friend and lead singer, Michael Hutchence. Their love and sympathy go out to Michael Hutchence's family. They ask that the media please, in this time of extreme grief, act with courtesy and grace, and respect both Michael Hutchence's family's privacy, as well as their own.

At this point in time they have no further comment.

PRESS STATEMENT
BY KELLAND HUTCHENCE AND PATRICIA GLASSOP
(Michael Hutchence's Parents)

On behalf of the entire Hutchence family, we are extremely shocked and deeply saddened by the sudden death of our son, Michael.

Michael was an inspiring talent who touched many people around the world with his work and will be greatly missed.

To us, and everyone close to him, he was a vibrant human being, with an immense heart full of love.

As we try to come to terms with our tragedy, we ask that the media respect the memory of Michael and leave us to grieve in peace.

They didn't.

On Monday, November 24, a tick after 6.30am, Paula Yates and Tiger Lily arrived in Sydney after a 22-hour flight from London on which she was heavily sedated and not a little distressed. The same day, Britain's *Daily Express* ran a story in which Paula was alleged to have said "Bob Geldof murdered Michael Hutchence … That bastard killed Michael. He is called Saint Bob. That makes me sick. He killed my baby [Michael]. We have had three years of this."

The comments were amongst several she apparently made during the flight. She had a captive and attentive audience. Speaking of the dress she had bought for the wedding, Yates said: "Now the dress is being dyed black. I'm going to wear it to the funeral with pride. Michael obviously flipped. He was worn down by three years of torture.

"People think he was a hell-raiser, prancing around in those black leather trousers. But underneath it all he was a sweet innocent boy. He was a wonderful father," she said. British newspapers said Hutchence sent a dozen red roses to Yates less than 24 hours before he was found hanging from a leather belt in his hotel room.

The flowers carried a note saying "All my beautiful girls, all my love Michael". The bouquet arrived in London after Yates had left for Sydney with their daughter Heavenly Hiraani Tiger Lily.

With her arrival the stake-outs began. The Sir Stamford Hotel in Double Bay where Paula was staying – 24 hours a day; Kelland Hutchence's home; Kym Wilson's home; Michael's brother Rhett Hutchence's home; less frequently watched but visited regularly were any known Sydney addresses for the members of INXS, in particular Kirk Pengilly's Potts Point residence.

Wherever the family moved they found cameras and microphones in their faces. It was truly pathetic. They didn't have anything to say. They were too damn griefstruck. Paula, however, beat the paparazzi at their own game, avoiding being photographed or seen from the time of her arrival at the hotel until the day of the funeral.

On February 23, 1998, Paula's story of these grim hours finally surfaced in *Woman's Day*. In an exclusive (then) interview, Martin Townsend wrote, "On the day before his [Michael's] death Paula was in court for a custody hearing. She had hoped to take her girls and join Michael for a three-month break in Australia where she had been offered work: a documentary about Australia as seen through an Englishwoman's eyes, a top rating breakfast show, plus two cover photo shoots for *Vogue* magazine.

"It would have been her first work since Paula and Michael began their relationship. He could hardly wait to see them in Australia. 'He thought that for three months, just three months, we would have a life,' she says.

"Then came the hammer blow: the hearing was adjourned and Paula was unable to take her three eldest daughters out of England. She knew she could not be parted from her children for that period of time. And she knew it would devastate Michael. 'I left the court and I turned to my barrister and said, "This will kill Michael" and . . . he died a few hours later.'

"Paula has tears in her eyes now, and through the sobs, her voice is choked with anger. 'How much can you take? What did we do? I loved him too much, we loved each other too much.'

"In their last telephone call, Michael and Paula discussed names for a baby girl they planned. Paula says she would definitely have had another girl. Michael, who was raised in and adored the Far East, favoured Shanghai; Paula liked Violetta.

"At the end of the call Michael said, 'I love you and I love Tiger and I'm gonna ring Bob and beg him to let the girls come.'

"In the middle of that night the doorbell rang at Paula's home, waking Paula, who was asleep in bed with Pixie, seven, Peaches, eight, and Tiger [Fifi, 14, was at boarding school].

"'I went downstairs and my friend Belinda [Brewin] walked in,' says Paula, 'and she was just sobbing. She said, "I've got terrible news for you – Michael's dead," and I punched her right in the face. It was awful. I was crying and saying, "How can you say something like that to me?" It was just like I was dead from then on . . .' "

On arrival in Sydney, Paula went straight from the airport to the mortuary.

Townsend writes: ". . . Paula's voice is barely a whisper now.

"'Tiger and I went in and just stayed with Michael. I was relieved to get to him, actually. It seemed like the longest 24 hours of my life just to get to someone. I got to him too late, but I got to him. Tiger saw her dad and then I sent her out and I stayed with Michael.'

"She adds, 'I had never seen anyone dead and I didn't even realise that they're that cold. It's really weird, they are like ice. I made the mortuary send out for a duvet and I wrapped him up in it. Tucked him in.'

"Did she hold him? 'Yes. I spent a long time with him. I just kept trying to look after him.' She talked to him. 'It was the most private time I'll ever have with Michael, ever. I would have taken him home with me. But it's all so strange because your automatic reaction is to want to make it better and you can't make it better; you can't do anything. The powerlessness is just . . . unimaginable.'

"The tears are flowing again. She had barely arrived in Sydney when a senior policeman, 'in that fantastic Australian way', told her that there had been no girl in the hotel room when Michael died. 'But, you know, I was always kind of impressed with Michael's ability to be very faithful to me and the girls because it's not easy when everyone thinks you're handsome.'

"She has no hesitation in dismissing suicide as the cause of death. 'I don't believe he would have left Tiger deliberately. I truly don't believe that, and I'm not just saying it to make me feel better or [to] try to make Tiger feel better in the future. I just know him.'

"The other theory, rejected by the coroner, was that Michael died accidentally in the midst of some kind of sexual experiment. Is this something he would do? There is a long pause, but Paula's answer is forthright. 'I don't think there' s anything on earth Michael wouldn't do.'

"Paula would prefer that verdict to suicide. 'I suppose it would be easier to bear, in a weird way, easier than thinking of someone you loved that much being in such despair.'

"What does she think happened in that hotel room? 'I think he was beside himself. With anger and a loss of hope, and pain, and missing the girls. And I think he was drunk'.

"Michael then spoke to Bob Geldof 'and . . . whatever happened, happened. I think it was a lot of things meeting head on. But I don't think he meant to die. And nor does anyone who knew him as well as me. A cry for help, a cry for understanding. But not a "Bye-bye Tiger". Never, never, never.' "

Everybody seemed have to an opinion about Michael's death. It became *the* topic of conversation, especially in lifestyles of the rich'n'famous country: one of their own had died. Why? Elsewhere, it was still the topic of conversation but on a more germane level. Devastated fans cried lonely tears and wrote long poems and tributes about the death of fantasy, of idol worship, of love never to be expressed. Others remembered their youth and a man who had – more often than not – provided a soundtrack to their own lives.

Among those tributes a couple stand out: from U2 and Duran Duran.

On Sunday, November 23, the day after Michael's death, U2's PopMart tour rolled in to San Antonio. But this was to be a show with a difference and one that set a standard for the rest of the tour, particularly when it reached Australia in February 1998.

Bono and the band's tribute to his old friend began during 'Pride (In The name Of Love)', a tribute to Martin Luther King, during which Bono sang 'Waltzing Matilda', the traditional Australian ballad. Between songs Bono spoke to the audience, saying, "This is for Michael Hutchence, a great singer and a great friend. We'll miss him." And with that the band broke into 'Still Haven't Found What I'm Looking For'. Two songs later during the equally moving 'Staring At The Sun' from their massively underestimated *Pop* set, Michael's face was projected on the giant screen that is such a feature of PopMart. Even then U2 weren't finished, substituting the normal closer 'One' with 'Wake Up Dead Man'. The band left the stage, the lights came up and as the audience left INXS' anthem 'Never Tear Us Apart' pumped through speakers.

A day earlier in Cleveland, Simon Le Bon of Duran Duran dedicated their concert and specifically, the song 'Save A Prayer', to Michael's memory, spoke of his "best friend" and asked the audience to remember Paula and Tiger Lily.

In England a few days later the eight-year-old Catherine Wheel, a complex, heavy, song-based alternative rock outfit that has recently come of age, also dedicated a song to Michael Hutchence.

When it came to words, British music writer Miranda Sawyer's obituary in *The Observer* to the "unbelievable, appalling, shocking" death of her friend left – as it should – a smile on the face: "Michael wasn't cool – you'd see him fall flat on his face during a TV rehearsal; he wasn't discreet – he revelled in wild living, outrageous gossip, call-the-lawyer situations. But he was the most fantastic rock star. He was born for leather trousers. He was a brilliant night out. And he was proving to be a great night in, staying at home caring for his new much-loved family. Michael was a big, beautiful man, with a big, beautiful heart. The world is a smaller, grimmer place without him."

A less publicised but nevertheless interesting hypothesis about why Michael wasn't feeling so good about life in the months leading up to his death was voiced in an article INXS: A Life by Steve Dow that appeared in *The Age* (November 29, 1997).

"Psychiatrists have coined a term that seems to fit Hutchence's alleged depression aptly. Dr Edwin Harari, a St Vincent's Hospital consultant psychiatrist, says many VIPs have a narcissistic vulnerability, either because of early traumatic childhood experiences or their genetic makeup. For such people, success works as an antidote. As long as they're doing well, they can regulate depression through success.

"Harari says Hutchence could be a case of the 'collapsible man of prominence', whose emotional reserves are low for when things go awry. As well, high-profile people are often flitting between cities, so if they suffer depression, they tend to take the medication and run, failing to knuckle down to therapy. 'Yet what they really need is to be treated like everyone else.'"

And what about the Prozac question. Dow writes, ". . . most psychiatrists say the use of Prozac reduces the chance of suicide among depressives, rather than increases it. But it is only effective in the right dosages, with right counselling and, in some cases, rest and admission to hospital.

"It is highly unlikely, if Hutchence took Prozac, that the drug itself triggered his decision to put a belt around his neck – unless he had experienced a rare dangerous reaction had he combined it with an old-style tricyclic anti-depressant (this could have caused confusion or even led to a coma), or mixed it with alcohol, magnifying drunkenness, or with amphetamines such as ecstasy, impairing his judgement, even reversing Prozac's task."

The Coroner later found Michael had a cocktail of alcohol, cocaine, Prozac and other prescription drugs in his blood (see Chapter 12).

Michael Hutchence knew drugs, he pushed it to the limit when he felt like it. And he knew the safety line. That night and morning he was either so distraught and so distracted that he went over the line and over the edge or he intentionally tried to moderate his state – one way or another – and failed. What happened inside Michael's head, alone in Room 524, between 6am and 10am is impossible to say. And why he couldn't find somebody to help him when he most needed help, a shoulder, a hand, an arm, whatever, is even more difficult to explain. Why, for instance, when all else had failed, didn't he call his family?

In *The Daily Telegraph* (UK) article of February 3, 1998, his father spoke of the day his son died. ". . . That night, he [Kell] suddenly became anxious about his son. Then at 6am, he awoke with a strong urge to call him. 'But Michael was always a late riser, nocturnal. I thought: he'll only get bad-tempered if I ring and wake him up, so I didn't.'

"He waited until 11am, but then, 'the phone just rang and rang.' Soon afterwards, a reporter was on the line. 'He asked if I had anything to say about Michael. I said: "About the new tour?" And he said, "Oh, I'm sorry," and hung up.' Kell remembers his heart suddenly pounding with fear. Within minutes, two policemen appeared at the door to tell him his son was dead.

"It was not the first time that he had learnt something about his son's life from a reporter before the official channels had a chance to inform him. When drugs were allegedly found under Paula's and Michael's bed in London, he read about it in the papers. 'It was all lies,' he insists. But what of Michael's own admissions that he took drugs and even 'carried liquid ecstasy around in a cookie jar'? 'I never knew about any incident where he was a druggie,' he counters. 'I'm not saying his crowd didn't take a little bit of this and that, but I don't think it was ever to any great extent. I never had to confront him.'

"Later Kell comments, 'Mike just loved having a ready-made family, and the kids loved him. Paula is a great mother and she also has a terrific sense of humour. I know that she and Michael used to meet a lot of her pretty famous friends in London – artists, writers. In some ways, she opened up a new field for him, in the arts.'

"For all that, Kell does not believe that Michael and Paula were about to get married. 'I asked Michael whether he was, and he said: "No plans yet, Dad, and you'll be the first to know." I don't think Michael was in the mood to get married yet.' Would he ever have married? 'I doubt it. He didn't really believe in marriage very much. I suppose kids from failed marriages often feel that way.'

"Not a man given to great introspection, Kell refuses to elaborate on his own divorce, saying only that his son found it 'very upsetting'. Was that one of the reasons behind Michael's relentless touring – and hell-raising interludes? 'I don't know,' he says sadly."

Marry the medical comments in Dow's article with the Coroner's report, Kell's replies and Paula's beliefs, and see what picture you get. A mess, a gargantuan nightmare of a mess in which beauty still reverberated – but only just, a Jackson Pollock or Pro Hart painting. How happy was the happy man everybody contentedly captured in the hours before his death? How thin was the veil between Michael's joy and the fears that were literally tearing him apart. I think Paula Yates knows the answer to that. She is probably the only person who truly understood what was going on deep, down in the dark corners of Michael. This was the ultimate bittersweet symphony. Paparazzi persecution drove Michael to the edge of insanity and Paula to failed suicide. They were the children of broken homes and dramatic out-of-control lives, thunderous splashes of Kodachrome and monochrome, flung together in passion and love and fear and desperation and loneliness – and that persecution forced them closer and closer together. They were almost one. She knows. And she doesn't have to share it because, perhaps, it is the one thing the world cannot take from her. That and Heavenly Hiraani Tiger Lily.

Back in the real world a funeral had to be organised. A

fitting funeral. Michael's mother, Patricia Glassop, brought in entrepreneur and celebrity manager, Harry M. Miller, to handle all inquiries on her behalf. And, it seemed soon after, quite a bit else. Astoundingly, Miller organised a deal with the Seven Network, allowing cameras into St Andrew's Cathedral (in the heart of the city where the funeral was to be held) and the rights to an international broadcast.

Extraordinarily, the members of INXS, Paula Yates and Michael's closest friends, only found out the details in the press the day before the funeral.

A horrified INXS immediately issued a brief statement via Shawn Deacon:

FUNERAL ARRANGEMENTS
INXS Media Statement

All arrangements for Michael Hutchence's funeral have been made by Michael's parents, and at this time we, the band members, must respect their wishes.

It got worse. *The Daily Telegraph* (December 13) looked back on those ridiculous hours: "Miller told the world the Anglican cathedral would be closed to the public and media. His comments incensed the Very Reverend Boak Jobbins, a man of measured words whose cathedral doors are open to everyone all the time – whether Miller wheels and deals over them or not.

"Ever the spielmeister, Miller berated the media at a farcical press conference the next day by telling them their stories about the 'closed service', based directly on his press release the day before, were wrong.

"More than 60 members of the media from around the world stood under the eastern suburbs railway line outside Miller's Woolloomooloo office as he reinvented history. The English press couldn't believe his front. The Australians, who had seen it before, rolled their jaded eyes."

Meanwhile, the fans each day added to a small shrine of flowers, a car number plate [INXS 01], pictures, words and memoirs that grew outside the Ritz Carlton Hotel. At least something seemed genuine.

10

Into My Arms

Dignity.

There is so little of it these days.

Even five months later, this day – the day Michael Kelland Frank Hutchence went away – remains the cruellest cut of all. Big boys and girls do cry. So they should. They did on November 27, 1997, when the coffin containing the late Michael Hutchence passed so slowly by, borne on the shoulders of his band mates and brother Rhett, the strains of 'Never Tear Us Apart' a stately embrace.

It was a moment of pure pathos. It was hard to believe that he lay inside.

Michael had been everywhere else for over an hour in this lofty ethereal cathedral – except the one place where he should have been . . .

Dignity.

At last there was dignity. The circus stopped for an hour. No, it didn't stop. It was cut off. The circus waited outside for the televised service – Paula, INXS and Michael's closest friends remained deeply opposed to and horrified by his mother's decision – to the end.

Inside the church a family much larger than Michael might ever have imagined said goodbye.

November 27 was a brute of a day. A hot, stifling, insensitive day. As we drove into the city's centre where St Andrew's Cathedral lives in the shadow of the Town Hall, nestled under an armpit and pushed back slightly from the road, business men in soaked singlets and shorts jogged through nearby parks, their faces a smile of pain. "I can do it. I will do it," an endless loop in their heads as they fried for fitness; there are many forms of shortening your life.

St Andrew's looks like it belongs alongside the busy streets in the city's retail heart. Its small gardens offer some tranquillity in the roar of the race to succeed; the footpaths that form diagonals around its edges hum and clicker-clatter while the big buses continually block out measures of light as they pass or slow to stop and pick up and spill. At night, it is almost unnoticeable; a ghost of the spirit waiting for another call.

It is formal, venerable, historic and composed. A place of serious intent and content of those who fill its wash of pews.

Michael loved churches. He told Paula so a decade ago. In fact, part of their chapter was engraved in a church.

In her autobiography, Paula writes; "Michael Hutchence stood in a Fifth Avenue church on Palm Sunday waving a palm frond. At first glance you might not have been able to tell that Michael was a love god, but he certainly stood out from his fellow worshippers with his post-Morrison glory of falling curls and his regulation off-duty-sex-symbol black leather suit. With the exception of the palm frond, which could have been a 'new man' sensitivity totem, Michael Hutchence looked like the logical conclusion of popstar attitude. A sort of rock star composite. A blend of attitude and sexuality in a way that is dangerous, appealing and admirable. I'd been sent to interview him for *Time Out* magazine. It was 1988, which had been a bad year for me . . .

". . . Don [Ateyo, then editor of *Time Out*] and I had been to the NEC to see INXS and I cried all the way home because Michael had a girlfriend. Don was most impressed, which is why I was sent to do the interview. I'd not seen Michael for a couple of years before that concert, but I sometimes spoke to him on the phone or we'd have a cup of tea if he was in London. And he was still on my fridge door.

"Michael Hutchence is seductive. He has none of the appeal of English pop stars who look like they couldn't threaten a jam roll and spend their spare time at home with their mums writing thank-you letters to fans for furry purple gonks. Michael is seriously alluring, in an old-fashioned, *louche* and loose-limbed way. His sex appeal is careless and seemingly lacking narcissism. There's an odd dichotomy between the visual, which is a heady cross of Dolores del Rio and dream boy, and the man who speaks, who is shy and sensitive.

170

"Being in church always makes me nervous. I stood there waiting to be struck down by a bolt of lightning. 'Look how lovely the ceiling is,' I said. Michael looked up, squinted, looked down again, took his shades off and slowly looked up again. 'I just love churches,' he crooned, 'and art galleries. They make me cry. I've cried in every major art gallery in the world.'"

At 1.30pm, the front entrance of the St Andrew's Cathedral was shut off; there was still an hour before the funeral was due to start. The 30 metres of concrete that separates the thick wooden double doors from the street had become a courtyard framed on both sides by a solid press of quiet fans and closer to the entrance, cameras, cameramen and photographers. All poised and waiting. An usher explained as soon as Michael's coffin was taken inside the cathedral, we could enter. The coffin: it sat there by the doors on its bier, draped in flowering irises and a single tiger lily. It looked like Mike had popped out for a smoke before the main event got under way. Soon enough the ushers raised it gently to their shoulders and stepped Michael out of the sun. We followed a minute later.

I don't know how many of you have been through a paparazzi flashbulb welcome: you are actually blinded for a few moments. The space immediately in front of your eyes ceases to exist as the retina completely loses focus. The most natural reaction is a desire to hit somebody. I didn't understand that until 1.38pm that afternoon. Half-blinded I entered the cathedral with an undignified stumble, completely missing seeing the usher just inside the door who had a checklist of guests and a seating floor plan. Just like the door list at a gig. Wendy dragged me back and we did the requisite name bit.

Shown to the pews reserved for guests we sat about two-thirds of the way to the front of the cathedral, just behind the rows reserved for the official party and close friends. On the end next to the aisle.

To be honest churches make me nervous as well. Mostly because I'm a heavily lapsed Anglican with a conscience who does believe in a greater something but doesn't see why it should be worshipped. And as for organised religion . . . well you take your choices. Whatever you need to get by is okay – as long as it doesn't screw up anybody else.

That said, I'm no heathen. But the two photographers with huge, fat, telephoto lenses perched on tripods that were aimed at the front rows seemed precisely that: foreign objects that needed surrounding by antibodies and ejecting. They watched and waited.

In the stepped up pews that run parallel to the main walls of the body of the church sat the curious and the fans who'd arrived early enough to get a seat. The curious are easy to distinguish. They are the 50-plus older men and women who gossip as every person of note arrives. A point here, an 'oh look over the back' there. Celebrity spotters who are there simply to tell their friends they were there. The fans simply nod or look intense, drinking everything in: for some this is the closest they've ever come to a zoo full of icons, heroes, would-be-stars and starry won't-ever-bes.

It is quiet; calm, surreal in the way such buildings with their towering ceilings of glass and tile are pointed – heaven sent – to their God.

Kylie Minogue arrived early wearing a short black dress with a discreet veil, and displayed a quiet grace as she walked towards the front of the church. A black-suited Helena Christensen arrived much later, her lovely face ravaged with tears. In between them came the other women who figured prominently in Michael's life: Michelle Bennett, Kym Wilson, and the band's manager Martha Troup. All were gracious, sincere, united by a shared grief for a man they loved and respected. There is an implicit understanding between such people, an understanding that needs no words.

And just before the family, Nick Cave, his great mate and Tiger Lily's godfather. St Nick of The Bad Seed looked like he belonged here.

Paula arrived just after 2.30pm dressed in a low cut Chinese-style black and floral print dress [by Collette Dinnigan] with Tiger Lily perched on her right hip. She carried herself with strength and dignity. Inside the church she moved to the front righthand pew with her friend Belinda Brewin next to her and St Nick just a few seats to her right.

On the other side of the aisle were Michael's family – Kell and stepmother Susan, his mother Patricia Glassop and her husband Ross, his half-sister Tina Schorr and brother Rhett and their families.

That aisle seemed like a no-man's land – until, a few minutes later Paula picked up Tiger Lily and walked over to Kell and kissed him on the cheek. He leaned over and kissed Tiger Lily who smiled brightly when Paula tickled her tummy. The sheer poetry of the moment wasn't lost on anyone – except the cameramen whom Rhett had asked to leave moments after entering the Cathedral.

Paula then moved to Patricia and Ross, and the two women kissed – perhaps the closest they have ever been or will ever be.

From the speakers INXS' 'By My Side' begun to play, a mellifluous haunting anthem that ushered in the choir and clergy.

If you'll excuse the impudence, I'll flash back now to what I wrote that night; if it seems overly sentimental it was meant to be. And still is. It was 1am the next day and making sense of making sense was a bitch [or bastard]. "Perhaps, at this late hour, when reflection has ebbed and flowed in the nine hours since this quixotic, sensitive, burning star took his final bow and went out with all the style to which he has been accustomed and, in many ways, made his own, it is time to talk some of simple yet intrinsically deep truths.

"Death is final and it is real. As The Very Reverend Boak Jobbins, Dean Of Sydney, said during his address, death is a shadowy figure that stands just behind us all – he stretched out his hand to his right as if to touch the essence of his own shadow. Sometimes it comes very close and you can feel its breath on your neck, your shoulder; at others it is a little more distant, yet never distant enough to be completely forgotten, dismissed from reality. 'A sinister figure in black, patiently waiting, knowing that in time each one of us will meet him.'

"And death changes life and lives. For everybody in the cathedral and for millions of fans. What he didn't say is it brings with it realities, courage, emotion and honour that define what we are as people.

"Within the ancient walls of St Andrew's Cathedral the greatest traits of man and woman rose from the pit of despair and in the face of overwhelming grief came together to bid adieu to a favourite son who passed far too early yet in death

173

said as much as he said in life.

"Today, from everywhere, Michael Hutchence's generation – his extended family – came together with his personal family; extended family because when everything hurts, music and its sons and daughters are a family beyond definition. There is nothing like the family of which they are a part. It is as unspoken as it is deep and indefinable.

"The people who danced and sang at the INXS secret show at the ABC's Gore Hill studios nearly 10 months ago were the same people, now amongst many others, who cried openly, or sat silently remembering and understanding that in Michael was a double-edged reminder of their own mortality.

"Peter Garrett, Martin Rotsey and Rob Hirst of Midnight Oil, Nick Seymour (Crowded House), Angry Anderson (Rose Tattoo), Jimmy Barnes, Richard Clapton, Wendy Matthews, Kate Ceberano, Jason Donovan, Dave Gleeson (The Screaming Jets), Billy Thorpe, Reg Mombasa and Peter O'Doherty (Mental As Anything), Jim Hilbun (The Angels) ... the list of those who as well as being musicians were friends, compatriots and whose lives Michael touched and who said farewell is a greater testimony than any other. And that's not to mention all the people from the many sectors of the industry through which he moved.

"One helluva family that mourned with humility and dignity. And supported one another.

"Even from afar. To the left of the altar and the coffin rested a giant claddagh – an Irish symbol, denoting love, friendship and loyalty – from Bono and his wife Ali. In the pews sat Tom Jones.

"And there was Nick Cave whose rendition of 'Into My Arms' was so poignant and powerful it defined the very essence of everything this funeral for a friend stood for. Even as one slightly crazed member of the public leapt to his feet mid-song, started to yell 'Michael is dead, Michael is dead', whirled a belt in the air, and moved to the edge of the upstairs balcony [in front of where he was seated] apparently intent on leaping, Nick didn't miss a word or a beat; he just sang a little louder. 'Into my arms, oh Lord, into my arms'. Only those in the Cathedral shared this private and intense moment: Cave had asked Channel 7 that the performance not be televised to honour a promise he had made to Paula. This tall, skinny, enigmatic and complex man gave it his all. There are some wickedly deep and mysterious places in Nick Cave but this rendition came from some soul-house few will ever find (and most should never look for). Many became one and it seemed to last forever; not just a few minutes when it seemed possible to believe in a beneficent God.

"And Kylie. She has become very strong and very wise. Looking into her eyes, perhaps she, more than anybody else, understood why Michael was gone. As the procession filed out, Kylie was deeply aware.

"A few feet in front of her, the tears finally came in great scuds to Paula as Michael's voice filled St Andrew's Cathedral. Broken hearts are not easily mended and this woman's has been ruptured – despite what the cynics might think.

"And Heavenly herself. She is aptly named. As her mother sobbed and the procession moved so slowly to the storm-darkened daylight that beckoned through the doors, Heavenly gazed into the eyes of all around her. At 16 months she is extraordinarily bright, extraordinarily alert. Extraordinarily her father.

"But, most of all, Michael . . . this was all Michael. The flash-bulbs that exploded in the eyes and the whirr of cameras as you entered and left the cathedral, the claustrophobic sensation of people jammed in a place from which they could escape but not without running the gauntlet, the intense scrutiny, the madness of the man in the gods, the metaphysical sense of mortality and immortality dancing with each other, kissing one another's lips, the thin line between rock and religion, the knife edge that defines the only resting place between rock and a hard place. Yes, it was all so much Michael. Even those television cameras broadcasting live around Australia and to the UK were a gross reminder of the grossest aspects of his life.

"Andrew Farriss in his eulogy got it in just one sentence: Michael gave his everything to music, to the band, to his fans, to life.

"He had given his life away.

"Michael Kelland Hutchence is gone; the memories have only just begun."

Looking back at these words now, they seem like they were

written on a cloud hovering a metre off the ground while desperately trying to get a foot back down.

It wasn't easy. The funeral had ended with a bang, a massive clap of thunder, an unearthly cosmic smash, that pounded the cathedral just as Michael's coffin was carried out of the door to the waiting hearse. It couldn't have been timed better. And then the rain came down. And I'll never forget seeing Kylie look up at the sky and smile.

A little later we stood outside under a tree with a thoughtful and philosophic Jim Hilbun. He was glad he'd come. As the rain drizzled and washed and the stretch limos and chauffeur-driven sedans fizzled through the puddles and free flowing gutters bearing the famous away, the flashbulbs still splattered and the cameras still ate film and the fans still stood where they'd been all day. "It's perfect. It's so Michael Hutchence," Jim said. "Look at it. He's gone out the way he'd want to."

It would thunder Michael again. Three months later to the day. On February 27, 1998, U2's PopMart found its way to the Sydney Football Stadium and some 38,000 fans. Jon Casimir was there for *The Sydney Morning Herald*. 'Cas' who isn't the biggest fan INXS ever had, generously e-mailed in the details of U2's tribute to Michael which had been announced earlier in the week. U2 had invited the remaining members of INXS to attend as guests and they were joined by Kylie and Helena.

They had been working up to this moment throughout the Australian tour. Ten days earlier at the tour-opening show in Perth, Bono introduced 'One': "This is for Michael Hutchence. This is for how you feel when you don't get the chance to say what you wanted to say." Dino Scatena reporting for *The Daily Telegraph* (February 18) wrote, "Bono has recently spoken of a sense of guilt at not being on hand when Hutchence reached out for help in the hours leading up to his suicide last November.

" 'This is his country, this is his house and we can't help thinking about him when we're here,' Bono said at a press conference after the [Perth] concert.

By Friday there was a buzz of approval competing with a buzz of anti-shlock. A fine, humid, unpleasant day had deteriorated (if that's possible) rapidly, clouds building like mountains in the direction of the concert well before dusk. It was going to rain. By 8pm, it was thundering in central Sydney. Looking out from the windows on the 27th floor of the IBM building where the *Herald* editorial stable heads for the line each day, great sheets of lightning erased the sky over the stadium. Everything was perfectly right.

Here's what Jon had to say: "It was right at the end, after 'Mysterious Ways' and before 'One'. The rain had stopped pelting. Bono walked out to the end of the catwalk, turned around and looked at the stage, the PopMart screen brought up an image of Hutchence in five coloured panels (*à la* Andy Warhol). Bono began to sing 'Sleep tonight . . . sleep tonight', the Edge accompanying with a little gentle picking of the guitar. Bono sang about a verse of this song (whether it was a song or just meanderings, I'm not sure). By the chorus, it had become 'Let it rain, let it rain'. Then, still turned to the screen, he sang/spoke:

> *I just wanted to say goodbye*
> *To a great singer*
> *And a great friend*
> *I just wanted to say goodbye*
> *I just wanted to say goodbye*
> *In front of his mates*
> *In front of his family*
> *In front of his band*
> *I just wanted to say goodbye*
> *So goodbye Michael*

"Then the band played 'One'.

"And as the crowd filed from the stadium, 'Never Tear Us Apart' blared over the monitors."

Michael took another bow. A hard rain fell.

11

The INXS Interview

In the aftershock of Michael's death, the remaining members of INXS became amongst the most sought after people in the world. That in itself is a tragic reflection of our ways and times. Amongst those who wanted to talk to them were writers representing publications who wouldn't have given a damn about INXS in normal circumstances. The whole world was running with Michael Hutchence stories and everybody wanted a piece of the action.

In this situation the band decided to grant one interview. The accompanying press release from INXS publicist, Shawn Deacon, read:

"What follows are edited excerpts from a lengthy interview conducted in Sydney, Australia on Monday, December 8, 1997, by Australian television journalist, George Negus, with the five members of INXS. (The interview was released to the media on the morning of December 15.)

INXS Management contacted Negus and asked him to speak with the band after they had been inundated with local and international media interview requests for their reaction to the recent death of the band's lead singer, Michael Hutchence.

As you would understand, the five members, Garry Gary Beers, Andrew Farriss, Tim Farriss, Jon Farriss and Kirk Pengilly – still in a state of shock and deep grief at the loss of their close friend and professional colleague – were reluctant to submit themselves to such a flood of interview demands.

The practical solution to this situation was for the band to produce a one-off, generic interview made freely available and non-exclusively to all media outlets.

The members of the band hope that you, the media, appreciate why they have taken this course of action and thank you for your forbearance."

178

The following was transcribed from the audio interview tape by Mercury Records.

George: I've been trying to think how to start this and for the life of me, where do you start? What was the difference between Michael and the myth if you like? You guys knew him, the rest of us didn't.

Kirk: Yes, the thing that always in some ways actually annoyed me often was Michael was actually very shy and too many times that was taken as him being sort of aloof or arrogant in a way. As a person he was very genuine, very warm, extremely giving but, you know, I think in a public sort of persona he was a shy guy even though there's many nights I can think of that he certainly didn't appear shy. He'd play up to it but deep down he was.

Tim: There'd be nights where Michael would just sort of say right then which was good or bad timing, I'm not sure, "You know, I'm not sure I feel up to this tonight." So, you know, this sort of thing and I'd say, "Mate, you're always up to it, don't worry, just relax, you know." Michael could sit on a stool all night and still be one of the most charismatic singers and performers I've ever seen.

Garry: He was really enjoying performing again. He'd gotten through the how big a superstar or how big a popstar and all the negative press etc and he, like the rest of us, was really enjoying being what he is.

Andrew: The man understood emotional human depth in how to convey that and communicate it. He understood that and I worked with him in it and I know how talented he was. I said to Martha [Troup], the group's manager, the other thing that astounded me with him ... a lot of people would get a pencil and paper and they would write out how they feel and then go back with an eraser and they'd rub out "No, I don't think so". The amazing thing with him, he used to shock me sometimes, he'd write a set of lyrics and he'd never go back. It just came out exactly like his thoughts but it used to be very scary because the thing was, what you saw was really exactly what he was thinking and that was often his means of communication. I think he was a great communicator with the modern medium of television and audio and all of it and like, and I'll say me, I can't speak for the rest of the fellas, but I know like me, with him he probably had things he was afraid of or things he had to deal with or whatever but I think I would agree with the fellas, I don't think the band was one of them.

It doesn't matter how much you think you know someone there's always what you see and what you don't see with somebody and there's things in there that I know. There's little jigsaw pieces that I can never quite put into place and it doesn't mean we weren't getting on or didn't see eye to eye or he didn't talk or whatever, I just think he felt that it was his own life.

Jon: I lived with Michael for about six years in Hong Kong, perhaps seven years in Hong Kong and I think I shared one of the rarest moments anyone ever shared with him without being involved with [him as] a woman or anything like that, just a couple of guys hanging out. When he finally actually settled down it was really, really nice to see him actually relaxed.

Tim: You know, I feel more like Michael was one of my brothers than a friend or working pal.

George: Well, it was nice of you to let him join the Farriss Brothers band. Ha, ha, ha, ha.

Tim: I nearly tossed him out once actually.

George: Why did you almost toss him out?

Tim: Well, 'cos he never carried the gear after shows, you know, and we'd all have to lug it out and Michael would be busy talking to people and that sort of thing.

Kirk: He liked the limelight, you know, and that's why he sort of initially chose to live in London and whatever else, um, I think a lot of the time he thrived on it but then I guess it just started to kind of backfire.

Tim: I think there was a certain element of Michael that felt that he would always get through it and come out on top in the end, you know, and I think that there was just certain elements of his life that he couldn't get on top of and that's what really bugged him. He was able to in any other way; with his music, with whatever. He was always able to, as we all are, get on top of it but there were certain aspects there . . .

George: Because it was, to an extent, beyond his control.

Tim: Beyond his control in a sense.

George: You are saying how up he was and then his Dad the night before, or the night of his death was saying that he was again re-assuring his father that he was okay.

Tim: Well, I guess that's one of the danger signs isn't it? When someone keeps reassuring you how positive and good they are feeling ... now I'm starting to realise that they're people to be worried about you know. It's the people who can tell you they're not happy and there's something wrong with their life you know, that maybe they've got a better chance you know, it's this kind of facade or something.

George: I feel a huge empathy with you guys because not only are you having to deal with the loss of Michael, it's going to be very difficult for you to avoid all the carry-on subsequently and all the theorising and all the scuttlebutt and the muckraking and god knows what.

Garry: Well things are starting ...

George: How are you going to deal with that? What is your own mechanism for handling what you know is going to be on?

Tim: Well, there's a certain just numbness and loss already with ... and I'm still grieving Michael's loss as a friend and family member that I have this barrier just where it just doesn't touch me anyway because they are only saying what they don't know about Michael; they don't know him the way we did, and what we know and ... we have the truth to guard us against whatever anyone else says and that's something no-one can replace and something that will always be with me so, you know, in a sense of course, it hurts and it makes me angry. The fact of the matter is I knew him that well, we knew him that well, they didn't.

George: There's been squillions of words written about what's been going on in Michael's life. What were his demons that you guys could detect?

Tim: Well personally, I feel that after the last few conversations I had with him the thing he wanted most of all was to be able to have Christmas here in Australia with his family.

Kirk: It was definitely nights in the last year on tour, yeah, I know quite a few nights that I spent with Michael and whatever, he'd open up to what had been going on in his life and you know, I mean some of it was pretty jaw-dropping stuff, you know, but he still always seemed to have strength with it all.

George: Paula Yates, if she's quoted correctly, she seemed to feel that he'd had enough of what was going on in their life.

Tim: Well, that's their private life. It's something I don't think is fair for us to comment on you know. We just want to make sure you know, Tiger is okay and Paula's okay. I mean, I feel like Tiger's my niece and I think we all feel the same way, we all have a responsibility to make sure she's looked after well and you know, as far as I'm concerned, that's my main priority.

George: Why do you think people have such mixed feelings about Paula and why have they had mixed feelings about their relationship? I don't want to harp on it . . .

Tim: I guess because in many ways there's been so much sorta rubbish written in the media about it all, that pumps it all up and the fact that in England they didn't have much of a private life and I think that's really something that we can all be fortunate enough that we have in a way – that Michael didn't in so many ways – is that we actually had other lives, you know, where [as] Michael was always if you go to a club or something there'd be photographers or this that and you know he just . . .

Jon: He needed, like everybody does, some sort of sanctuary to go to and I think the band were his sanctuary. I think in a sense that when that door was closed and there was only six guys in the room, only us will ever know what that was like and anyway . . .

Tim: The other thing is nothing makes you more sick to the guts than reading about someone who really hardly knew him at all selling their story about how they knew Michael. I mean, what are they going to say? They can't say that much; they hardly knew him, you know. I mean, where's that at? To me it makes me furious and just sick you know.

Andrew: Even back then I'd been calling him up and he was working on some solo stuff and I'd say, "Are you right, are you okay mate?" because this stuff looks pretty crazy to me and he said, "I'm fine but all I wanna do is work with you fellas again. Let's do it."

George: A most difficult question – I mean does it matter to you to ever know how he died and why? Can you go on doing what you're doing, being who you are, remembering Michael the way you want to remember him without knowing for sure what happened in those fatal hours?

Tim: Not really, no you know, I still . . . there's a large part of me that can't believe he took his own life, um, perhaps it's just denial but there's a part of me that refuses to believe it. Maybe that's for good or bad I don't know. It's just the way I feel.

Andrew: I think the way to think about it is I remember the day when we were at the rehearsal studio being told that Michael was dead. I remember my first reaction was just tremendous loss. Not why and I still feel that and I will always feel that and I think the why – a bit like anyone that I've lost that's been close to me in my life – isn't tremendously important, it's the loss of the person that's important.

George: The reasons become irrelevant.

Andrew: Yeah – to me – yeah.

Garry: And they're his reasons – I don't fully understand it.

Tim: There's just one thing I do wanna say and this is that I think the world should be very careful about taking anti-depressants – that's all I think. I think the whole thing is a very grey area and people should respect when they're putting things like that into their bodies just exactly what they're doing.

George: Do you feel that played a big part?

Tim: I don't know. I know there's been a lot of recent things, things like anti-depressants and alcohol mixed together making people suicidal and I think the world's got to take a deeper look at it and make sure that you know, we're not giving these people who need . . . [who] have a chemical imbalance in their brain emotionally the wrong things. It's a sickness, it's not a decision they make with a clear head – it's a chemical imbalance, it's a disease just like you don't hold someone responsible for dying of cancer – you know it's the same sort of thing – that's the way I see it. I can't be angry at Michael because if he did take his own life, I feel he was sick.

George: What are your finest memories going to be?

Tim: Well, one of the memories I was gonna say just before we did this show somewhere on the East Coast of the USA and Michael had started off the show doing 'Elegantly Wasted' in his *costume de homme* suit – you know with the little rip just the way he liked it – and ended up wearing, just wearing his wife-beater and pants you know, and he strolls down in front of the audience, and he's standing on this table and he looks up at the bar and he goes, "Martinis for everybody!" including this couple whose table he's standing on. This is the weirdest gig we've ever played in our lives and, ah, then he started and I've never seen him do this before, he started talking to the people who were sitting at the table and it turned out they'd just gotten married and he says to them, "Oh – they've just got married and this is just what you wanted on your wedding night. Michael Hutchence standing on your table."

George: He was a consummate performer wasn't he?

Tim: Yeah, he loved it.

Jon: The element of absolute terror on stage – you really had to have it together sort of – that's cool that's okay – he'd be about to blow that thing up . . . he's running under the stage now and we'd lost him for three songs and he's underneath some enormous structure while the 20,000 people are going, "Where is he?"

Garry: The other side of Michael is that he didn't really have the greatest eyesight in the world and the fact was he was actually performing to the first 15 rows, so every show was quite intimate to him.

George: So it was a club act!

Garry: Yeah – that's why he went out and there was one particular night where he got contact lenses and he went out there and just stood there and went, "There are 25,000 people here."

Jon: I need to just feel sorry for any guy that would sit in the front.

Andrew: He would flirt with everything and everybody . . . you know, danger was just one of them.

George: That was certainly the reputation.

Andrew: He was always happiest with the idea of becoming . . . he wanted to become more indie . . . he didn't just want to be the centre of attention.

Tim: He was never that comfortable with the enormous success – he actually preferred being the underdog.

Andrew: Even though it seems incongruous to say it now. That's why he liked Nick Cave so much . . . it's why he loved people who were a little underground or indie. He was always up on new music, new trends, new developments in things. I think, and there's a lot of people in the music business who paint a portrait of themselves as being dangerous, um, you know, who live life to the max, "living on the edge" type personalities that dress in a dangerous fashion and all that sort of stuff – but they're all actors or actresses – Michael was real. He was always doing something extraordinary.

Garry: He just really enjoyed life. He really enjoyed living life.

George: The sort of guy you're describing, I mean, it's hard to know whether we're talking about somebody whom you should say "Michael was made for rock'n'roll or rock'n'roll was made for Michael". It's hard to imagine Michael Hutchence doing anything other than what he did.

Garry: He probably could have done anything he put his mind to. He's a very smart man but he did sort of slip into the rock'n'roll lifestyle pretty well.

George: What would he say now?

Garry: I have no idea.

George: What should he tell us we should be asking?

Garry: Oh, I don't know. I think he's probably said it all. I don't know. I've got a feeling if he had the choice again he wouldn't do what he did, so maybe he'd have something to say about . . .

Tim: Appreciating life a bit more.

George: You just said to me before you feel like playing some music again.

Tim: Yeah, totally – a lot – I'm not sure I'll be that good at it mate, that's what I feel like doing.

Garry: To me selfishly, that's one of the hardest things I've had to come to grips with is that we're not the five of us on stage behind Michael.

George: Yeah, tell me about that – I mean as Kirk puts it, six against the world. How about five? How much difference is it gonna make?

Kirk: Well it won't obviously be the same, you know, whatever we do.

Tim: We know perhaps better than anyone with Michael's career what he would've wanted us to have done and we're gonna try and do the right thing by him whatever we do.

George: What would he have wanted you to do?

Tim: Well I think he'd want us to probably take a long break!

Garry: And if he didn't we will anyway.

Kirk: I mean as far as we're concerned, *Elegantly Wasted* as a release and what we still had planned to do with it, we'll still go ahead with. I mean we had always planned to release the next single which is 'Searching', which funnily enough is one of Michael's favourite songs on the album, but we'd always planned to release that single and we're still going to do that.

Tim: Because Michael is no longer with us we can guarantee it, this for sure doesn't mean that he would want us to in any way inhibit what he wrote and the legacy of his life to be taken to the people. I'm sure more than ever he'd want that [*Elegantly Wasted*] to be seen and to be heard by people and we'll do our darnedest to make sure it happens.

Kirk: The hardest thing that we're going to have to probably face in the near future – perhaps the next year or whatever – is there's going to be a lot of things come out of the woodwork you know, unauthorised books, whatever else. I think for me that's gonna be a difficult situation for us because one of the things that we have always tried to do and always wanted to maintain is the integrity of the band.

Jon: Mike's in all of us saying we'll be there and a funny thing I've noticed about close family members or someone like Michael who passes away, I feel intuitively a sort of part of them sort of comes into you a bit. I don't know if anyone else feels the same way but there's certain parts of the relationship that you share especially with that person. That you're giving back that gift in a sort of spiritual way.

Tim: Little things that he hated and the little things that he loved.

Jon: So when the five people here . . .

Tim: Those things he just sort of blew away at the time now have a lot more meaning you know and will stay with us.

George: I mean there are going to be lots of 10s, 100s, 1,000s, millions throughout the world of INXS fans and Michael fans not feeling anything like you're feeling at the moment but their own version of it. What do you say to them?

Tim: Well, it's very difficult for me, I can't speak on behalf of all of us but to read a lot of the tributes and a lot of things that people are saying at the moment – it's still too soon for me to be able to read it before I lose it. But I would like to say to all the people who've written so many wonderful and kind and beautiful poems, little stories and tributes, you know, you've made Michael very proud and it touches us all very deeply and on behalf of him we thank you.

George: Guys, I didn't know where to start so I don't know where to stop either. Thank you.

To this point in time (April 1998) INXS have not conducted any further media interviews.

12

Everything

On February 6, 1998, the NSW State Coroner, Mr Derek Hand, ruled that Michael Hutchence had committed suicide.

Mr Hand found that Michael had a cocktail of "alcohol, cocaine, Prozac and other prescription drugs" in his blood, that there was "no forensic or other evidence to substantiate" speculation that his death was caused by "an act of auto eroticism" (the most commonly favoured theory was that Michael had died while practising auto-erotic asphyxiation) and that the cause of death was hanging.

The report should have put a full stop to speculation but it didn't. In April 1998 it is possible to find any number of people who believe that Michael did not commit suicide and that the report's content in terms of the finding was influenced by his family. No evidence has been brought forward to support any such claims.

Paula Yates became the first person to publicly question Mr Hand's findings when on March 29, 1998, on the TV show *60 Minutes,* she said she refused to accept the coroner's finding of suicide in the death of Michael.

Paula said she was seeking legal advice to have the finding by Mr Hand overturned. "In no way do I accept the coroner's verdict of suicide," she told the Nine Network programme. "I will be making it abundantly clear that because of information that I and only I could know about Michael . . . I cannot accept the verdict. And I won't have my child grow up thinking that her father left her, not knowing the way he loved her."

Mr Hand found that Hutchence was in a "severe depressed state" due to his relationship with Yates and her custody battle with Sir Bob, combined with the effects of the substances in his body.

Paula also rejected rumours that Michael never wanted their daughter, Heavenly Hiraani Tiger Lily, saying the pair endured a year of fertility tests before having the child.

She said although Hutchence was depressed, Tiger was his great joy and reason to live and the couple were planning to marry as soon as the custody dispute with Geldof was finished: "He'd asked me to marry him. I think we would've already done it by now, I'm almost certain we would have done it around Christmas."

Deeply affected by the divorce settlement and custody battle over the three daughters she had with Sir Bob, Paula almost died from an overdose of pills and alcohol last year. She said it was a plea for Geldof to end the dispute. "I was dead . . . not for very long fortunately, not very long at all," she said.

On claims that she was involved in a battle for Hutchence's $36 million estate, Yates said he left his affairs in good order and his main concern was to take care of their daughter.

"Tiger and I have 60 per cent, that was his will. It's like any father would probably make when he has a child," she said. "I have no fight with anyone, I don't need to fight with anyone about anything. I need to get through the next hour, that's what worries me. I wouldn't dream of fighting."

Paula also said that Michael thought suicide was the most cowardly act in the world. "I just don't think he killed himself, I really don't," she said. "He did in the end but I think it was accidental and I knew him so well.

"The coroner didn't meet him or know him and he would not have left our baby, he just loved her . . . so he wouldn't have left her – never, never, never, never, never."

Whether Paula Yates, the woman who refuses to give up the honourable memory of her man and refuses to let love lie bleeding and forgotten, has any evidence to reveal that could possibly result in the coroner's finding being overturned remains to be seen. But if she has, it seems strange she did not bring it to Mr Hand's attention during his inquiry into Michael's death.

The following is the complete, unedited transcript of the Coroner's report:

INQUEST INTO THE DEATH OF MICHAEL KELLAND HUTCHENCE

I have received a completed police brief into the death of Michael Kelland Hutchence on 22nd November, 1997, at Ritz Carlton Hotel, Double Bay. I am satisfied that the cause of death was "hanging". I am also satisfied that there was no other person involved in causing the death.

The question of whether the death was a suicide or not has to be considered. The deceased was found at 11.50am naked behind the door to his room. He had apparently hanged himself with his own belt and the buckle broke away and his body was found kneeling on the floor and facing the door.

It has been suggested that the death resulted from an act of auto eroticism. However, there is no forensic or other evidence to substantiate this suggestion. I therefore discount that manner of death.

With regard to the question of suicide I have to be satisfied on a strong balance of probabilities before I am able to come to such a conclusion. There is a presumption against suicide. Having considered the extensive brief I am satisfied that the standard required to conclude that this death was a suicide has been reached for the following reasons:

(1) Michelle Bennett, a former de-facto of the deceased, received two telephone calls from him on the morning of the 22nd November. The first was on an answering machine and Mr Hutchence sounded "drunk". During the second call at 9.54am the deceased commenced to cry and according to Ms Bennett sounded "very upset". She was concerned about his demeanour and for his welfare and told him she would come immediately. However, when she arrived at the hotel she was not able to rouse him by knocking loudly on his door nor by ringing him. She wrote a note and left it at reception. Ms Bennett stated that Mr Hutchence never expressed previous inclinations regarding suicide.

(2) The deceased's father, Kelland Hutchence, dined with him the previous night. The deceased was in good spirits, however appeared very worried in regard to the outcome of a custody suit in London. Mr Hutchence could offer no explanation as to why his son would take his own life.

(3) Ms Kym Wilson and Mr Andrew Rayment were with the deceased in his hotel room from sometime after 11pm and left about 5am. According to Ms Wilson the deceased appeared to want both of them to remain with him to offer support if the result of his custody hearing was unfavourable. His mood was described as "elevated, however pensive when discussing court proceedings". All three persons consumed alcohol, including vodka, beer and champagne together with cocktails during this time.

(4) Whilst Ms Wilson and Mr Rayment were in the room Ms Martha Troup, the deceased's personal manager, rang from New York. Then later at 9.38am she received, via voice-mail, a call from Michael Hutchence in which he said: "Marth, Michael here. I f . . . ing had enough." She rang the hotel immediately and the telephone rang out. A further call was received at 9.50am on Ms Troup's telephone answering machine. The deceased sounded as if he was affected by something and (his voice) was slow and deep. This call worried Ms Troup and (she) spoke to John Martin, the tour manager for INXS, about her concerns. Mr Martin refers to a note received from the deceased stating that he was "not going to rehearsals today". The rehearsal was to be the last one prior to the start of the tour and was quite important.

(5) Ms Paula Yates provided a statement. She provided background to the custody dispute between her and Sir Robert Geldof. She stated that she rang the deceased at some time prior to 5.38am on the 22nd November and he told her he was going to beg Geldof to let the children come out to Australia. She had told the deceased that the custody matter had not been finalised and was adjourned until the 17th December and she would not be bringing the children out. Ms Yates stated that the deceased sounded "desperate" during the conversation.

(6) Sir Robert Geldof received two telephone calls from the deceased, the first at about 6.30pm London time on (the) evening of 21st November. It was of a short duration and Geldof asked the deceased to call back. The second call was received by Geldof about 5.30am on 22nd November, Sydney time. This call was of some length. Geldof refers to the deceased's demeanour as being "hectoring and abusive and threatening" in nature. He refers to the deceased as "begging" to allow him to let the children come to Australia. He did not sound depressed during the conversation. A

friend of both Geldof and Paula Yates, Ms Belinda Brewin, confirms the substance of the conversation between the two. A statement obtained from a Gail Coward, the occupant of the room directly next to the deceased's room, alludes to her hearing a loud male voice and expletives emitting from the deceased's room about 5am that morning. I am satisfied that she was hearing the telephone conversation between the deceased and Geldof.

(7) A statement obtained from the mother of the deceased, Mrs Patricia Glassop, confirms her opinion that the deceased was in a depressed state.

(8) In December 1995, Michael Hutchence was first prescribed Prozac by Dr J. Borham, a London medical practitioner, to treat a pre-existing depressive problem. He was last so prescribed on 1st November, 1997. A London psychiatrist, Mr Mark Collins, was consulted by the deceased on 17th October, 1997 in regard to a minor depression being experienced by him. According to the doctor there was no hint of suicidal thinking by the deceased.

(9) An analysis report of the deceased's blood indicates the presence of alcohol, cocaine, Prozac and other prescription drugs. On consideration of the entirety of the evidence gathered I am satisfied that the deceased was in a severe depressed state on the morning of the 22nd November, 1997, due to a number of factors, including the relationship with Paula Yates and the pressure of the on-going dispute with Sir Robert Geldof, combined with the effects of the substances that he had ingested at that time. As indicated I am satisfied that the deceased intended and did take his own life.

I am also satisfied that this death is one in which nothing will be gained by holding a formal Inquest. The identity of the deceased, the date and place of death and the manner and cause of death are clearly set out and the time and expense of holding an Inquest is not warranted and therefore such will be dispensed with. May I offer to the family of Michael Hutchence my sincere condolences on their sad loss.

INQUEST DISPENSED WITH.

(D.W. HAND)
NSW STATE CORONER
Glebe. 6th February, 1998

13

We Are Thrown Together

Dignity went out of the window immediately after the funeral.

Even in death Michael was torn apart again, literally, as the remaining members of the Hutchence family went to war.

It only took a few minutes: the thunderclap as the coffin was carried from the cathedral became the ringing of the bell for hostilities to commence.

The Daily Telegraph (February 14, 1998) reported: "As they left St Andrew's Cathedral in a limousine bound for a crematorium, Kell told [Patricia] Glassop he was disappointed by the cameras and other aspects of the funeral. Three independent sources say the grief-stricken mother responded in a physical manner."

If that was the first blow, the Hutchence legacy since has been head-butted, knee-capped and dragged through the slush of self-interest.

So complicated is the fall-out between the various members of his family it would make a book – or a soap opera – in its own right. By February 1998, it was easy to determine the factions: Kell, Rhett and Paula versus Patricia and Tina. By March 1998 it was easy to find people not only willing to confirm that but also to leak details of the familial strife. Why? Because many people – after respecting the family's feeling and sentiment for several months, only to see various members bleed to the highest-bidder – had just had enough of it all. That was enough. By April 1998 the underlying sentiment in Sydney was let Michael rest in peace. But even that was spiritually impossible.

Michael was in three places at once: his earthly remains – his ashes – split in three. Kell wanted Michael's ashes scattered in Sydney Harbour, but admits (*The Daily Telegraph* UK, February 3): " 'I was unable to reach an agreement with the other people involved.'

"Do you mean Paula and your ex-wife?

" 'I'd rather not say who. But as a result, poor old Mike's been divided into three urns.' "

Kell kept good to his vision and scattered his one-third of Michael's ashes off Sydney Harbour. Paula and Patricia also have one-third each. In London and on the Gold Coast, respectively. It's horrific.

But that, sadly, is only the beginning.

This book is neither here to revel in the fallout of emotion nor to judge anybody. There are two sides – in this case, at least – to every story. This was never a strongly-bonded family. Once the substance that held it together – which now appears to have been Michael – was no longer around to provide at least a viscous material then the fabric and structure simply fell apart.

The psychology of the emotions involved is deep and complicated. Remember this is a family that first broke up early in the piece. Later, they had to deal with Michael's fame – and that was never easy. In such situations brothers and sisters often become lost in their famous kin's shadow. And dealing with the grief, guilt and Russian roulette of emotions that come with the death of a loved one is an endless grey zone where 'what if' and 'but' repeat endlessly to no horizon.

Yet such has been the public airing of inter-family woes it's hard to remain unaffected or unbiased.

Money . . . money . . . money . . .

Kell sold his story first to *New Idea* through his appointed negotiator Lyndon Sayer Jones who then set up a second deal with Channel 7. And we're talking big money here. The following amounts are in Australian dollars. At least one six-figure sum (about $170,000). Rhett's story was also put on the market. A financially-troubled Paula initially sold her story to *Hello!* magazine in the UK for about $1.1 million and followed that with several other major deals including the *60 Minutes* interview for which she was allegedly paid $60,000. Her most recent deal was selling the exclusive rights to the March 31 christening of Heavenly Hiraani Tiger Lily to the British magazine *OK!* for an undisclosed sum, although her friend Belinda Brewin said Paula would not profit from the deal. The money paid for the pictures would be used for the then 20-month-old Tiger Lily's education.

Meanwhile, Patricia and Tina were shopping around a book about the Michael they knew and his death: a somewhat different story – it is said – to that proffered by Paula, Kell and to a lesser extent Rhett.

How different became apparent with the February 16, 1998, edition of *New Idea*. In a story by Julie Hayne, Tina shattered what thin threads of feeling may have held these people together. So vicious was her attack on Paula, that Rhett – who had remained quiet and removed from the general shedding since his brother's funeral – was forced to respond.

Marcus Casey wrote in *The Daily Telegraph* (February 14,1998), "She [Tina] lashed out at Yates and criticised Kell and Rhett in a magazine interview. Yates' custody battle with former partner Sir Bob Geldof, Tina said, was to blame for the state of mind which led to Michael hanging himself with his belt.

" 'He was boxed in, trapped in the relationship and wanted out,' " Tina said. She said she felt 'a deep void, sadness, anger and incredible pain.' Her truth didn't gel with Kell's and he was furious, firing off a fax to Tina while the magazine tried to sell the story to Fleet Street.

"In doing so – and especially with her timing – Tina widened the gap even further and strained tense inner relationships to near breaking point, putting half-brother Rhett into a position he didn't want to be: making a public reply. One which, ironically, healed wounds in the relationship between Kell/Rhett and Yates.

"In a statement released to *The Daily Telegraph*, Rhett stated that his and Kell's main concern was the security of Tiger Lily and Yates, with whom they have had arguments. 'I am deeply saddened and embarrassed by what my step-sister Tina has said publicly about Paula and Michael's relationship,' Rhett said in the statement.

" 'I believe this will hurt Michael's daughter, Tiger, very much, as the woman being so cruelly discussed is her mother – her only surviving parent. I know Michael would be horrified by members of his family publicly speculating about his private life and hurting Tiger in this way. It seems he has become an easy target for gossipmongers, as he is not here to defend himself.'

"After being approached by *The Daily Telegraph*, Rhett spent

24 hours pondering whether to make a statement. The 35-year-old didn't want to fuel the public fire, to indulge in 'blame and hatred'.

"But in his search for the dignity he wanted restored to Michael's memory, Rhett wrote the statement calling on Tina to act from 'love and compassion'. It was in the hope this act would settle the issue and free it from public curiosity.

"Was it Tina's right to discuss her feelings about her family? 'Put it this way,' a close and longtime friend of Michael said this week, 'if you added up all the days Michael visited Tina in the last 15 years, you might just scrape together a week. They were not close at all, and I don't think Tina can say she's the one who really knew Michael.

" 'This makes me so upset, I think it's sick. Michael's family has always been pretty mixed up, and I just wish they'd stop all this and let the poor f . . . ing guy rest in peace.' "

Another close friend of Michael's put it even plainer: "Tina didn't know – really know – Michael at all."

Reading Tina's story it is reminiscent of the attack on Paula [and Michael] by her former publicist Gerry Agar who worked with her at the time of the opium and porno pictures incident of September 1996.

Writing first-person for *Woman's Day*, Agar says: "Paula ultimately wanted people to stop being mean to her. I felt sorry for her, but told her she'd have to do what I said, and that she had done some ridiculous things.

"She soon got very dependent on me and I became over responsible, acting as her agony aunt and psychoanalyst . . .

"She told me she had already had quite a few other affairs while married to Bob. She was always making up things, so you never know what was true. Paula was brilliantly persuasive and, despite being bright himself, Michael Hutchence always believed her. He was always very impressed by name dropping and it increased his interest in her."

She also accuses Paula of tipping off the press the time Michael attacked a photographer in a hotel. "She wanted them to get caught because he wouldn't finish with his girlfriend, Helena Christensen. She would get a member of staff to make the call because the papers would recognise her voice. Paula did the same thing with so-called wedding plans. She would tip off the tabloids, saying they were getting married, without even asking Michael."

Agar writes later, "In my opinion, Michael Hutchence's sexual kinkiness and drug taking escalated through the headiness of his relationship with Paula. She always went along with his desire to go near the edge and she was, if you like, his equal . . ." and ". . . I remember taking Michael Hutchence aside and talking about drugs. He told me about his childhood and said it had screwed him up."

There is much more about the finding of the drugs and pictures, the police raid a few days later, Agar's making a statement to the police and the subsequent threats she claimed she received. "We [herself and Anita Debney, Paula's nanny who had worked for Paula and Bob for 13 years] were being called and harassed and told by this chap we would never be safe anywhere . . . I suffered cuts and bruises when I had to dive away from a car that came driving straight at me.

"I also had a devil's head put on my car and had my tyres slashed constantly, as well as receiving threatening calls. Luckily I've got tapes of some of these.

"In one threat in the week after the drugs raid, a man told me that I wouldn't be safe anywhere if I didn't retract my statement. The police were angry, but I retracted my statement."

Gerry Agar concluded by saying she wasn't surprised that Michael was now dead.

The story is blunt and loaded with accusations. Consider the timing though: it was printed after Michael's death – and for what price. Who knows the agendas in all of this. Keep an open mind when you read all the stories in this book.

Tina is equally blunt in the *New Idea* article.

" 'It is fair to say that Michael was very unhappy with Paula at the time of his death. Michael had no intention of marrying Ms Yates.'

"Not only were there no wedding plans, but says Tina, Michael was actually looking for ways to end the relationship. 'It was not common knowledge,' she says. 'However, people in Michael's inner circle knew he had been trying to get out of his relationship with Paula.'

"Tina wants to set the record straight about her brother, his death and what she says are Paula's false claims that Michael planned to marry her ... Tina, an author and mother of two who has lived in Los Angeles for the past 25 years, shared the same mother with Michael, Patricia Glassop, who later married Michael's father, Kell Hutchence.

"Tina claims to have witnessed the rock star's relationship with Paula from the start. 'Michael was happy with Paula in the beginning,' Tina says. 'He loved her children, he has always wanted a family of his own. But he was concerned about going on the road with a family.' Tina first became aware of Michael's unhappiness a year before his death.

"'In November, 1996, he spent a considerable number of hours at my house, where we discussed our children,' she recalls. 'He was such a proud dad, displaying photographs of his adored Tiger. It was not his intention to be an absent father.' But, when talk turned to marriage, Michael seemed uncomfortable. 'I asked him about marriage and he withdrew,' says Tina. 'He said he was not ready, he just did not know about taking that step.'

"On a subsequent visit to Tina's LA home, nothing had changed. 'Again, in July last year, he said the same thing. Paula visited him in Los Angeles at that time and it was obvious that they were not a perfect match,' she says. 'I understood his reservations, I witnessed several Paula's in a matter of minutes. She could change from timid to intimidating. In fact, Michael told me he wished he could have the same Paula back that he had fallen in love with.

"Early on in the relationship, I was determined to like Paula. After all, she was Michael's choice and I respected this,' says Tina. 'Actually, I liked the "shy" Paula. But when she moved into the "storytelling" Paula, tipping off the press on their every move, I quickly moved into "tolerance", I guess in respect for him.

"Tina says Paula's manipulation of the press reached its peak last year when she intentionally leaked that she and Michael were planning to wed on the tropical island of Bora Bora, a move which Tina says greatly upset Michael.

"'In October, 1997 Michael had his agent Martha Troup,

release a statement emphatically denying a story Paula had planted, pertaining to a wedding on Bora Bora,' Tina reveals. 'He called me to assure me the proposed wedding was just a story. He was upset because he felt that family members would have their feelings hurt if they thought they were being left out of an important event.'

"During that conversation, Michael also revealed to Tina that he was planning to move to Los Angeles after leaving Paula. Indeed, Tina says that just before his death he told her he wanted to end the relationship because he found it 'very destructive' personally . . .

". . . 'The only woman I have ever heard him say he would wed is Michelle Bennett,' reveals Tina.

"Meanwhile, Paula is rumoured to be heading to Australia next month (March 1998) to spend some time with Michael's father and Tina's stepfather Kell (which she did). The two have been in almost constant contact since Paula returned to London after Michael's funeral.

"The news of Paula's visit to Kell comes as a shock to Tina. 'Frankly, that surprises me,' she says. 'The night before the funeral they had a hell of a fight.' Since Michael's death, Kell and Paula have publicly feuded over many aspects of Michael's estate . . .

"Amidst her heartache, Tina has had to endure a very public mourning period. 'Truthfully, some of the stories sadden me, especially coming from the family. It is painful and embarrassing.'

" 'There have been many lies, even from family members,' Tina says bitterly. Tina and her mother must now deal with their loss and regret. 'Our lives are changed forever,' says Tina. 'I feel a deep void, sadness, anger and incredible pain. To think that my brother had nowhere to turn, when he was loved so much.' "

The will

Michael's estate is believed to be worth about $36 million including a solid share/property portfolio.

Under the terms of the will, his daughter, Heavenly Hiraani

Tiger Lily, would get 50 per cent while the other half would be shared equally between Kell, Patricia, Tina, Rhett and Paula. [Friends Of The Earth and Greenpeace are also said to get $100,000 each].

Paula as much as confirmed this breakdown in her *60 Minutes* interview: "Tiger and I have 60 per cent, that was his will. It's like any father would probably make when he has a child."

But that would be too simple.

The Sydney Morning Herald journalists Ian Verrender and Kate McClymont spent a month investigating Michael's estate. Their conclusion made the front page of *The Sydney Morning Herald* on February 21, 1998.

Verrender and McClymont claimed that Michael was technically bankrupt and had relinquished ownership of his assets in attempt to minimise tax. They wrote: "The man who now legally controls all Hutchence's assets – and who has discretion over who receives anything – is an elusive Queensland barrister named Colin Thomas Diamond.

"During the past five years, Diamond established an intricate web of trusts and holding companies stretching through Hong Kong, the British Virgin islands, Monaco, Australia and Europe.

"So well hidden are the assets and so murky is their ownership, that members of Hutchence's family are preparing legal action in an attempt to recover them.

"But attempts to unravel the web so far have been complicated by the fact that Diamond – and his business partner, Andrew Paul, a Hong Kong tax specialist – are also executors of the estate."

This article, an accompanying piece on Mr Diamond, an explanation of how discretionary trusts work and a subsequent 4000-word feature that delves even further into "Michael's Missing Millions" – as the headline dubs them – painted a picture of confusion over the will.

The Sunday Age (March 1, 1998) shed further light on Mr Diamond and the controversial will, adding that although Kell Hutchence is named beneficiary of at least one trust company in the web, along with many of Diamond's family, Patricia Glassop and Tina appeared to have been shut out.

More importantly, though, were the quotes by Mr Diamond's

ex-wife Robyn who claimed: " 'Michael set the whole thing up to protect Tiger so that she would inherit one day. She's a little baby and he made Colin sole executor because Colin knows the family story.' "

"She [Robyn] said the problems over Michael's will stemmed from members of his family 'wanting more than they were given'.

" 'I think they were given something but they want more,' she said. 'Tiger is Michael's family, which everybody seems to be forgetting.'

"And she said initial problems between Colin and Hutchence's lover, Paula Yates, had been resolved. 'He and Paula are talking and they are sorting things out for Tiger's benefit,' she said. 'They had a bit of a kerfuffle shortly after the death but now they are fine.' "

The Daily Telegraph (February 14, 1998) had earlier reported: "In recent years Michael laughed when people talked about the money he made from music," a friend said. "He'd laugh his head off and tell them the truth: that most of his wealth had come from shrewd investments. Colin Diamond and this other guy from New Zealand did a brilliant job."

And as usual there are two sides to every story: no matter how small. *The Sydney Morning Herald's* 'Michael's Missing Millions' feature (March 28, 1998), concludes: "Colin and Stephen Diamond have been in contact with Hutchence's father, Kell. And they have brokered a truce with Paula Yates. But both refuse to deal with Hutchence's mother, Patricia Glassop. It is a situation that has left her overcome with anguish.

" 'I feel like I have lost Michael twice,' she told the *Herald*. 'His houses have been closed down and his personal effects have been locked away. I do not even have one of his shirts to remind me of him.' "

The Daily Telegraph (February 14, 1998) records: "Glassop surprised several friends and colleagues of Michael's recently with her calls about chairs, mirrors, and other furniture. Did they own that chair Michael left at their place nine years ago, or had Michael given it to them? For 10 years Michael's Sydney bodyguard looked after and paid for maintenance on a Harley Davidson the singer kept here. Glassop asked for it back."

Ironically, *The Sydney Morning Herald*'s front-page lead into that March 28 feature carried the headline "Family anguish: let Michael's will be done".

A friend of Michael's commented a few days later, "It is being done, just as he wanted. Look at who is complaining and who isn't."

However, that theory obviously held little sway with Patricia Glassop or Tina Hutchence. In *The Sydney Morning Herald* of April 18, Verrender and McClymont reported that the two women had gone on the offensive against the executor's of Michael's estate, launching legal action aimed at recovering his "missing fortune".

Mrs Glassop, and Ms Hutchence, launched the proceedings in the Queensland Supreme Court against Colin Thomas Diamond and Andrew Morrison Paul – co-executors of Hutchence's bankrupt estate – and a string of companies. The companies are registered in Queensland, the United Kingdom, France and the British Virgin Islands. Many are controlled by discretionary trusts which deliver absolute power over the assets – including property and bank accounts in Australia, Europe, the Caribbean and Hong Kong – to either Mr Diamond or Mr Paul.

Verrender and McClymont wrote: "Mrs Glassop and Ms Hutchence are seeking orders for the administration of the estate and have demanded that the executors hand over accounts relating to it.

" 'They also seek declarations that certain assets held by the other corporate defendants were in fact beneficially owned by Michael Hutchence at the time he died and that these assets form part of his estate available for distribution to all beneficiaries in accordance with the terms of his will,' they said in a statement through their solicitors. Mr Paul was served with a writ at his Hong Kong office on Thursday night but process servers have so far not tracked down Mr Diamond, who lives on a farm north of Auckland in New Zealand but moves regularly between Hong Kong, Tokyo, Jakarta and Sydney . . .

"According to documents distributed by the executors to Hutchence's beneficiaries in February, he did not own or have any interest in three Gold Coast properties worth more than $4 million, a villa in the south of France, a house in London, and a number of expensive cars and a hotel development in Indonesia.

"Also absent from the estate was income from the sale or publishing of music recorded and written by INXS and Hutchence, although a British Virgin Islands company, Chardonnay Investments, is believed to hold amounts of cash generated by recorded music sales.

"Two Queensland companies, Nexcess Pty Ltd and Sin Can Can Pty Ltd, own properties and cars that have not been included in Hutchence's estate, while a United Kingdom company, Nextcircle Ltd, owns a Gold Coast development property thought to be associated with Hutchence."

So play it again, Sam, what will it be? *Give Peace A Chance, Imagine* or *Instant Karma . . .*

14

Shine

What about INXS?

Indeed, what about the band who now faced the most difficult decision of their five lives. A major player in this drama for 20 years, they were brutally cut out of the script by a chain of events that made major players of bit part actors.

Now they are probably in a no-win situation. Whatever decision these talented and private men make, it will sit well with some and poorly with others. It is a conundrum which could be dwelled upon forever. In some ways there is no perfect answer.

So what about INXS? They are getting on with life and coming to terms with the loss of a friend. And they are getting back out there.

These are talented men and musicians who have nothing to prove. They conquered the world. They do not have to again. They have always been – and remain – a positive force for life, equality and fairness, for the everyday man and woman.

Garry Gary Beers played at the recent Sydney benefit for former lead singer of Dragon, Marc Hunter, who has throat cancer. Jon Farriss has just done some drum clinics in Perth and has been working with Richard Lowenstein who is directing a short film promoting tourism in Victoria. Jon appears in various roles including driving a sports car and playing golf. A 30-second grab will be used as a TV ad. Incidentally, Lowenstein is also coming out of his self-imposed ban on music video work to direct the video for *Skin*, the first single from Ollie Olsen's stunning new dark, synthesiser driven, whirlpool (think MC 900 ft Jesus meets Portishead meets Garbage meets the Ozric Tentacles) Primitive Ghost fronted by the whispering, corrosive Baby Lemonade. Kirk recently finished production duties on an EP for his brother Drew's South Australian-based band, Coo.

And INXS recently met with their manager Martha Troup to consider options.

According to their publicist, Shawn Deacon, you'll probably know the answer to all those 'future' questions already. But there are up to 80 unreleased INXS tracks in the vaults and some of those are likely to make it to disc later in '98. It is believed that Andrew Farriss has already begun working through this material.

As for any new material INXS may wish to record should they stay together ... well, initially they will have to negotiate a recording contract. Their former label Mercury dumped them shortly after Michael's death but retained the rights to their back catalogue up to and including *Elegantly Wasted*. A spokesman for Mercury (Australia), Tom Enright, said this would also include all unreleased material recorded by the band prior to Michael's death.

Determined to keep clear of the ruck'n'maul that followed the tragedy, the band members only ventured into the press twice: for the interview with George Negus, and to deny a story published by *The Sun-Herald* on December 14, 1997, under the headline "Wanted: lead singer".

The story, which didn't carry a byline, read: "INXS, the rock band devastated by the death of Michael Hutchence on the eve of a comeback tour, is planning a world-wide hunt for a new lead singer.

"Band members have spoken with advisers and are already considering a bizarre secret audition over two weeks at music studios either here or in London to try out possible replacements for the charismatic star.

"It has not been decided whether they will advertise in the music press or rely on word of mouth and invite applications in the way AC/DC found singer Brian Johnson after the death of Bon Scott in 1980.

"A close friend said: 'Michael wasn't the band. They are all members of the band, and he would have wanted them to carry on."

The story met a sharp rejoinder by way of a press release the next day.

"The manager of INXS, Martha Troup, and the five band members, Tim Farriss, Andrew Farriss, Garry Gary Beers, Kirk

Pengilly and Andrew Farriss, wish it to be known that the band is not auditioning for replacement singers following the recent death of their close friend and professional colleague, Michael Hutchence, as reported in this weekend's Sydney *Sun-Herald.*

"The article that ran in the newspaper has released an unprecedented flood of media and public inquiries [some wanting to audition] which the band feel is necessary to stem.

"The band is still in a deep mourning phase of grief and request that media speculation about their future plans be put aside for the time being. They have currently made no other plans other than to take a big break."

While those future plans are decided, it should be said that the five remaining members of INXS acted with dignity, poise and compassion throughout what must have been the most heartbreaking, frustrating and anger-provoking time of their lives. If only others could have followed their lead.

Solo

There are plenty of theories doing the rounds about what would or could have happened to INXS in 1998 had Michael still been alive, but one thing seemed certain, and its impact is hard to judge – Michael would have released his first solo album. Talk about the set first surfaced in 1996 with details firming up over the following year. By late '97, Michael was talking freely about an album that veered away from the established INXS sound and into more edgy and experimental territory.

The most detailed insight came after his death when Gil Kaufman of *Addicted To Noise* (January 29, 1998) spoke to producer Andy Gill. Kaufman wrote, "It's a very different image of the late Michael Hutchence than the profile of the unsettled, emotionally off-centre rock star that has emerged over the last three months: perched on the edge of an unmade bed in his home in the south of France more than a year before his death, the face of INXS is hard at work on his own music, intensely focused, spending hours at a time, day after day, experimenting with vocals for his début solo album.

"Producer Andy Gill watches from across the room and records dozens of different takes and vocal ideas that never seem to stop coming as Hutchence jumps from one idea to another with an internal rhythm only he can understand.

" 'He was very inventive,' the former Gang of Four guitarist said of the nearly eight months of studio time that he spent producing for and working with Hutchence between 1995–1996 and from which he was able to offer some insight into the charismatic singer. . . .

"The untitled album the pair was working on – for which they recorded close to 16 tracks, including 'Get On The Inside' and 'A Straight Line' – is in limbo now . . . Both Gill and longtime INXS manager Martha Troup said this week that the album, Hutchence's first solo venture, was clearly at the forefront of his energies.

" 'He wanted it to be a big deal,' Troup said. 'It meant a lot to him, just like being in INXS meant a lot to him. He loved his music.'

"Gill shared production duties on some of the tracks with Danny Saber of Black Grape. Saber also recorded a handful of tracks with Hutchence in LA less than a week before his death. Bomb The Bass' Tim Simenon worked on early demos with the late INXS frontman in 1995, as well as lending a hand during some of the Gill sessions.

"Gill said there are at least nine or 10 songs he worked on with the singer that are nearly complete and mixed and three more with vocals that have yet to be mixed.

"Hutchence was cagey, Gill said, but sweetly shy about asking him to be involved in the project. 'He rang up and asked was I interested in doing some guitar stuff on the album,' said Gill, whose cinematic wails of post-punk distortion have placed him among the influential guitarists of the early '80s.

"Once Gill had agreed, he said Hutchence rang back five minutes later and asked, 'Actually, would you like to write some songs with me?'

"The pair then spent six months, on and off, writing songs, which time they became close, said Gill, who added that he was continually impressed by Hutchence's tireless work ethic.

" 'In many ways we were very compatible,' Gill said. 'I always thought he was a brilliant singer/performer and [he] really invested a lot of himself in the record.'

"Both Gill and Troup described the songs on the album as autobiographical, several of them dealing with Hutchence's frustration and confusion about an ongoing struggle with former Boomtown Rats leader Sir Bob Geldof over custody of the three children Geldof fathered with Hutchence's lover, Paula Yates.

" 'It was the one thing that really got him down,' Gill said about the struggles with Geldof ... 'He would go on about it and to him it seemed like he felt Geldof still treated Paula as his property and he was going to great lengths to make it difficult for Michael and Paula to have any life and happiness together,' Gill said.

"While Hutchence didn't necessarily address his personal problems explicitly in the lyrics, the songs – which Gill described as 'a bit darker than INXS, sort of like an interesting mix of grainy, gritty, almost industrial things with almost symphonic, orchestral sounds' – were clearly personal, he added.

"Explaining that she is in the process of going through tapes now and deciding which songs need work, Troup said one of the completed songs already sounds like a hit. 'There are around 25 songs with some kind of vocal,' she said. 'Some are funny, some darker, some serious, but there's this one ballad, a beautiful, incredible song that is just a definite hit. It's a beautiful track you just want to hear again and again.' It was unclear yet whether the album will be released, as originally intended, by early summer, Troup said.

"And while family, friends, fans and the curious wait to hear what Hutchence left the world, the image of this dark-haired icon sitting on the edge of his bed, improvising, digging, reaching out for the perfect song, keeps coming back for Gill.

"Hutchence would fight his way through the songs with Gill queuing the track in the background and then sitting back as the singer clamped down on his vocals. 'I'd have the track going and we'd do it again and again,' Gill said. 'He'd do dozens of vocal takes, work on lyrics a bit . . . He didn't just sing one thing and say "that's it". Something would work and then he'd be off again on a tangent with a different approach.

" 'It was difficult to keep track of it all,' Gill added. 'He'd really focus on it and just keep pushing it and working on it.' "

Remarkably, Michael had no solo contract and negotiations with several companies were said to be taking place in April '98. There is little doubt that the album – which would have been eagerly anticipated if he was alive – will now be one of the most prized – and analysed – records of the year.

The only time Michael ever broached the topic of solo albums with me, he said, "I'm not rushing to do one. It'll come when the time is right. I want it to be the best record possible. It has to be. I don't like it when people in bands put out half-hearted efforts and it looks like they're just cashing in on their success. You know, the kind of record that's in reality a collection of songs their band don't want to play or don't like, yet don't have much to distinguish them either. I've got a lot of ideas and I want to get them right. I want to take some chances."

Time will tell how close he got to his dream.

Christened

This is amongst the strangest, eeriest, most inexplicable things about the whole Hutchence affair: there was so much for Michael to live for in 1998. He dared to dream and this year several of those wishes appeared likely to be fulfilled: a new acting career, a solo record, and the continued growth of his daughter including her christening.

Paula arrived back in Sydney in late March with the purpose of christening Tiger Lily in her Michael's homeland. It wouldn't be without drama.

On Tuesday, March 31, 1998, Heavenly Hiraani Tiger Lily was christened in a traditional service at St Peter's church in Watson Bay, on the inner-city outskirts of Sydney. The 25-minute service was attended by about 20 guests including Kell and Rhett Hutchence. There were no hymns, no speeches and Tiger Lily did what all baby's are expected to do at such moments – she cried.

However, the day after the service a 19-year-old security guard was charged with assaulting a photographer from *The Daily Telegraph* newspaper, Brendan Esposito. Detectives claim that the guard pushed Mr Esposito off a wall just before the service began. The photographer fell heavily, injuring his back. The guard was one of six hired to keep the media and public away from the christening.

Paula Yates' friend Belinda Brewin denied subsequent reports that a European magazine had paid for the guards. Ms Brewin said she had hired them and had the receipts to prove it.

She also said *OK!* magazine had bought the exclusive rights to the christening.

After the service Paula and Tiger Lily were smuggled out of the church by separate doors. *The Daily Telegraph* (April 1, 1998) reported that "in the excitement of the moment the christening certificate was left behind on a church pew".

A picture of that certificate appeared in *The Daily Telegraph*. It shows clearly that Tiger Lily's "sponsors" – godparents – are Ms Brewin, INXS' manager Martha Troup, the executor of Michael's estate, Colin Diamond, Nick Cave, Josephine Fairley, Andrew Young and Catherine Mayer.

That afternoon the high-profile restaurant Mezzaluna, in Victoria St, Potts Pt, close to where Kirk lives, was the scene of a party attended by Paula, Ms Brewin, the INXS guitarist and other unidentified members of the christening party.

Out the front it looked like a scene from a high security operation. On the opposite side of the road to the restaurant's entrance a white Mercedes waited for Paula. Valet parking attendants in white, looking like formally dressed seamen from the nearby naval base, stood on either side of the door. Directly in front of it, a van with sliding doors sat perfectly positioned. Two security guards, immaculately attired in sombre suits, scanned the footpath and street and immediately got out as I walked by the restaurant's entrance, returning to the van after I passed. Later they were seen escorting Kirk home down Victoria Street.

Five months after Michael's death the song remained the same.

Feud

As if it could get any worse.
    It did.

Michael's mother, Patricia Glassop, called in the police.

The story was broken by *The Daily Telegraph* (April 7, 1998) which reported Police in two States had been drawn into a bitter feud between Paula Yates and Mrs Glassop.

"The latest in a series of alleged incidents led to a police welfare check of Hutchence's child . . ." wrote police reporter, Charles Miranda.

"Police also investigated phone calls allegedly made to Mrs Glassop by Ms Yates and heard from Ms Yates' lawyer of an apparent feud over the Hutchence will.

"Police visited Ms Yates' apartment during her stay in Sydney last week to check on the welfare of 20-month-old Heavenly Hiraani Tiger Lily.

"The child was found to be 'in good spirits and obviously well cared for'.

"The details of the visit to Quay West apartments at the Rocks on March 30 is contained in a confidential police report obtained by *The Daily Telegraph*.

"During the visit, police spoke to Ms Yates' travelling companion, Belinda Brewin, and her New York based agent, Martha Troup.

"The Rocks area officers, including an acting inspector, reported after the visit they were completely satisfied with the child's welfare.

"The visit was two days before Heavenly Hiraani was christened at St Peter's Church in Sydney's Watson Bay.

"The one-page document, marked 'Confidential' and 'Media Status: Strictly Not for Press', appears to have stemmed from information received from Mrs Glassop.

" 'Surfers Paradise police station advised that over the last two days telephone calls of a threatening nature were made allegedly by Paula Yates to Mrs Patricia Glassop, Main Beach, Surfers Paradise (mother of the late Michael Hutchence),' the report reads.

"Another pargaraph reads: 'There was concern that Ms Yates may harm her child, Heavenly Hiraani Tiger Lily, daughter of Paula Yates and Michael Hutchence.'

"Under the headline 'Comment', the report concludes: 'There is no concern for the welfare of the child.'

" 'Surfers Paradise Police advised and will inform Patricia Glassop.'

"Barrister Andrew Young spoke to Rose Bay police the same day after The Rocks police visited the child regarding an alleged dispute between Mrs Glassop and Ms Yates over Hutchence's will.

"The officer in charge of the matter, Acting Inspector Danny McConville, is on leave and not available for comment.

"Police have also launched an investigation into how *The Daily Telegraph* obtained the document, a copy of which they seized from the newspaper.

"A lawyer for Mrs Glassop last night said there was no contest over Hutchence's will."

The article was accompanied by a tear-out of the document.

And amidst all these bitter tears, a young girl who will never know her father smiled sweetly and radiantly in every picture that appeared.

15

Afterword

There was a story in the paper the other day about the death of Australia's first naturally born gorilla at Taronga Zoo in Sydney. Ten days after his death the grieving gorilla mother continued her vigil, nursing her dead baby son.

The last paragraph read, "The 10-strong western lowland gorilla community at the zoo is dealing with their grief privately. The gorilla section of the zoo has been closed."

How ironic: we afford the animals we cage the dignity of grieving in private, yet the people we cage we continue to stare at, make fun of, subject to the worst indignities, invade their lives – because of and despite their sorrow.

This book does not purport to be the definitive story of Michael Hutchence. It is an observation and a tribute.

There is no guilty party in this book.

Paula Yates did not kill Michael Hutchence. Her greatest crime was leaving a British hero she no longer loved for a man who was her soul mate – just as many couples split from all walks of life because one or the other has lost that loving feeling. Her second greatest crime was threatening the tenuous and fragile balance of a troubled family that had its own agendas with their one shining star. Paula Yates fell in love. That isn't a crime. I've never met her, perhaps one day I will. I'd certainly like to. She is strong, yes, and dangerous. And maybe some of her actions are questionable. But who the hell are you, I or the tabloid and gossip media to judge? She is also a divine actress, the mistress of the flick of the head, the roll of the eye, a smouldering intensity, a pure innocence that is a lethal sexuality. So what? She's a woman and, I fancy, awfully proud of it.

Sir Bob Geldof didn't kill Michael Hutchence. He simply did what any aggrieved father under threat would do. He tried to protect his children and ensure he had reasonable access to them. His actions were right and proper. When his ex-wife tried to take his children on a tour of Australia with her lover and his band, he objected. Who wouldn't? If Sir Bob is the devil as Michael claimed, then he is a devil haunted by his own conscience and also the knowledge that after 18 years he hadn't done enough to keep the woman he loved. The war of words and actions between Sir Bob and Paula is the drama of separation, of love spinning over the thin line that separates it from hate and turning its roses to thorns.

Kym Wilson didn't kill Michael Hutchence. The theory that if Kym had stayed with Michael in his moment of need, then he'd be alive today is as ludicrous as charging Kell Hutchence with the death of his son because he didn't act on his gut impulse and ring him at 6am when he awoke and thought something was wrong. Kym Wilson was simply going about her life. She wasn't contracted to be Michael's nursemaid. He was a big boy.

Kell Hutchence, Tina Schorr, Patricia Glassop, and Rhett Hutchence, individually or collectively, did not kill Michael Hutchence. Michael had dealt with his family problems for many years. They had become no better or worse at the time of his death.

The tabloid and gossip media didn't kill Michael Hutchence. Not directly. They operate on supply and demand. If there is no demand then they have to change what they supply. Without demand there are no advertisers and without advertisers there is no paper or magazine. Until the relentless need for more and more sensation is either diminished by reader disapproval [which seems unlikely] or legislation is introduced to control chequebook journalism and set boundaries within which such publications must operate then the gross exploitation of an individual's privacy will continue. I believe firmly in the freedom of the press but not to the extinction of basic human rights.

So who did kill Michael Hutchence?

Michael Hutchence killed Michael Hutchence. That he did is a desperate reflection of how out-of-control the world around him had become and the end result of the pressures brought to bear on him by most of the above: thousands of actions, consequences, coincidences and reactions. Michael was trapped in a world of his own making. The life he lived.

At 37, Michael Hutchence was a lonely man caught up in a massive personal dilemma. He was *the* man and he wasn't. Paula summed up Michael better than anybody when she said, "People think he was a hell-raiser, prancing around in those black leather trousers. But underneath it all he was a sweet innocent boy."

Michael wanted to please everybody and he nearly pulled it off. His family, Paula, his friends, his bandmates. He kept them all happy for a time. But he also knew he couldn't do it for much longer.

His star was waning. And Michael was a true star. He loved the spotlight, worshipped the limelight, revelled in the attention. Yet he also knew the damning reality that INXS were unlikely to ever reclaim the glory days of the late 1980s when they were the biggest band in the world and he an attraction worthy of comparison with Jagger, Morrison and Bono. He also knew that his relationships, particularly that with Paula, was affecting his relationship with the family that until then he had treasured the most: his brothers in INXS.

Michael also saw an opening, a way to keep his star shining: the movies. The sniff of screen superstardom beckoned. Not many have done it, made that transition successfully, but Michael could have. He was that talented.

But at what cost? INXS would probably suffer and combined with his nearly completed solo album, the man who tried so hard to put his bandmates in the spotlight would hog it again. And what if his solo album was critically acclaimed? Where would that leave INXS?

His new family: Paula, her three daughters with Sir Bob, and Tiger Lily were a huge distraction. The band had already made allowances for him. That is implicit in the interviews with Tim and Kirk. That they continued to support and love him speaks much louder than words will ever do for Andrew, Jon, Tim, Kirk and Garry.

And the pressure of the tabloid media and gossipmongers was never ending. He wanted to shield his family . . . sorry, his families from it. But how does one man fight an army?

That battle alone is more than enough for one spirit, yet Michael chose also to fight a battle which while honourable was not his. He chose to stand for Paula and tackle Sir Bob. How many

215

boyfriends talk to their girlfriend's ex-husband, interfere in the fallout of a broken relationship, yet alone actively fight them? There is little doubt Michael felt Paula was being treated awfully by Sir Bob. But, in the end, the court was always going to have the final say. What Michael did was so noble, yet so damaging because he left himself so exposed, so vulnerable.

In November 1997, Michael Hutchence was on the edge of so many dilemmas. He saw answers but with each answer he saw the potential for more pain, more loss.

He returned to Australia happy on the outside, carrying a dream: three months with his band, his woman and his family. Surely, it wasn't too much to ask for. But the last few years had taken their toll and he'd changed. Those changes inevitably distanced him from the people he had been closest to. Michael had found heaven and hell – and there was only person who understood him, really understood him. And he needed to be with her. Like it or not, when Paula Yates was with Michael the world made sense. Maybe it was a sex-crazed, drugged out, million miles an hour world, but there's every reason to believe that in it Michael found joy, particularly when he held their daughter in his arms.

There are questions that remain unanswered: in those final moments when Michael desperately needed a friend, why didn't he call Kell with whom he'd always been close? Why didn't he call Paula? Was the truth too much to bear? How could he turn his back on the child he loved so passionately? Had he already made up his mind? Was it suicide or an accident? What was it a friend could tell him but his lover or his parent couldn't? How depressed was Michael Hutchence and how serious was his condition?

And so horribly a gentle, beautiful, sinner, reprobate and full-blooded rebel yell screamed into oblivion alone and full of questions that had no answers, and answers that asked too many questions.

Confused, despairing and wasted, Michael Hutchence hit overload that morning and simply tore himself apart.

At least, that is what I believe – and I could be completely and utterly wrong.

– Mike Gee, Sydney, April 6, 1998

Appendix 1

THE ORDER OF THE FUNERAL SERVICE

WITH THANKSGIVING FOR THE LIFE OF
Michael Kelland Hutchence

22nd January 1960 – 22nd November 1997

Thursday, 27th November 1997
2:30pm

ST ANDREW'S CATHEDRAL
SYDNEY

Human beings have experienced the mystery of death, and the pain of grief, since time immemorial. Every society has developed rites to mark the passage from life through death, and to commemorate the dead. Today we do that through this service.

The wounds of grief need time and care to heal. The service may help this process, by enabling us to acknowledge our loss, give thanks for the life of Michael, make our last farewell, and begin to take up life once more.

Christians believe in God, the source and giver of life. God's good news proclaims Jesus Christ to be our living Lord, who laid down his life for us. He knew death, yet triumphed over it, drawing its sting, and was raised by God to new life. Christians affirm the presence of the Spirit of Christ, who helps us in our weakness. Yet we, with all mortals, still face death. Those who put their trust in Christ share the sufferings of their Lord, even in the midst of God's love and care.

In this service we proclaim the Christian hope in the face of death – Jesus Christ, whose resurrection is the promise of our own.

217

ORDER OF SERVICE

Before the service begins, "By my side" by INXS will be played. (The people stand as the Choir and Clergy enter the Cathedral).

GATHERING IN GOD'S NAME

THE GREETING The Very Reverend Boak, Jobbins, Dean of Sydney

SCRIPTURE SENTENCES (Sung by the Choir) Croft

I am the resurrection and the life, saith the Lord: he that believeth in me, though he were dead, yet shall he live, and whosoever liveth and believeth in me shall never die.

John 11: 25–6

I know that my Redeemer liveth, and that he shall stand at the latter day upon the earth. And though after my skin worms destroy this body, yet in my flesh shall I see God: whom I shall see for myself, and mine eyes shall behold, and not another.

Job 19: 25–7

We brought nothing into this world, and it is certain we can carry nothing out. The Lord gave, and the Lord hath taken away; blessed be the name of the Lord.

1 Timothy 6: 7, Job 1: 21

PRAYER (Led by Bradley Watt, said by all)

Loving God, you alone are the source of life.
May your life-giving Spirit flow through us,
and fill us with compassion, one for another.
In our sorrow give us the calm of your peace.
Kindle our hope, and let our grief give way to joy;
through Jesus Christ our Lord. Amen.

The people sit.

THE REMEMBRANCE

EULOGY Richard Wilkins
Music Journalist

MUSIC "Into my arms"
Nick Cave

218

TRIBUTE   Andrew Farriss
                             INXS

TRIBUTE   Tina Schorr, Rhett Hutchence

THE MINISTRY OF GOD'S WORD

PSALM 121   (Sung by the Choir)

I lift up my eyes to the hills: but where shall I find help? My help
comes from the Lord: who has made heaven and earth. He will not
suffer your foot to stumble: and he who watches over you will not
sleep. Be sure he who has charge of Israel: will neither slumber nor
sleep. The Lord himself is your keeper: the Lord is your defence
upon your right hand; The sun shall not strike you by day: nor shall
the moon by night. The Lord will defend you from all evil: it is he
who will guard your life. The Lord will defend your going out and
your coming in: from this time forward for ever more. Glory to
God; Father, Son, and Holy Spirit: as in the beginning, so now, and
for ever. Amen.

BIBLE READING   1 Corinthians 15
                    The Very Reverend Boak Jobbins

HYMN   (The people stand)   Crimond

1   The Lord's my shepherd, I'll not want.
     He makes me down to lie
     in pastures green, he leadeth me
     the quiet waters by.

2   My soul he doth restore again;
     and me to walk doth make
     within the paths of righteousness,
     e'en for his own name's sake.

3   Yea, though I walk in death's dark vale,
     yet will I fear none ill:
     for thou art with me; and thy rod
     and staff me comfort still.

4   My table thou has furnished
     in presence of my foes
     my head thou dost with oil anoint,
     and my cup overflows

5   Goodness and mercy all my life
     shall surely follow me:
     and in God's house for evermore
     my dwelling-place shall be.

ADDRESS   The Very Reverend Boak Jobbins,
                           Dean of Sydney

ANTHEM

Deep river, my home is over Jordan. Deep river, Lord I want to
cross over into camp ground. O God's children, O don't you want
to go to the heavenly feast in that promised land, where all is
peace? Walk right into heaven and take my seat, and throw myself
at Jesus' feet.

The people sit or kneel.

THE PRAYERS

PRAYERS   (Led by Canon Jim Holbeck)

THE LORD'S PRAYER   (Said by all.)

**Our Father in heaven, hallowed be your Name, your kingdom
come, your will be done on earth as it is in heaven. Give us today
our daily bread. Forgive us our sins as we forgive those who sin
against us. Lead us not into temptation, but deliver us from evil.
For the kingdom, the power, and the glory are yours now and for
ever. Amen**

THE GRACE   (Said by all.)

**The grace of our Lord Jesus Christ, and the love of God, and the
fellowship of the Holy Spirit be with us all evermore. Amen**

THE BLESSING   **The Dean**

     The people stand as the procession leaves the Cathedral.

     At this time "Never tear us apart" by INXS will be played.

Please remain in the Cathedral until after the family and other
                    chief mourners have left.

**St Andrew's Cathedral Choir, directed by Michael Deasey, Organist
and Master of the Choristers.**

Organist: Mark Quarmby.

Appendix 2

EULOGY BY ANDREW FARRISS

A life so vital and gifted and full of promise, as God created from the first. Who knows what goes through a man's thoughts, except his own spirit that is within him. Only he and the Lord know. He answers every prayer. His mercies are new every morning and a new light will dawn.

The following is a saying from the indigenous peoples of the world. You have noticed that everything a man does is in a circle and that is because the power of the world always works in circles and everything tries to be round. The sky is round and I have heard that the earth is round like a ball and so are the stars.

The wind in its greatest power whirls. Birds make nests in circles for theirs is the same religion as ours. Even the seasons form a great circle in their changing and always come back again to where they were.

The life of a man is a circle from childhood to childbirth and so it is in everything where power moves.

I would like to thank all the people that helped us make this possible today and your kindness and support is gratefully accepted. We would like to thank all those who have sent flowers and condolences. It has been very much appreciated.

I would like to share with you on behalf of myself and the members of INXS some thoughts about our friend and workmate Michael Hutchence. We met as school friends, we played music because we loved it.

Together with Michael we experienced some very hard times and some very good times. The hard times made us stronger and the good times we will always cherish. As a songwriting team for more than 20 years he and I had written hundreds of songs together.

His lyrics are the soul and depth which have touched millions of people around the earth.

He had exceptional communication skills. Michael was one of the greatest singers and stage performers of his generation. We are so proud to have worked and played with such a talented and gifted man.

Over the years INXS have had every type of media imaginable – the best and the worst.

That is human nature. Some have chosen to judge Michael harshly. But tragically they chose not to tell one glaring truth. Michael had spent almost his entire adult life performing and giving 110 per cent of his being to entertaining people around the world.

He gave himself away to bring enjoyment and happiness into other people's lives. What price is happiness?

Michael was a sociable guy and yet he took life seriously. He had great courage. He stood up to those he felt he needed to stand up to. He loved to travel and explore the world. He loved Australia. He loved his friends.

He loved his family. He was a caring father and a passionate family man. He loved music and he loved his fans. We ask that the band's fans and for those who are touched by his death not to react in any ways to hurt themselves. Michael would not have wanted that.

We will remember him with love and affection. We will all miss you Michael. God bless you.

(This extract from *The Daily Telegraph*, Friday, November 28, 1997)

Appendix 3

EULOGY BY RHETT HUTCHENCE

A part of me died the other day and strangely a part of me was born, and then there is the part that will carry the memory of my brother Michael forever in my heart.

Michael and I were only two years apart when we grew up arm-in-arm. From the very beginning all the signs were there that Michael was destined to lead an extraordinary life. When he first opened his soulful eyes, he had two loving wonderful parents Patricia and Kelland from whom he inherited gentlemanly charm, accommodating nature and charisma.

With the help of our sister Tina, who played an integral part, feeding, helping, bathing, caring and being, when finally Mike came along our family was complete.

I have an early lyric book of Michael's in which when he first started writing [and] there is a list of 10 things he wanted to achieve in this life. The first one was to conquer the world. I can't remember what the other nine were but I'm sure he achieved them too.

Michael was a poet, a singer and a gifted performer. He touched the lives of everybody he met, even people he never met.

It hasn't been easy being Michael's brother, it's strange, it's been fantastic at times and other times the hardest, but having Michael for my brother I wouldn't have had it any other way.

My heart goes out to Paula and beautiful, darling girl Tiger, and the other girls, to the band, to his friends and people who have known Michael and lost a tremendous friend.

Thanks to the support from friends, the love I'm receiving at the moment is helping me through this.

I cannot stress enough the importance of friendship and love in today's times.

The other night I went and spent some time at the room, his room at the Ritz, to see if it had any answers.

It seemed a sad room, it definitely wasn't Michael.

224

And if Michael, who loved Oscar Wilde, would have identified with the famous poet's last words "either this wallpaper goes or I do" then I understand.

On behalf of Michael I would like to thank my family for the love they gave him and together these words may have meaning for us all.

To mourn too long for those who we love is self-indulgent, but to honour their memory with a promise to live a little better for having known them gives purpose to their life and some reason for their death.

Rest in peace Bro. I love you. I will miss you.

(This extract from *The Daily Telegraph*, Friday, November 28, 1997)

Appendix 4

EULOGY BY TINA SCHORR

On November 28, 1996, my brother was in Los Angeles and he spent Thanksgiving with us and it was a wonderful Thanksgiving. We held hands around the table and we gave thanks for all our blessings.

Today, November 27, 1997, is also Thanksgiving Day. I give thanks for being blessed to have my brother. The kindest most deeply sensitive, loving man.

I received a fax today from Gibson Kemp and I think the band would certainly like to hear this.

Do not stand at my band and weep, I am not there, I do not sleep, I am a thousand winds that blow, I am the diamond glints on snow, I am the sunlight on rice and grain, I am the gentle autumn's rain, when you awaken in the morning hush, I am the swift uplifting rush, a quiet bird's encircled flight, I am the soft stars that shine at night, do not stand at my grave and cry, I am not there and did not die.

(This extract from *The Daily Telegraph*, Friday, November 28, 1997)

Appendix 5

The former lead singer of Cold Chisel and Australian solo star, Jimmy Barnes, shared many a drink and stage with Michael and INXS. Most notably, the two vocalists roared, ranted and rolled at each other on the storming 'Good Times' single. Jimmy wrote this poem as a tribute to Michael.

The Gift

To Michael

I will light a candle
To show you the way
Just one of many, but it will shine brightly
So you can see
Follow the love that shines from it
And the respect that makes it burn
It comes from me
I will light the incense
That will make you calm
And take you messages of peace
So you will know that no one judges
And that all is well
Go on your way
You great explorer
With your gentle, searching, gracious heart
And take with you your
Courage and passion
Slay those dragons and
Rescue your maiden with Love songs
Like the true hero that you are
I honour you and am blessed
To have known you,
Albeit for such a short time
And I look forward to hearing

Your tales and adventures
When next we meet my friend
Until then I will miss You

With Love from my Heart,
Jimmy

Appendix 6

DISCOGRAPHY

The following discography of INXS recordings, while detailed, is by no means comprehensive. There are rare and obscure releases in most territories that are not listed and many of the band's major releases are available on up to three different labels. So head down to your local secondhand shop, collector's fair or garage sale and start digging: you never know what you'll find. Good luck.

Singles

Simple Simon/We Are The Vegetables (Deluxe/RCA)
Just Keep Walking/Scratch (Deluxe/RCA)
The Loved One/The Unloved One (Deluxe/RCA)
Stay Young/Lacavocal (Deluxe/RCA)
Night Of Rebellion/Prehistoria (Deluxe/RCA)
The One Thing/Space Shuttle (WEA)
Don't Change/Go West (WEA)
Here Comes II/To Look At You/The Sax Thing/You Never Used To Cry/Here Comes II – double single pack in gatefold sleeve (WEA)
To Look At You/The Sax Thing (WEA)
Original Sin/In Vain–Just Keep Walking (WEA)
I Send A Message/Mechanical – flip-back envelope picture sleeve (WEA)
Burn For You/Johnson's Aeroplane (WEA)
Dancing On The Jetty/The Harbour (WEA)
What You Need/I'm Over You (WEA)
This Time/Sweet As Sin (WEA)
Kiss The Dirt (Falling Down The Mountain)/Six Knots–The One Thing (live) – with triple gatefold fold out picture sleeve (WEA)
Listen Like Thieves/Different World (WEA)
Good Times/Laying Down The Law (Mushroom)
Need You Tonight/I'm Coming Home (WEA)
New Sensation/Do Wot You Do (WEA)

Devil Inside/On The Rocks – with poster (WEA)
Never Tear Us Apart/Move On (WEA)
Suicide Blonde/Everybody Wants U Tonight (WEA)
Disappear/Middle Beast (WEA)
Bitter Tears/The Other Side – with sticker (WEA)

12" Singles
(All with picture sleeves unless mentioned. EV= extended version)

The One Thing (EV)/Space Shuttle–Phantom Of The Opera (WEA)
Black And White (EV)/Long In The Tooth–Any Day But Sunday (WEA)
Original Sin (Dance dub) (WEA)
Burn For You (EV)/Burn For You (remix)–I Send A Message (EV) (WEA)
What You Need (EV)/What You Need–I'm Over You (WEA)
Listen Like Thieves (EV)–Listen Like Thieves (instrumental)/Different World (EV)–Begotten (WEA)
Need You Tonight (Mendelsohn mix)–Need You Tonight–Mediate/I'm Coming (Home)–Move On–Kiss The Dirt (Falling Down The Mountain) (WEA)
Need You Tonight–Mediate/I'm Coming (Home) (WEA)
New Sensation (Nick 12" mix)/Guns In The Sky (Kick Ass Mix)–New Sensation (Nick 7" mix) (WEA)
Devil Inside (remix version)/Devil Inside (7" version)–On The Rocks – with poster (WEA)
Suicide Blonde (7" mix)–Suicide Blonde (Milk mix)/Suicide Blonde (Devastation mix)–Everybody Wants U Tonight (WEA)
Disappear (extended 12" mix)–Middle Beast/What You Need (Coldcut force mix) – with poster (WEA)
Shining Star/I Send A Message (live)–Bitter Tears (live)–The Loved One (live) – in gatefold sleeve (East/West)

Compact Disc Singles

Suicide Blonde (7" mix)–Suicide Blonde (demolition mix)–Suicide Blonde (earth mix)–Everybody Wants U Tonight (WEA)
Disappear (extended 12" mix)–Disappear–Middle Beast–What You Need (Coldcut force mix) (WEA)
Bitter Tears (12" Lorimer remix)–(instrumental)–Disappear (alternative mix)–The Other Side – with sticker (WEA)
By My Side (movie mix)–Faith In Each Other (live)–Soothe Me – very limited edition without picture sleeve but with poster (East/West)
By My Side/Soothe Me (East/West)

230

Shining Star/I Send A Message (live)–Bitter Tears (live)–The Loved One (live) (East/West)
Heaven Sent–It Ain't Easy–11th Revolution–Deepest Red–Heaven Sent (gliding version) (East/West)
Taste It (club mix)–(12" mix)–Not Enough Time (East/West)
Baby Don't Cry–Questions (instrumental)–Ashtar Speaks–Baby Don't Cry (vocal and orchestral mix)–(orchestral mix) (East/West)
Beautiful Girl–Strange Desire (original recording)–In My Living Room– Ashtar Speaks–Wishing Well (instrumental) (East/West)
The Gift–Need You Tonight–Kiss the Dirt (Falling Down The Mountain)– What You Need–Burn For You (East/West)
Please (You Got That)–Born to be Wild–The Gift (extended mix)–The Gift (Bonus beat mix) (East/West)
Time–Communication (live)–The Gift (live)–Please (You Got That) (live)– Taste It (live) (East/West)
Freedom Deep–Please (You Got That) (club mix)–Cut Your Roses Down (sure is pure mix)–Viking Juice (the butcher mix) (East/West)
The Strangest Party (These Are The Times)–(Apollo 440 mix)–Wishing Well (courier extended mix)–Sing Something (East/West)
Elegantly Wasted – a one-track promo accidentally shipped to record shops (Mercury)
Elegantly Wasted (radio edit)–Need You Tonight–Original Sin (epic adventure), I'm Only Looking (Morales bad yard club mix) (Mercury)
Elegantly Wasted (radio edit)–(shagsonic remix)–(shagsonic dub)–(G force & Seiji remix) – comes with 4 collectors cards (Mercury)

Albums

INXS – with an inner sleeve with lyrics (RCA/Deluxe)
Underneath The Colours – gatefold sleeve with lyrics (RCA/Deluxe)
INXSive 1980–82 (RCA/Deluxe)
Shabooh Shoobah – with a lyric sheet and a limited poster (WEA)
The Swing – initial copies in a die cut picture sleeve: all copies came with an inner sleeve and gatefold sleeve (WEA)
Listen Like Thieves – gatefold sleeve and lyrics sheet inner (WEA)
Kick – with a gatefold sleeve and an inner sleeve with lyrics (WEA)
Kick – rare limited tour release with reversed gatefold sleeve and sticker (WEA)
Kick – picture disc in hard plastic outer sleeve with sticker – excellent collector's item (WEA)
X – with inner sleeve with lyrics
Welcome To Wherever You Are – with inner sleeve/lyrics and different cover to CD/cassette version (WEA)

Compact Discs

INXS (Mercury)
Underneath The Colours (Mercury)
INXSive 1980–82 (Mercury)
Shabooh Shoobah (Mercury)
The Swing (Polygram)
Listen Like Thieves (Polygram)
Kick (WEA)
X (WEA)
Live Baby Live – rare box set with a CD, video, booklet, postcards, bio, t-shirt and poster (WEA)
Live Baby Live – standard release (WEA)
Welcome To Wherever You Are – has different cover to the LP and cassette (East/West)
Welcome To Wherever You Are – with totally unique 'desert' picture sleeve (East/West)
Full Moon, Dirty Hearts (East/West)
The Greatest Hits (WEA)
The Greatest Hits – in limited slipcase with bonus CD: *All Juiced Up* (features remixes and alternate mixes) (WEA)
The Greatest Hits – reissued with different track listing after moving to Mercury Records who now own the entire back catalogue (Mercury)
Elegantly Wasted (Mercury)
Elegantly Wasted – limited numbered slipcase with six tracks live CD: *Live in Aspen 97* (Mercury)

Selected Promo Releases

Merry Christmas Song (no label) – fan club only 7″ – issued to US and Aust fan club members only. Valued at $250 (Aust) in April '98
Dancing On The Jetty/The Harbour–All Voices – promo only 12″ to promote the film *Strikebound,* interview is with the entire band (WEA)
New Sensation (Nick's 12″ mix)–(extended mix)/New Sensation–Guns In The Sky (extended mix) – white label promo only 12″ (WEA)
Never Tear Us Apart/Move On – the disc is numbered TEAR ONE (WEA)
Mystify/Mystify – white label promo only 12″ (WEA)
Mystify/Mystify – white label test pressing 12″ some copies of which have rubber stamped labels. Carries a different catalogue number, KICK-2, to the version above (WEA)
Dekadance EP – one of the most sought-after INXS releases. Featuring

Original Sin, I Send A Message, Burn For You, Dancing On The Jetty, Melting In The Sun, Love Is (What I Say) and *Jackson* (with Jenny Morris), the vinyl version has the six different covers that the cassette sports. There's also a short biography on the rear of the sleeve explaining that it is a Promotional Only 12″ to help sell the cassette. The version of *Jackson* here is unique and doesn't feature the long intro on the tape. Mint copies can fetch up to $150 (Aust) (WEA)

What You Need (Coldcut force mix) – promo only 12″ (WEA)

Kiss The Dirt (Falling Down The Mountain)/Six Knots–The One Thing (live) – promo only 12″ (WEA)

Living INXS featuring the tracks *One By One/Listen Like Thieves:* another collector's favourite, this vinyl 12″ was issued to promote the video tape *Living INXS.* There's a write-up on the rear of the picture sleeve explaining the release of the single and the concert from which it was culled. Mint copies were fetching $120 (Aust) in April '98 (WEA)

Cassette Biography 1977–1985 – another much sought-after item, the cassette features an interview with the entire band on one side and eight tracks on the reverse. Best of all it has a massive gatefold sleeve, one side of which shows a map of the world with selected tour dates and venues while the other has a short bio. Mint copies sell for $80 (Aust) (WEA)

INXS: The Ultimate Collection – nearly as sought after as the tape above, this 22-track 'best of' features nearly the entire *Kick* album. $60 is the starting price for mint copies (WEA)

X – Lovely promo only box set featuring the full *X* cassette plus postcards. The box is wrapped by a red ribbon pulled across it in the form of an *X*. Changes hands for about $75 (Aust) (WEA)

Disappear (extended 12″ mix)/What You Need (Coldcut force mix) – promo only 12″ (WEA)

Bitter Tears (Lorimer remix)–(extended 12″ mix)–instrumental/The Other Side – white label promo 12″ only (WEA)

Bitter Tears (Lorimer remix)–Bitter Tears (instrumental) – white label promo 12″ only (WEA)

By My Side/By My Side – 7″ white label promo only

Faith In Each Other (live) – light blue flexi disc given away with the October 1991 issue of Dolly Magazine

The Stairs (live) – promo CD to release the *Live Baby Live* album (East/West)

New Sensation (live) – promo CD to release the *Live Baby Live* album (East/West)

Heaven Sent, Not Enough Time, Taste It, Baby Don't Cry, Beautiful Girl – these five CD singles were released to promote *Welcome To*

Wherever You Are. All are one-track discs and all come in digi-packs with custom sleeves. Each is worth about $35 (Aust); the full set fetches a minimum of $150 (Aust) but the asking price is on the way up (all East/West)

The Gift, Please (You Got That) – both promo only singles for the *Full Moon* album (East/West)

Please (You Got That) (E-smooves club mix)–(E-smooves Needful dub mix)– (Downtown dub mix) – white label 12″ only promo

Taste It – a double 12″ pack called the *Mix It Yourself 12″*. $40 (Aust)

Elegantly Wasted – advance CD of album in white cardboard cut-out slick. Disc bears catalogue number ADV 1997 1 – $50 (Aust) (Mercury)

Elegantly Wasted – promo only set beautifully presented in rectangular shaped flip-top with full colour cover shot of scene from the *EW* video and cover shoot. Inside 17-page full colour booklet with biography, band quotes and many pix is stuck to the flip-top cover. Disc sits in bottom half of flip-top. Minimum $80 (Aust) in April '98.

*Note that prices for INXS collectible items are increasing all the time due to Michael's death and the subsequently active market place.

Michael Hutchence Solo

Late 1960s: *Jingle Bells* – Santa Claus Xmas Doll (Jingle Bells record insert) – Hong Kong made LP

1982: *Speed Kills/Forest Theme* – both with Don Walker (Cold Chisel) from the *Freedom* original motion picture soundtrack (WEA, re-released 1996 Origin)

1985: *Sex Symbol/Jungle Boy* by Flame Fortune (whose back-up band The Rocking Love Gods included Andrew Farriss), available as coloured vinyl 7″ and 12″, co-produced with Andrew Farriss (Polygram)

Session work with Beargarden leading up to the release of their two singles that year – *I Write The News* and *Sea, Salt and Sand* (both Virgin) and their self-titled mini-album (WEA)

1987: *Dogs In Space* – original motion picture soundtrack available on both vinyl (CBS [Aust], Atlantic [US]), CD (both Atlantic and Mercury), cassette (Atlantic). 7″ single from the album was *Rooms For The Memory*, 12″ had additional track (WEA)

Glory Road by Richard Clapton features Michael on backing vocals on two tracks, *The Emperor's New Clothes* and *Angelou* (WEA)

1988: *Motorcycle Baby 12"* by Ecco Homo (great track) was co-produced by Michael and also features him on backing vocals and in the video as are Tim and Jon Farriss (RooArt)

1989: *Max Q,* on which Michael is the vocalist, co-writer (six tracks) and co-producer (with Ollie Olsen). Available on a variety of labels on vinyl, CD and cassette formats. The three singles from the 11-track album – *Way Of the World, Sometimes* and *Monday Night By Satellite* – were all released in 7", 12" and CD formats and there are plenty of different pressings to collect. Promo items include a *Max Q* 5-track CD sampler.

1991: Backing vocals on *Take You Higher* from the chart-busting album *Love Versus Money* by Noiseworks (Columbia)

1994: Lead vocal on *Under My Thumb* from the compilation album *Symphonic Music Of The Rolling Stones* with the London Symphony Orchestra (RCA)

1994: Lead vocal with NRBQ on *Baby Let's Play House* from the tribute album *It's Now Or Never – The Tribute To Elvis* (Mercury)

1995: Lead vocal on *The Passenger* from the *Batman Forever* original motion picture soundtrack (Atlantic)

1996: Lead vocal on *Spill The Wine* from the *Barb Wire* original motion picture soundtrack (London)

Lead vocal on *Red Hill* from *One Voice: The Songs of Chage & Aska* compilation (EMI)

Lead vocal on *The King Is Gone* from *No Talking Just Heads* by The Heads (UMA/MCA)

1996/97: Work on his début solo album primarily with Tim Simenon (Bomb The Bass), and Andy Gill (Gang Of Four). See Chapter 15.

[The basic information for this discography appeared in the June/July/August 1997 edition of *The Australian Record Collectors* magazine. Additional material from *Who's Who Of Australian Rock* (3rd Edition) compiled by Chris Spencer and Zbig Nowara, Five Mile Press, 1993]

Appendix 7

INTERNET GUIDE

So you are all set up, ready to surf but have no idea where to go to find INXS on the internet. It's easy. There are copious megabytes devoted to INXS sites, Michael Hutchence tribute sites, soundbites, streaming video, interviews, news, reviews and pictures galore just waiting for you.

Rather than try to list all the sites (which is impossible because they're are always beginning, ending, moving, changing address), here are four excellent sites which will start you on your path to being saturated in INXS.

The official INXS home page can be found at **http://www.inxs. com** – the first base for fans because it is the official page and a moving tribute to Michael.

To plumb the depths of INXS there are two excellent reference sites: An Excess of INXS – **http://www.umdnj.edu/~kotharne/ inxs.html** – is run by Neil Kothari and has it all. The latest news, the most complete discography on the 'Net, copious archives of interviews, reviews and general articles, links galore, guitar TABS, music for sale, fan resources, a chat room and a message board. If it's INXS it will probably be in this award-winning site somewhere. Put aside several hours if you really want to get the feel of Neil's outstanding and much-loved site.

Another very good site is **http://www.inxskick.com** which offers excellent links to INXS material all over the 'Net, makes its information available in six languages and also takes you straight to the INXS material archived in major media sites.

When you've surfed your way through the fact and philosophy of INXS then visit **http://web.wt.net/~stazya/** (If your browser cannot handle frames – AOL's Webcrawler cannot – then try **http://web.wt.net/~stazya/stazya/reach.html**) which is the home of the Reaching Out To Others Pages (ROTO). When you hit the front page simply hit the link in the left hand panel "to INXS Fans". Compiled by Stacy "Stazya" Ambler in December 1997 – and regularly updated – the ROTO Pages are a central source for tribute page links with descriptions for each, chat room links and information, other INXS outlets and crisis hotlines.

Amongst the ROTO pages are links to nearly 70 fan tribute pages for Michael Hutchence: if you want to understand what Michael meant to his fans and the genuine grief and loss his death has caused then look no further. A heartwarming and very special collection of pages dedicated to all INXS fans.

And if you're a sucker for punishment then visit the 60-pages of INXS at **http://www.thei.aust.com/music2/splatdex.html** (THE iZINE) where you'll find all the official press releases that followed Michael's death, articles, tributes, news and interviews. And, yes, I declare an interest.

If you want to get even more deeply involved then you should join . . .

The INXS List

The home of INXS devotees from 15–50, the INXS list is the only place to go if you want to be part of the worldwide expanded family that is INXS fans on the Web. The email-based conversations, topics and trading are delivered straight to your email letterbox: you can be silent and lurk or you can join in and get to know the folks.

To subscribe, address an email to **listmgr@digitalcastle.com**

The *body* of your mail message should consist ONLY of the commands:

> SUBSCRIBE INXS-List First_LastName (ie SUBSCRIBE INXS-List Big_Fan)

Please note that these are case sensitive commands, and must be reproduced exactly as shown above.

So, it's that easy. Just a few steps and the world of INXS on the 'Net can be yours. Go surf.

Appendix 8

BIBLIOGRAPHY and RECOMMENDED LISTENING

The author recommends the following books which proved invaluable sources of information in the writing of this book.

The Virgin Encyclopaedia of Popular Music (Concise Edition) by Colin Larkin (1997, Virgin Books)

Rock – The Rough Guide, Edited by Jonathon Buckley and Mark Ellingham (1996, Rough Guides Ltd)

Babel by Patti Smith (1978, Fourth Impression, G.P. Putnam's Sons New York)

Arthur Rimbaud – Collected Poems (Penguin Classics), Introduced and Edited by Oliver Bernard (1986, Reprint, Penguin Books)

The Trouser Press Guide To '90s Rock, Edited by Ira A. Robbins (1997, Fifth Edition, A Fireside Book published by Simon & Schuster)

The Great Rock Discography by M.C. Strong (1996, 3rd Edition, Unwins Ltd)

Who's Who Of Australian Rock, Compiled by Chris Spencer and Zbig Nowara (1993, 3rd Revised Edition, The Five Mile Press)

Paula Yates: The Autobiography by Paula Yates (1995, HarperCollins)

The Secret History of Australian Independent Music 1977–1991 by Clinton Walker (1996, Pan MacMillan Australia Pty Limited)

The Guinness Book Of British Hit Albums Edition 7 by Paul Gambaccini, Tim Rice, Jonathan Rice (1997, 7th Edition, Guinness Publishing Ltd)

INXS – The Official Inside Story Of A Band On The Road, text by INXS with Ed St John (1992, Mandarin – a division of the Octopus Publishing Group)

Talking Dirty by Susan Chenery (1997, Sceptre, published by Hodder Headline Australia Pty Ltd – a member of the Hodder Headline Group)

The author would also like to recommend recorded works by the following groups and artists that provided an invaluable soundtrack without which this book would never have been written:

The Verve, Radiohead, Spiritualized, Blur, Pulp, Morcheeba, Tortoise, Trans Am, Can, Neu!, Sand, Faust, Delerium, Stereolab, Moby, Regurgitator, Split Enz, Crowded House, The Mavis's, Kylie Minogue, Nick Cave and The Bad Seeds, Bowery Electric, Labradford, Stars Of The Lid, The Legendary Pink Dots, Laika, Cul De Sac, Ivy, Blue Oyster Cult, Grateful Dead, Neil Young (and Crazy Horse), The Dandy Warhols, The Divinyls, Telstar Ponies, Grey Area, Bob Dylan, Catherine Wheel, Sky Cries Mary, Andy Prieboy, James, Alpha, Loop Guru, Purple Penguin, Air, The Paradise Motel, Finitribe, Garbage, Joni Mitchell, Man, Max Q, The Strawbs, Screaming Trees, Emmylou Harris, Rickie Lee Jones, Tuatara, Giant Sand, Genesis, Tim Buckley, Jeff Buckley, Pink Floyd, Captain Beefheart, Frank Zappa & The Mothers Of Invention, OP8, Juno Reactor, Channel Light Vessel, Ministry, Soundgarden, Metallica, Miles Davis, Yo La Tengo, Leonardo's Bride, The Superjesus, The Kinks, The Mercy Bell, Hunters & Collectors, Madder Lake, McKenzie Theory, R.E.M., The Stranglers, Echo & The Bunnymen, Julian Cope, Pablo's Eye, Elvis Costello, Blondie, Sonic Youth, Clash, The Minutemen, Richard and Linda Thompson, Skinny Puppy, Bruce Springsteen, King Crimson, The Church, Flaming Lips, Velvet Underground, Nirvana, The Doors, Led Zeppelin, Deep Purple, The Who, Mountain, Joy Division, New Order, Jefferson Airplane, Moby Grape, Tori Amos, Janis Joplin, The Byrds, Smashing Pumpkins, Mark Hollis, Mazzy Star, Telstar Ponies, Madonna, Ani Difranco, Patti Smith, Ozric Tentacles, Kid Loco, Victoria Williams, Cornershop, and, of course, the music of INXS.